A Question of Place

A Question of Place

Exploring the Practice
of Human Geography

R. J. JOHNSTON

BLACKWELL
Oxford UK & Cambridge USA

First published 1991

Blackwell Publishers
108 Cowley Road, Oxford, OX4 1JF, UK

Three Cambridge Center
Cambridge, Massachusetts 02142, USA

Library of Congress Cataloging in Publication Data

Johnston, R. J. (Ronald John)
    A question of place : exploring the practice of human geography /
R. J. Johnston.
        p.   cm.
    Includes bibliographical references (p.   ) and index.
    ISBN 0-631-15603-8 — ISBN 0-631-18207-1
    1. Human geography—Philosophy.   2. Human geography—Methodology.
I. Title.
GF21.J64   1992
304.2—dc20   91-3229   CIP

British Library Cataloguing in Publication Data

A CIP catalogue record for this book is available from the British
Library.

Typeset in 10 on 12 pt Sabon
by Photo·graphics, Honiton, Devon
Printed in Great Britain by Billings and Sons Ltd., Worcester

This book is printed on acid-free paper.

Contents

Preface

There seems to be no consensus on what human geography is, or what are its objectives in analysis. . . . human geography is, I believe, in the midst of a major intellectual crisis.

Michael Dear, *The Postmodern Challenge: Reconstructing Human Geography.*

Although many geographers might see Michael Dear's (1988, p. 265) evocation of a siege mentality within their discipline as an overstatement, nevertheless there have been several signs of unease regarding the nature of contemporary geographical scholarship. Recent book titles such as *Remaking Human Geography*, *Remodelling Geography* and *New Models in Geography* are indicative of that unease. I agreed with much of the diagnosis of the disciplinary condition in my *On Human Geography* (Johnston, 1986c). The present book develops from that, not only by extending the diagnosis but also, and more importantly, by exploring a means for enhancing the role of geographical research and writing through the central concept of place.

A number of writers have identified the contemporary problem of geography – and specifically of human geography – as its shift away from a focus on the particularities of individual places. Too many researchers have been concerned to establish generalizations about the spatial organization of society – whether from within the 'spatial science' paradigm that was launched in the 1950s and 1960s or from within the Marxist-inspired 'uneven development' paradigm of the succeeding decades. This at any rate is the claim. But the main counters to those works have been writings which entirely ignore them. As a consequence they fail to set the understanding of places in the context of an appreciation of the wider structuring of society which acts as both constraint to and opportunity for those who are manipulating the fortunes of separate places. What is needed is an approach to the study of places which falls into neither the 'generality trap' which assumes the existence of general laws to which all are subject nor the 'singularity trap' that argues against the existence of any general processes.

The case for such an intermediate position has recently been put by Entrikin (1991) in his book on *The Betweenness of Place: Towards a Geography of Modernity*, where he argues persuasively for a geography that has:

> access to both an objective and a subjective reality. From the decentred vantage point of the theoretical scientist, place becomes either location or a set of generic relations and thereby loses much of its significance for human action. From the centred viewpoint of the subject, place has meaning only in relation to an individual's or a group's goals and concerns. Place is best viewed from points in between. (p. 5)

Unfortunately, Entrikin's powerful general argument is not accompanied by a suggested framework within which the sort of study that he advocates can be conducted: 'I do not offer a new "method" for the study of place, nor do I provide an instructional guide for how to go about such studies' (p. 4). He is not alone in this abdication; others who have argued for a reconstituted geography focusing on the particularity of place have similarly failed to provide a convincing paradigm or set of exemplars for those who would follow them. I take this up in more detail in chapter 2. This book clearly differs from those written from a similar standpoint, however, because it seeks to advance the study of place not only by arguing for it but also by suggesting how it might be done.

The result is not a comprehensive treatise on the nature of human geography, in which the study of place is firmly set within its constraints. Some arguments are taken for granted, such as the case for uneven development argued so persuasively in recent years by David Harvey (1982), Neil Smith (1984) and others. *A Question of Place* is an essay on what place is and how it can be studied by human geographers. The need for such an essay is brought about, it is argued, by the current fragmentation of geographical scholarship and the lack of any central focus which brings the disparate parts together – the theme of chapter 1. And so the book is presented as a contribution to a wider argument about the nature of the practice of geography, rather than as a summation of what the discipline is, could and should be. As such, it can have no conclusion; it is a starting point, not an end.

The ideas presented here have been developed over the last decade in a number of lectures and publications, on which the text draws but which it doesn't reproduce. I am grateful for all the invitations which have allowed me to try out those ideas. In particular, I would like to thank: the Council of the Institute of British Geographers, for inviting me to give the tripartite

Annual Joint Lecture in 1984; the Conference of Irish Geographers, who invited me to give a guest lecture in 1985; the then President of the Association of American Geographers (Risa Palm) for inviting me to participate in the Presidential plenary session at Detroit in 1985; the Colston Society of Bristol, which invited me to present the lecture at its Annual Dinner in 1986; the University of Canterbury for inviting me to give a plenary lecture at the fiftieth anniversary celebrations of its Department of Geography in 1987, and also for asking me to give a Faculty of Science Prestige Lecture; the Department of Geography at the University of Utrecht for inviting me to participate in its conference on the future of regional geography in 1987; the Swedish geographers to whom I gave a plenary lecture at their Geografdagarna in 1988; the University of Amsterdam, to which I gave a plenary lecture at the opening of the Faculty of Spatial Sciences in 1988; and the members of the Institute of British Geographers, who elected me as their President for 1990. All these invitations gave me the opportunity to try out some of the ideas that have since been refined for the present book. In addition, requests to write essays for books edited by George Benko, David Livingstone, James Simmie and Roger King, Derek Gregory and Rex Walford, and Janet Kodras and John Paul Jones, and requests from the editor of the *New Zealand Journal of Geography* and from the Australian Geography Teachers' Association, similarly allowed the ideas to be developed. Some ideas were developed in association with two former students – Mike Griffiths and Charles Pattie – and, while fully absolving them from all that is written here, I would like to acknowledge my great debt to them for their academic companionship during the late 1980s. My thanks also to Lucy Johnston for introducing me to the social psychology literature referred to in chapter 6.

Finally, my thanks to John Davey, who has been everything that an author can ask for in a publisher. I only wish that he could say the same in return!

Acknowledgements

All the illustrations in this book were drawn specifically for it by Graham Allsopp of the Department of Geography at the University of Sheffield, to whom I am deeply indebted for this and much other assistance in recent years. Most of them are reproduced from other sources, as credited in the captions, and every effort has been made to obtain permission to reproduce them, in some cases in modified form.

We are grateful to the following for granting their permission:

Dr Simon Duncan for figure 4.1.

The Association of American Geographers for figures 1.1, 1.5, 1.6 and 5.8 and table 1.1.

The Institute of British Geographers for figures 1.2, 1.3, and 1.4.

The American Political Science Association for figure 1.7.

The editor of *Antipode* for figures 4.2, 4.3, and 4.4.

The editor of *Economic Geography* for figures 5.15 and 5.16.

Edward Arnold for figures 5.2, 5.3, 5.4, 5.5, 5.6, 5.7, 5.9, 5.13, 5.14, and 5.17.

Blackwell Publishers for figures 3.1, 3.2, 3.3, 3.4, 3.5 and 3.6.

Prentice-Hall for figure 5.1.

Sage Publications for figure 3.7.

1

Introduction:
A Fragmented Discipline?

There is . . . in the Sauer archive in the Bancroft Library a note by him saying he knew nothing whatever about corals, but that he wished to know more. Today that kind of remark from an historical or cultural geographer would be almost unthinkable: for an economic or political geographer it would be out of the question. The walls have been built between us, and too many of us devote our time to despising the intellectual validity of what our colleagues are concerned with.

D. R. Stoddart, *To Claim the High Ground: Geography for the End of the Century.*

The last few decades have been characterized within academic geography in the United Kingdom and elsewhere in the English-speaking world by a number of plaintive cries that the discipline is fragmented. Stoddart's is just one example of the sorts of claim made. In it, he argues that many of his contemporaries are 'despondent, morose, disillusioned, almost literally devoid of hope, not only about Geography as it is today but as it might be in the future' (1987, p. 328).

The fragmentation of the discipline that Stoddart identifies is considered by him to be a 'bad thing', for two reasons. First, it offends the belief that geography is an integrating discipline, which brings together the sciences and the arts (and, to the extent that they are recognized, the upstart social sciences) to create syntheses of knowledge: geography unites (or should unite) what the disciplinary structure of academia splits asunder. According to Stoddart again (p. 329), 'too many of our colleagues have either abandoned or failed ever to recognize what I take to be our subject's central intent and indeed self-evident role in the community of knowledge' so that 'We call ourselves not just physical or human geographers, but biogeographers, historical geographers, economic geographers, urban geographers, geomorphologists. We each develop our own expertise, our own techniques, our own theoretical constructs'. He continues in the same vein (p. 330):

> The result is clear enough. Across geography we speak separate languages, do very different things. Many have abandoned the possibility of communicating with colleagues working not only in the same titular discipline but also in the same department. The human geographers think their physical colleagues philosophically naive; the physical geographers think the human geographers lacking in rigour. *Geography* . . . is abandoned and forgotten . . . There is a double danger in this situation. The first is that outside a more general framework physical geography loses its coherence. We become specialists in pedology, climatology, geomorphology, biogeography, drawn more to cognate disciplines than to any common core. . . . The second danger is even greater. Human geography as an exclusively social science loses its identity – it competes with sociology, economics, anthropology – but on their ground, not on ours.

By focusing on the parts only, and not seeing geography as a holistic enterprise, the rationale for the discipline is eroded from within. Stoddart wishes to renew the holistic enterprise, with a '*real* geography – a reasserted *unified geography* . . . and at the same time a *committed geography*' (p. 333), though, as Bird (1989) points out, he fails to tell us what that will look like.

Other observers are more measured in their tone, but are nevertheless as pessimistic as Stoddart. Harvey (1990, p. 431), for example, notes that:

> the academy has moved towards an increasing fragmentation in the division of labor within disciplines, spawned new disciplines in the interstices and looked for crosslinks on thematic topics. This history resembles the development of the division of labor in society at large. Increasing specialization of task and product differentiation, increasing roundaboutness of production and the search for horizontal linkages are as characteristic of large multinational corporations as they are of large universities. Within geography this process of fragmentation has accelerated since the mid-1960s. The effect has been to make it harder to identify the binding logic that is suggested by the word 'discipline'.

With this fragmentation is associated increasing pressure towards novelty in what researchers do, producing what he terms an increased 'turnover time' in ideas: 'Last year it was positivism and Marxism, this year structurationism, next year realism and the year after that constructivism, postmodernism, or whatever'. People are appointed to geography departments to fill narrow specialist niches, and:

> The best we can do is appoint specialists and hope that they have an interest in the discipline as a whole. Our seeming inability or unwillingness to resist fragmentation and ephemerality suggests a condition in which something is being done to us by forces beyond our control.

I agree with Harvey's analysis, hence this book. A major task essayed here is promotion of the concept of *place* as a central, integrating core for geographic work, although Harvey finds it no more important than any of the other brief fashions – 'The social search for identity and roots in place has reentered geography as a leitmotif and is in turn increasingly used to provide the discipline with a more powerful (and equally fictitious) sense of identity in a rapidly changing world'.

Alongside this *intellectual* case for geography is a second, more pragmatic argument – the *political* case for geography. Whereas the intellectual case is based on a belief in geography's place within an ideal structure of academic disciplines, and thus argues for its existence as a necessity, the political case begins with the present disciplinary structure and seeks to retain it, in particular geography's relative strength within it. Bennett (1989, p. 290), for example, writes of 'a real danger of the geographical priesthood remaining whilst the congregation departs. The subject will rightly no longer claim the share of students it has received in the past, and it will have lost its capacity to contribute useful knowledge to the research process, to policy debate and to practice' if the discipline's teaching and research activities are not restructured. In this second case, the fragmentation of geography is presented as political hostage to fortune; to the extent that individual geographers identify themselves more with members of other disciplines – publish in their journals, attend their conferences – than with other geographers so they offer academic politicians the opportunity to dismember geography as a discipline with its own academic structure and power base, and to locate geographers elsewhere, if anywhere at all (see, for example, Abler, 1987). The consequence, not too far in the future, would be the demise of gegography, which is welcome to those who believe that the academic division of knowledge is counter-productive (Eliot Hurst, 1985) but not, it is contended, to the great majority of practising geographers.

These two cases are presented here as separate, ideal types, with the implication that they are used independently of each other. In the abstract this is quite feasible; a political case for geography may be made, for example, without any reference to the intellectual case, purely as an exercise in defending some aspect of the status quo and without calling on any deeper justification. But this is unlikely to be the situation; even if the 'real' reason for somebody making the case for geographers uniting is a political one, it will undoubtedly be made, at least in part, on the grounds that the discipline as a whole must be defended because of its fundamental contribution to the advancement and propagation of knowledge.

While not denying the importance of the political argument, and the need for geographers to be ever-vigilant in the protection of their discipline (and hence of their own individual, career interests), the focus here is entirely on the intellectual case. Unless such a case can be sustained, then the political case must fall; there will come a time when it proves impossible to defend the indefensible, the existence of an academic discipline that has no intellectual rationale. The bulk of this book, then, is about the case for geography as a discipline occupying a viable niche within the academic division of labour. In order to make that case, however, it is necessary to begin with a brief review of the current situation, and the evidence of an undesirable fragmentation of the discipline. This is then followed by a review of similar arguments from within two other disciplines.

WHAT FRAGMENTATION?

Most of the current arguments about the undesirable fragmentation of academic geography are based on anecdotal evidence and beliefs rather than 'hard information'. The latter is difficult to obtain, if for no other reason than that the term fragmentation is hard to define: what constitutes a fragmented discipline, and what would characterize a united geography? Once those questions were answered, it might then be possible to design a research project which would inquire into the degree of fragmentation, and provide the basis for unification projects, if such were believed necessary. No such research project has been undertaken as a prelude to the present book, for two reasons. First, there is plenty of evidence that some geographers believe that there is a fragmentation problem, which in itself is sufficient to justify the task undertaken here. Secondly, and linked to that belief, I subscribe to that general view, although my definition of the problem differs from that of many others, as will become clear as the argument within this book develops. Nevertheless, in order to sustain the case that I will be developing here, some limited evidence is presented.

The structure of learned societies

Two recent analyses of the membership structures of the main learned societies for academic geography in the English-speaking world – the Association of American Geographers (AAG) and the Institute of British Geographers (IBG) – provide insights to the degree and nature of the fragmentation.

The AAG is nearly three decades older than its British counterpart, having been founded in 1904 (James and Martin, 1979); the IBG was inaugurated in 1933 (Steel, 1983). Each is now to some extent a federation of subdisciplinary groups, to which are entrusted much of the detailed organization of academic activity – notably the holding of conferences and other meetings, and the arrangement and conduct of sessions within the parent body's annual meeting. Information on the membership of those groups provides interesting insights on the internal fragmentation of the discipline.

Although the IBG was the first to introduce such groups – they are termed study groups – initial attention here focuses on the AAG's specialty groups. The AAG is a bigger organization (some 5400 members in the late 1980s compared to about 1500 in the IBG), has more groups, and has recently been the subject of a detailed study (Goodchild and Janelle, 1988).

Within the AAG, members are entitled to belong to three specialty groups as part of their subscription, and they indicate which each year by ticking the relevant boxes on the annual dues form. In addition they can belong to other groups if they wish, for a small additional subscription. In May 1984, at the time of Goodchild and Janelle's study, there were 35 groups operating; their titles and membership then are shown in table 1.1. They ranged in size from just 50 members (Native American – the title reflects an academic interest and not a racial categorization of the members) – to 531 (Urban Geography); interestingly, the second largest group was Cartography, which is relevant to most if not all other aspects of the discipline, and could be seen as an 'integrating forum'.[1]

The number of Groups that members choose to affiliate with provides an indicator of the degree of fragmentation within the discipline, as represented by the 5000 plus members of the AAG – remembering that they can associate with as many as three at no additional cost to their membership of the association. Goodchild and Janelle (1988, p. 12) report that just 32 per cent of the members identified themselves with the maximum of three, 47 per cent chose at least two, and 57 per cent at least one, with the implication that over 40 per cent of the members of the Association

Table 1.1 The Specialty Groups of the Association of American Geographers and their membership in 1984

Specialty Group	Membership
Africa	124
Aging	67
Applied	440
Asian	128
Bible	61
Biogeography	176
Canadian Geography	84
Cartography	483
Chinese Geography	82
Climatology	233
Coastal and Marine	134
Cultural Ecolocy	144
Energy	184
Environmental Perception	209
Environmental Studies	356
Geographic Perspectives on Women	150
Geography in Higher Education	167
Geomorphology	316
Historical	342
Industrial Geography	158
Latin American	202
Mathematical Models and Quantitative Methods	250
Medical	123
Native American	50
Political Geography	248
Population	256
Recreation	182
Regional Development and Planning	302
Remote Sensing	341
Rural Development	162
Socialist	96
Soviet	123
Transportation	208
Urban	531
Water Resources	283

Source: Goodchild and Janelle, 1988, p. 12.

chose to subscribe (at nil cost) to none. A substantial proportion of AAG members identified with no subdisciplinary group (or at least with none of those currently in existence), which presumably indicates either an antagonism towards the fragmentation of the discipline which some see the Groups as representing (the relevance of Almond's 'separate tables' metaphor – see below, p. 30 – is substantial here) or the lack of any Group serving a substantial minority of the members' interests. Countering that situation, about one-third of the members elected to join three Groups which suggests either that a further substantial proportion are not narrow specialists identifying with one subdisciplinary activity only or that there are several complementary groups serving particular constellations of research and/or teaching interests. Interestingly, Goodchild and Janelle report that the older the member the greater the probability that he or she was affiliated with no Specialty Group, which hints that the fragmentation of the discipline, as represented by the Groups, is very much a feature of the recent generations of graduates (who, on the whole, are more active within the AAG, especially in terms of presenting papers at its various meetings).

To explore the nature of the fragmentation further, Goodchild and Janelle undertook a statistical analysis (multidimensional scaling) which maps the relative locations of the Groups according to their joint memberships. The closer together two Groups are on the map, the more members they have in common. The resulting two-dimensional map – the simplest representation of a 35 × 35 matrix showing the common memberships of all pairs – is in figure 1.1. It suggests some clear divisions within the discipline in North America.

The first, and the most expected, division is between the physical and the human geography Speciality Groups. All of the former fall within one quadrant of the map – the 'southwest' – with only one non-physical geography Group (Geographic Perspectives on Women) at all close to them. (It may be that this is in part an artifact of the 2-dimensional solution, and that if a 3- or higher-dimensional map were derived, the last-named Group would be found some distance from the physical geography Groups.) The only other nearby Groups, suggesting cross-membership by physical and human geographers, are Water Resources, Recreation, Cultural Ecology, Environmental Perception, Environmental Studies, Cartography, Historical and Applied.

Countering the concentration of physical geography Specialty Groups is a cluster of human geography Groups in the 'northeast' quadrant, including Urban, Regional Development, Mathematical Models and Quantitative Methods, Political, Transportation and Industrial. (All but the last of these had over 200 members in 1984.) Only one Specialty Group which might be

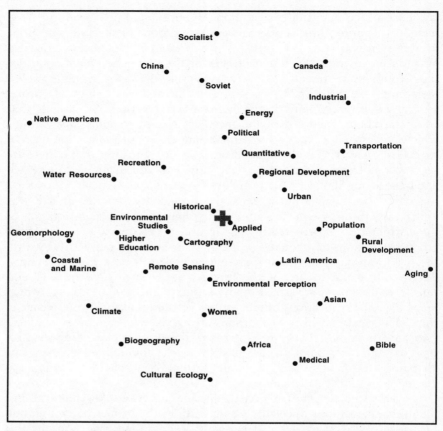

Figure 1.1   A two-dimensional map showing the relative locations of the 35 Specialty Groups in the Association of American Geographers in 1984, according to their cross-memberships. *Source*: Goodchild and Janelle, 1988, p. 13.

considered 'mainline human geography', is not in this quadrant: Population Geography is in the 'southeast', very close to Rural Development. (On whether population geography has been 'mainline human geography' in the 1980s – in the UK at least – see Findlay and Graham, 1991.)

Apart from this split between the 'mainline' physical and human Groups, the remainder of the map comprises a wide scatter of relatively isolated and, on the whole, small Specialty Groups. Only two, China and Soviet, are close together, indicating that in relative terms a susbtantial number are members of both. The Socialist Specialty Group is not too far distant from those two, but it is unlikely that many of the 'radicals' belonging to it are students of either of the world's main socialist states.

Goodchild and Janelle conclude that any integration within the discipline (as suggested by their data) is provided by what they call the 'resource and technical specialties' (1988, p. 13) which 'provide a hinge relationship between the broad human and physical divisions'. The central position of three Groups – Applied Geography, Cartography and Historical Geography – leads them to speculate whether these have replaced regional geography as the discipline's core. (They earlier note that 'the regional specialties are scattered over the space with no strong community of interest', and later conclude that 'areal specialists tend to concentrate their efforts on a single region and to have lower levels of interaction with those who study other regions ... the evidence suggests that interest in a region derives not from some general interest in regions but from the associated systematic specialty': 1988, p. 14). The centrality of Applied Geography is because it represents the 'discipline's outreach in the service of society' whereas that of Cartography reflects 'the importance of maps as one of geography's principal tools of communication and analysis'. (Why, then, does Mathematical Models and Quantitative Methods not occupy a more central position, given the arguments for the shared use of methods and paradigm among physical and human geographers over several decades?) The Applied Geography and Cartography Groups may indeed bring human and physical geographers together, but the case that they make for the centrality of Historical Geography – 'suggestive of humanistic concerns among geographers' – is less convincing.

Goodchild and Janelle further analysed the Specialty Group membership data by looking at the diversity of the links for each Group: a specialized Group was one whose members tended to be members of a small number of other Groups only, whereas a diversified Group was one whose members were distributed relatively evenly across the remaining 34 in their subscriptions to other Groups. They found that the physical geography groups were among the most specialized, leading Marcus (1988, p. 541) to wonder whether 'physical geographers are narrower in geographic perspective than other geographers, or simply that they choose to devote their cross-connecting time and energy to cognate disciplines rather than other geography groups?' The most diversified Groups, on the other hand, were those at the centre of the MDS map – Recreation, Historical and, notably, Geography in Higher Education, whose agenda should attract the interest of scholars of all research persuasions (though the Group had only 167 members and 108 cross-membership links with other Groups, and so comprised only a small minority of AAG members drawn from a wide range of interests).

Goodchild and Janelle's overall conclusion (based on other data and analyses as well as those briefly described here) identified the 'emergence of increased specialization in geography . . . aided by the integrating effects of new technologies' (1988, p. 24). These technologies could enhance generalization because they facilitate communication among specialists, but in turn raise potential problems of narrow specialization which Goodchild and Janelle hope an ecumenical organization such as the AAG can counter by bringing such diverse groupings together in productive academic intercourse. (As presumably individual American university departments of geography do, since these are diverse in the interests of their faculty members and are not specialized research groupings.) The links among those specialists suggest to them the continued importance of three of the four main traditions of geographic scholarship identified by Pattison (1964):

'man'-land (the 'central' specialist groups such as Historical and Environmental Studies);
spatial (the human geography systematic specialisms of the 'northeast'); and
earth science (the physical geography groups).

The fourth – *area studies* – is lacking, they claim. Certainly it does not occupy the central, integrating location that many argued for traditional regional geography, and the regionally-oriented Specialty Groups are identified as 'peripheral'. Instead, Goodchild and Janelle identify a further central theme represented by Applied Geography, Cartography and Historical, which may 'provide a core of intellectual and technical binding among the 'man'-land, spatial and earth science traditions' (1988, p. 24).

Why has this specialization come about, with the consequential lack of cross-disciplinary interests? In a response to the Goodchild and Janelle article, Marcus (1988) argues that it reflects the policies of academic institutions which 'force' scholars to specialize in order to advance along the academic career path:

As long as the reward system (merit, promotion, recognition) is biased towards the successful specialist, most will avoid the pitfalls that come with broadened curiosity.

Thus we get what he identifies as 'geography's dilemma: breadth versus depth':

Fewer geographers pursue or are trained across the range of human and physical topics, while many have abandoned all but lip service allegiance to the discipline's central core. Good specialized research often results, but the external (and increasingly internal) questions are: Is it geography and what is geography?

This leads him to conclude that 'Geography is presently walking a razor's edge between wide public acceptance and academic dismantlement' (1988, p. 542).

A similar analysis to Goodchild and Janelle's has recently been conducted on membership and cross-membership of the IBG's seventeen Study Groups (Johnston, 1990a). Members can affiliate with two Study Groups as part of their general subscription, and can join as many more as they like for a small additional charge. (Table 1.2 lists the Groups, their membership in early 1989 when the study was undertaken, and the number of cross-memberships.) Most take the opportunity of affiliating with two but, as table 1.2 shows, there is variation among the Groups in the degree to

Table 1.2 The Study Groups of the Institute of British Geographers and their memberships in 1989

			Membership		
Study Group		Total	Sole[a]	One other	Two or more others
1	Biogeography	57	6	43	8
2	Geomorphology	192	57	118	17
3	Developing Areas	191	19	127	45
4	Higher Education	55	4	31	20
5	Historical	205	18	149	38
6	History and Philosophy	63	4	27	32
7	Industrial Activity	140	4	92	44
8	Medical	74	3	43	28
9	Planning	206	5	134	67
A	Political	71	5	36	30
B	Population	144	4	96	44
C	Quantitative Methods	222	15	157	50
D	Rural	210	11	152	47
E	Social and Cultural	201	0	119	82
F	Transport	66	3	44	19
G	Urban	370	19	253	98
H	Women	58	0	21	37

[a] Sole members are those who belong to no other Study Group.
Source: Johnston, 1990a, p. 408.

which their members are likely to affiliate with others also. In general, it is the physical geographers, for whom there are only two Groups within the IBG, the Geomorphology Study Group and the Biogeography Study Group, who are the more 'isolationist'; they are the only two Study Groups with more than 10 per cent of their members not belonging to at least one other.

Linkages between IBG Study Groups were studied in a similar way to Janelle and Goodchild's analysis, using matrices (reproduced in Johnston, 1990a) showing the number of common members in each pair of Groups to produce maps of their relative location in intellectual space. Three maps are reproduced here, referring to IBG members who belonged to two groups only (figure 1.2), those who belonged to three or more (figure 1.3), and to all members (figure 1.4). On these, the closer two Groups are to each other the greater their common membership (relative to their total memberships).

Each of those maps shows the 17 Study Groups arranged in a circle

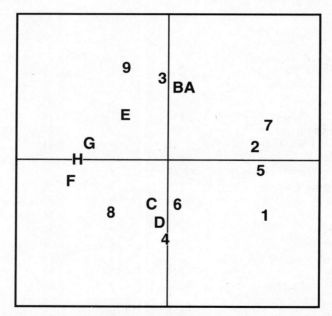

Figure 1.2 A two-dimensional map showing the relative locations of the 17 Study Groups in the Institute of British Geographers in 1989, according to cross-memberships for individuals who were members of two Groups only. A key to the Groups is given in table 1.2. *Source*: Johnston, 1990a, p. 411.

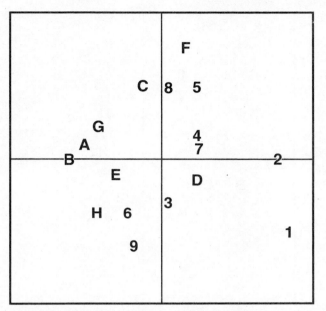

Figure 1.3   A two-dimensional map showing the relative locations of the 17 Study Groups in the Institute of British Geographers in 1989, according to cross-memberships for individuals who were members of three or more Groups. A key to the Groups is given in table 1.2. *Source*: Johnston, 1990a, p. 411.

around an empty centre, suggesting the existence, as far as these data are concerned, of a 'discipline without a core'. When all links are analysed (figure 1.4), the circle comprises 15 of the 17 Groups, with the other two – Biogeography and Geomorphology – outside it, in the 'far east'. In the 'centre-west' (or the 'centre-left') are four of the large 'mainstream' generalist human geography Groups – Political (A); Population (B), Social (E), and Urban (G) – together with the Women and Geography Study Group (H). The 'northwest' of the circle has the two 'mainstream' economic geography groups – Industrial (8) and Transport (F) – and next to this, in the 'northeast', are the Planning (4), Higher Education (5) and Rural (D) Groups. Between them and the 'southeastern' cluster – Developing Areas (3), Historical (6), History and Philosophy (7) – is the Quantitative Methods Study Group (C); the Medical Geography Group (9) lies somewhat isolated in the 'deep south'.

There is clearly a major division within the IBG between physical and human geography, with little cross-membership in Study Groups across

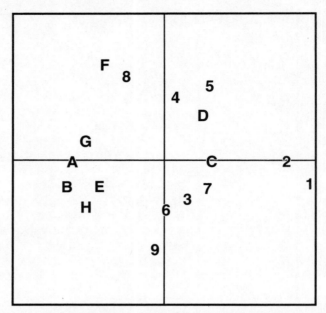

Figure 1.4   A two-dimensional map showing the relative locations of the 17 Study Groups in the Institute of British Geographers in 1989, according to cross-memberships for individuals who were members of two or more Groups. A key to the Groups is given in table 1.2. *Source*: Johnston, 1990a, p. 412.

that divide. This is not a surprising find, given the discipline's recent history. More relevant to the present discussion are the separate groupings of human geography Study Groups, which suggest that there are clusters of inter-related specialisms within the discipline, but relatively slight links between those clusters. Furthermore, there is no cluster in the centre of any of the maps, of Study Groups similarly linked to all others – or at least to those in the circle surrounding the 'empty core'. If there were such 'core' groups, they could be interpreted as those which to some extent integrate the discipline by bringing together geographers with wide specialist interests.

The absence of such core Groups is taken here to indicate a fragmented discipline comprising specialists with few common interests. It could be that the fragmentation is an artifact of the data and the Study Group structure of the IBG: many geographers are generalists in their intra-disciplinary interests rather than specialists, but do not reflect this in their Study Group memberships. To some extent, the absence of a core may be because 'integrating' Study Groups have not been established by the IBG. However, Groups are created as a result of members' requests, with relatively few criteria to be met, so the absence of some which might occupy the 'core' implies that there is no perceived need for such organizations. There are three Study Groups already in existence which might be claimed as already meeting a need for a core – the Higher Education, History and Philosophy of Geography, and Quantitative Methods Study Groups, each of which covers ground that is common to many specialist human geographers, and perhaps to some physical geographers as well. In addition, it could be argued that the Planning and Geography Study Group covers an area of interest which spans those of most, if not all, specialist human geography Groups, and it too might be expected to occupy a core position.

None of those four Study Groups is apparently seen as a 'home' for geographers with diverse other specialist interests, however. Two of them – Higher Education and History and Philosophy – have small memberships only (table 1.2), perhaps indicating that they are perceived as representing very specialized interests rather than being of general relevance: this is a much more plausible interpretation for the situation with History and Philosophy than Higher Education, however, for the latter's concerns with the pedagogic roles of geographers should be perceived as relevant to a large proportion of the membership. Both are relatively new Study Groups within the IBG, and their integrating role may therefore still be latent only, but there is little evidence of growth in membership or of interest in the research areas they represent.

The Quantitative Methods and Planning Study Groups are among the largest in the IBG, with more than 200 members each. The former is also one of the oldest, having been established in the early 1960s at the onset of the 'quantitative revolution' in British geography. At that time, quantitative methods were seen as a vehicle for integrating physical and human geography, and it is still the case that members of the BGRG (British Geomorphology Research Group) who are members of the IBG and of its Geomorphology Study Group are much more likely also to be a member of the Quantitative Methods Study group than of any other; the current figure is approximately one-quarter. (The BGRG is a separate body which predates the creation of Study Groups within the IBG. It has affiliations with other learned societies as well, and has many members who are not academic geographers and have no background in the discipline. The Geomorphology Study Group is a sub-set of the BGRG's membership who are members of the IBG.) Nevertheless, that cross-membership is insufficient to draw the BGRG into the main clusters of points, because it has very few links with any other Groups, other than the Biogeography

Study Group, which has very few links with any others, except BGRG and, to a much lesser extent, Quantitative Methods and Rural Geography.

Quantitative Methods does not occupy a central position within the map of British geography, as represented by IBG Study Group memberships, because its constituency does not cover the other specialist human geography interests equally. Very few members of the Women and Geography, Social Geography and Political Geography Study Groups are also Quantitative Methods group members, for example. Interestingly, its relative position on the three maps is quite different. On that for individuals who are members of two groups only (figure 1.2) it is in the 'south', close to Planning (4), Historical (6), Industrial (8) and Rural (D). At least the first two of those have few 'direct links' with Quantitative Methods (i.e. few cross-memberships); their proximity on the map indicates that each of the three has a relatively dispersed pattern of cross-memberships — there are no 'close neighbours', of groups with complementary interests that many might join, as is the case with E, G and H, for example. In the map for members belonging to three or more groups (figure 1.3), the Quantitative Methods Study Group is closest to Industrial (8), but far from 4, 6 and D. Finally, in the composite map it appears to occupy something of a 'bridging' position for three clusters: Planning (4), Higher Education (5) and Rural (D) to the 'north', Biogeography (1) and BGRG (2) to the 'east', and Developing Areas (3), Historical (6), History and Philosophy (7) and Medical (9) to the 'south'. That it is not central to all four clusters suggests that quantitative methods are of relatively little interest to Political (A), Population (B), Social (E — this grouping was recently renamed the Social and Cultural Geography Study Group), and Urban (G) geographers, nor to members of the Women and Geography Study Group (H).

This analysis assumes that as the IBG is the leading academic learned society for geographers in the British Isles, its members are representative of the situation for the discipline as a whole, so that the divisions indicated are typical of other aspects of the discipline's operations. Beyond the Institute, whereas some of those academic geographers (i.e. members of geography departments in universities, polytechnics and colleges) who are not members are undoubtedly drawn from all specialist interests, some specialist groups have clearly opted away from the IBG. The main grouping of climatologists, for example, is the Association of British Climatologists, which is affiliated with the Royal Meteorological Society but not with the IBG; it used to hold meetings as part of the IBG annual conference, but no longer does so because of a perceived lack of benefits (e.g. little else on the programme of interest to its members). Those interested in remote sensing and, more recently, geographical information systems (GIS) have also decided to develop affiliations elsewhere and although their concerns have in part been met both by the Quantitative Methods Study Group and by other groups with specialist interests in using the techniques, the main focus of their activity is clearly external to academic geography.

In general, physical geographers may have developed the better institutional links away from the main organizations of academic geography (the Biogeography Study Group has close links with the British Ecological Society, for example), in part because of their perceived separation from human geography and in part because of the scientific benefits obtained from such an orientation. For human geographers, the variety offered within the IBG is much greater, as is that outside it, but there is no obvious single alternative which seduces large numbers away from the IBG. The Regional Studies Association and the Regional Science Association offer links with other disciplines that attract some, as does the Agricultural History Society for a small number of others, but British human geographers have not developed strong institutional links with, say, the British Sociological Association or the Political Studies Association, even though some individuals are members of those bodies. For human geographers, the IBG and its Study Groups are their main institutional focus. Within it, they are major contributors to its fragmentation, suggesting that there is no apparent core of interests to which most human geographers would subscribe.

Citation patterns

Other evidence which illustrates this chapter's general theme is provided by the analysis of citation patterns in the geographical literature. This uses the citations to other works in a paper or book (i.e. the items in a bibliography) to quantify the impact of a particular piece (the number of times it is cited by other workers – one frequently cited is termed a 'citation classic'), the relative impact of different journals (the frequency with which items published in them are cited elsewhere), the relative impact of different authors (the number of independent citations to their work), and so on. Such data are compiled by the Institute for Scientific Information, and have been used by a number of geographers to investigate various aspects of their discipline's structure. Some have demonstrated the relative importance of particular items and individual authors within that literature: some geographers have their work cited much more than do others (for example, Whitehand, 1985 and Bodman, 1991); some pieces are much more frequently cited than others, and could merit the appellation 'citation classic' for example (Wrigley and Matthews, 1986); some are cited by certain groups within the discipline only.

One use of these data to investigate the fragmentation of geography is to explore whether they indicate the existence of separate networks of researchers who cite each other's work frequently but who neither cite that of others very much nor are frequently cited themselves by members of other groups. Such independent networks are often referred to as 'invisible colleges' within the discipline, that have relatively few external contacts: they are relatively self-contained groups within the larger whole, operating their own paradigms. In this context, paradigm refers to the details of the approach and methods used, rather than to the wider concept of a 'world-view' as to the nature of science (Johnston, 1991c).

The existence of such 'invisible colleges' is frequently assumed but rarely rigorously evaluated. Gatrell's (1984) study of the literature on spatial diffusion did not identify such a relatively closed grouping, for example; rather he concluded that 'although individual researchers . . . are engaged in spatial diffusion research, there is no sense of a research community, network of scholars or individual college' (p. 450). This was a study of only one specialism, however, and so not the basis for wide generalizations. Furthermore, whether or not the techniques used identify an 'invisible college' depends very much, as he stresses, on which items (papers and other publications) are included. If some are peripheral in their concerns, and if there are subgroups within the larger whole, then the absence of homogeneity is assured. For example, the study of disease diffusion, with close links to epidemiology – Cliff and Haggett (1989) – began as part of this wider field but has now, for reasons that Haggett (1990) sets out, somewhat distanced itself from other studies of diffusion.

An alternative use of citation data is to look at the impact of different journals: the more frequently a journal is cited, the greater the impact of the papers that it publishes on the development of a discipline. Wrigley (1983) introduced this method of analysis to the journal *Environment and Planning A*: this is a generalist international journal of urban and regional research with links to several other disciplines (economics, sociology, planning etc.), that covers several areas of human geography, though with a particular (perceived) emphasis on quantitative modelling, reflecting the interests of the founding editor, Alan Wilson. The data that Wrigley cites for 1981 show that the largest number of citations to items in geography and related journals were mainly to articles in long-established, generalist journals such as *Annals of the Association of American Geographers* and *Transactions, Institute of British Geographers*. However, when the number of citations is related to the number of citable items to produce an 'impact factor', more specialist journals such as *Economic Geography, Geographical Analysis, Regional Studies* and *Urban Studies* are awarded the highest scores, suggesting that the most influential pieces – those cited most by other workers – on researchers publishing in *Environment and Planning A* are placed in the specialist rather than the generalist journals. This could reflect one or more of: differences in submission patterns to different types of journal – where do you send your best papers?; differences in editorial policies between different types of journal; and differences in reading habits.

Whitehand (1984) performed a similar analysis of geography journals, looking at their impact in each of five years (1978–82) – the impact was defined as the number of citations in year x relative to the number of items published in the two preceding years. He selected 16 generalist geography journals, seven specialist geography journals and four journals covering fields which overlap geography. The largest impact score in 1982 (1.127) was achieved by a specialist journal, *Journal of Biogeography*, and both all seven of the specialist journals and all four of the cognate journals outscored eight of the general geography journals. Some of the latter have restricted markets (e.g. *Soviet Geography, Canadian Geographer*, and *Geographische Zeitschrift*), and some have a wider market than academic geography (e.g. *Geography, Journal of Geography*). Nevertheless, specialist journals such as *Economic Geography* (impact score, 0.891), *Journal of Historical Geography* (0.697), *Earth Surface Processes and Landforms* (0.579) and *Geografiska Annaler Series B* (0.462) very substantially outscored not only such general journals as *Geographical Journal* (0.244) but several of them outperformed *Geographical Review*. Overall, the 'big league' English-language generalist journals performed best – *Area* (0.815), *Annals* (0.813), *Transactions* (0.800), *Professional Geographer* (0.687) – and held top positions in each of the years studied (except *Area*, for which only 1982 data were available). But a relatively specialist journal – *Geographical Analysis* (0.813) – occupied second place in 1982, first place in 1981, and second place in each of the two preceding years.

Overall, Whitehand's data suggest that the generalist geography journals are not pre-eminent within the discipline, and that the most cited pieces of geographical work are not necessarily placed there by their authors – another indicator of fragmentation in the discipline? (A further indicator was the relative absence of physical geography articles submitted to both leading IBG journals, a situation bemoaned by their editors – Wrigley (1988, 1990), McDowell (1989), Sparks (1990) – and perhaps changing somewhat in the early 1990s.) Whitehand's (1990) later analysis shows that the situation changed relatively little in the mid-1980s, with the top two positions for 1984–7 inclusive (covering all citations to work published in the journals concerned) occupied by *Annals and Transactions*, and a third – *Progress in Human Geography*, launched as a journal in 1977 only – occupying fourth place in the study of 1987 citations. But specialist journals also occupy high places in the 1987 analysis – *Political Geography Quarterly* ranked second (impact factor 1.400) behind the *Annals* (1.469); *Environment and Planning D: Society and Space*, a relatively specialist journal for those interested in modern social, cultural and political geography and with links to social theory, ranked fifth (0.891), and *Journal of Historical Geography* (0.872) came next. Older-established journals, such as *Annals* and *Transactions*, have a larger 'backlog' of materials to cite, however. If only articles published in the previous three years are used to compute the impact factor, then *Political Geography Quarterly* achieves first place (1.565 compared with 1.524 for the *Annals*).

An alternative way of looking at the impact of various journals is their 'trading relationships'. Gatrell and Smith (1984) introduced this to geography with a study of 22 journals, half of which are 'generalist' and publish articles from most, if not all, branches of the discipline; the remainder were human geography journals. For each of two periods – 1970–2 and 1980–2 – they produced a 22 × 22 matrix of cross-citations (i.e. each cell showed the number of times that papers published in one journal were cited in another). They were then able to calculate an import/-export ratio for each journal: a ratio different from 1.0 indicated that there was an imbalance in the trade between the two. Similarly, they could obtain an overall trade ratio for each journal: the number of times papers in it were cited in the other journals divided by the number of times papers in other journals were cited in it. Finally, they looked at self-citation rates, the proportion of all citations in a journal's articles to papers in all 22 that were to papers in the same journal.

They reached two main conclusions regarding the overall trading relationships of journals. First, in both periods the main 'net exporters' (i.e. the journals whose papers were cited more frequently in others than papers in others were cited in it) were of two types: general geography journals such as *Annals* and *Geographical Review*; and the regional science journals. With regard to the latter, geographers cited more work published in regional science outlets than regional scientists cited papers in geographical journals. (This is evidence of a relationship between geography and other disciplines noted elsewhere – geographers cite work reported in other disciplines much more than vice versa; Laponce (1980). Note also Wrigley and Matthews's (1986) finding that geographical work is little cited outside the discipline, and Hay's (1985a, 1985b) with regard to articles resulting from PhD thesis research that articles in non-geographical journals are more likely to be cited outside geography than are those in the discipline's 'mainstream' journals.) The most important work – or at least the most visible and hence the most cited – was apparently placed in the main generalist journals, according to the first of Gatrell and Smith's conclusions. Between the two time periods, however, the relative position of this group of journals declined, with all having a lower ratio in 1980–2 than 1970–2 (that for *Geographical Review* fell from 3.96 to 2.40, for example). More specialist journals increased their trading position, on the other hand; *Antipode*, for example, became a net exporter (a ratio of 0.03 in the first period but 2.50 in the second), as did *Economic Geography, Geographical Analysis* and *Regional Studies*; *Environment and Planning A* increased its export trade substantially. Over the decade, it seems, geographers were increasingly placing their more important pieces in the more specialized journals.

The self-citation rates indicate the degree of 'isolation' or 'introversion' of a journal (relative only to the other journals studied), thereby reflecting either its dominance by an introverted specialist group or its distance from the rest of the geographical literature. Several types of journal had relatively high rates: those on the fringes of geography, with links to other disciplines too – journals such as *Urban Studies, Regional Studies* and *Environment and Planning A*; regional journals – such as *Scottish Geographical Magazine*; journals which carry a considerable amount of 'commentary' and 'debate' – notably *Area*; and 'fringe' geography journals, such as *Geographical Journal*, which carries 'low proportions of papers written by academic geographers, who would have access to, and knowledge of, a wide geographical literature' (p. 302).

Gatrell and Smith used multi-dimensional scaling to produce maps of the relative location of journals in the pattern of intellectual trade, as demonstrated by citations, in the same way as the maps in figures 1.1–4 were derived. For 1970–2, the map (figure 1.5) shows the 'generalist' American journals in the centre, occupying what they term the 'core of the disciplinary space', with the various specialist journals on the periphery (the regional science journals are in the 'west', linked to the core by *Economic Geography*). Ten years later, the general pattern is the same (figure 1.6), but with some significant differences from the previous decade: *Geographical Review* has moved from core towards the periphery; *Environment and Planning A* has moved into the centre, linking the main British and American journals; the regional science journals have become more peripheral (suggesting their lesser impact on geography as a whole in the early 1980s relative to the early 1970s); and the Dutch journal

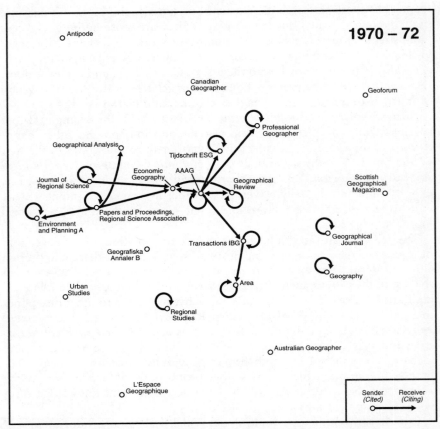

Figure 1.5   A two-dimensional map showing the relative locations of 22 geographical journals in 1970–2 according to cross-citations. The 25 largest citation values are shown by the arrows: they link the journals which apparently have most in common, although in 12 of the 25 cases the citations are to other papers in the same journal. *Source*: Gatrell and Smith, 1984, p. 303.

Tijdschrift voor Economische en Sociale Geografie has moved even closer to the core, reflecting its stronger international flavour than that of, say, the comparable Australian and Canadian journals. Overall, Gatrell and Smith note 'a general "migration" outwards from the center' (p. 305) – which could be yet further evidence of the growth of a discipline without a core – and the growing peripherality of the journals associated with the

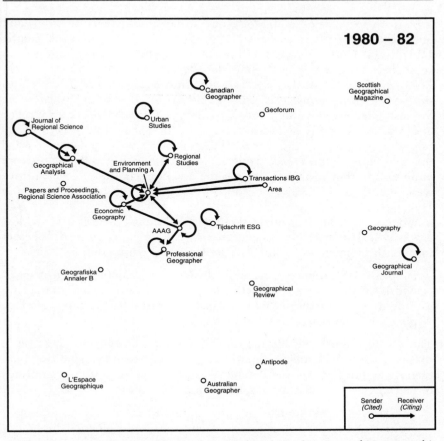

1980 – 82

Figure 1.6 A two-dimensional map showing the relative locations of 22 geographical journals in 1980–2 according to cross-citations. The 25 largest citation values are shown by the arrows: they link the journals which apparently have most in common, although in 12 of the 25 cases the citations are to other papers in the same journal. *Source*: Gatrell and Smith, 1984, p. 304.

oldest geographical societies in both America (*Geographical Review*) and Britain (*Geographical Journal*).

Students of citation data also look at the impact of particular items and of individuals; on the latter, see Whitehand (1985), and Bodman (1991). Frequently-cited items are termed 'citation classics', and Wrigley and Matthews (1986) identified the 'classic' journal articles and books published by geographers up to 1984. Looking only at the articles, their list of the top 21 – all published prior to 1972 – included three published in the

Annals (in 1961, 1964 and 1969), one in the *Transactions* (in 1965) and one in the *Geographical Review* (also in 1965). The last-mentioned (Taaffe, Morrill and Gould, 1963) was ranked fifth. The top three appeared in specialist, non-geographical journals (*Papers and Proceedings of the Regional Science Association, Transportation Research* and *Transactions of the American Geophysical Union*), and the fourth was published in the Swedish human geography journal, *Geografiska Annaler B*. (Later Wrigley and Matthews (1987) identified three items that should have been in the 'top 21': two were in the *Annals* and their inclusion would have pushed the sole entry from *Transactions* to joint 24th place.) Of more recent publications, they identified the 'top ten potential classics', of which three were published in *Transactions*, one in the *Annals* and one in *Progress in Human Geography*.

What do these findings imply about the publishing practices of individual academics? Turner (1988) sought an answer in a paper entitled 'Whether to publish in geography journals'. He began by noting that:

> Subfields, departments, and individuals in geography seem to vary widely in the extent to which they publish in geographic journals. Indeed, some of the most distinguished geographers use the discipline's outlets only sparingly. (p. 15)

Those who publish outside the discipline do so, he suggests, because in that way their work makes a much wider impact, thereby enhancing both their own and, perhaps, the discipline's status more than if they published in the relatively uncited geographical journals – thus:

> For virtually any subfield of geography, a set of non-geography journals exists that offer a size of audience and potential dissemination through citations (impact factor) that cannot be matched by geography journals . . . [and] The visibility of physical geographers is particularly enhanced by publishing in major non-geography journals. (pp. 16–17)

Presumably, if geographers publish in non-geography journals their fellow geographers will find that work and cite it, and non-geographers will have it brought to their attention: if they publish in geography journals, on the other hand, only other geographers are likely to find and cite it, because non-geographers tend not to refer to the discipline's literature.

Turner found significant differences within geography by dividing the individuals studied (the staff of the 'top eleven PhD programs in the U.S.') into three groups: earth scientists/remote sensors; nature-society; and all others. On average, 89 per cent of the citations to the first group's works were to publications in non-geography journals, compared to 71 per cent for the second group and 58 per cent for the third. In general, therefore, the geographers studied gained more recognition for their published work if it was placed in a non-geographical outlet than if it was accepted by one of the discipline's own journals. To get substantial impact for their work, geographers tend to publish either in specialist, non-disciplinary journals or in the journals of other disciplines. This carries dangers for geography, according to Turner:

> it may promote centrifugal tendencies that fragment the discipline or at least isolate some branches of the discipline. The earth science and nature-society subfields already may publish their best research and the large majority of their research in non-geography journals. Once accustomed to this mode, they may find it easy to abandon the 'mother' discipline altogether. (p. 18)

(Not that it is always easy to 'break in' to another discipline's literature, as Gudgin and Taylor (1979) show.)

Evidence of the relative popularity of specialist and generalist journals is provided by Lee and Evans's (1984) survey of the ranking of 34 different geography journals by American geographers. The respondents used a scale ranging from 5 (excellent) through 4 (good) and 3 (adequate) to 2 (less than adequate) and 1 (poor). The *Annals* ranked second with a mean score of 4.29 from those who rated it and *Geographical Review* fourth with 4.19, but most of the top-rated journals specialize within certain branches of the discipline only. Many of the highly-rated journals were known to only a small proportion of the respondents, however, because of their specialist nature. Lee and Evans looked at differences between groups in their rankings and found, for example, that the *Geographical Review* was more favourably regarded by those who graduated prior to 1958 than by younger geographers – who were also more likely to respond more positively to *Antipode*. Further:

> Physical geographers showed more significant differences in rankings than any other group. In general, they were enthusiastic about physical geography journals but critical of most general publications and journals treating human geography topics. . . . This tendency to view favorably journals in one's subfield may be widespread. Similar results were reported in political science . . . and psychology. (p. 299)

Lee and Evans subsequently (1985) extended their work to cover American geographers' evaluations of both geography journals published in other countries and non-geography journals. Of the 65 journals ranked, the top nine, with mean scores of 4.36 or higher from those who rated them, were all non-geography, physical science journals, followed by *Earth Surface Processes and Landforms, Geographische Zeitschrift* and *Progress in Human Geography.* As in the study of American geography journals, the more specialist outlets are known to a relatively small number of geographers only, and when the rankings are weighted according to the respondents' familiarity with them, then general journals – such as *Canadian Geographer, Transactions, Geographical Journal* and *Tijdschrift* – come to the top. Again, they found that 'physical geographers are more critical of journals, both within and outside their subdiscipline, than are researchers with human geography interests' (p. 402), but more important is the implicit finding that, as Turner suggests, individual specialists within geography departments tend to orient themselves either to the journals of other disciplines or to specialist journals within geography.

General geography journals do not seem to be particularly popular with geographers as places in which to publish their major works and as sources to scour for citable material, therefore. Nevertheless, all geographers in British universities were asked in 1989 to identify their 'best two' publications in the preceding five years. An analysis that I did of those data for the Conference of Heads of Geography Departments found that more of those who listed papers in refereed journals claimed that their best work had been published in the IBG's *Transactions* than anywhere else, and the sixth most cited outlet was the *Geographical Journal.* (The specialist *International Journal of Remote Sensing, Earth Surface Processes and Landforms, Environment and Planning A* and *Regional Studies* occupied second to fifth places.) They were also asked to 'star' any items 'which were considered to be of major significance in the field'. Again, *Transactions* was the most mentioned, suggesting that people tended to put their very best work there (or they believed that those evaluating what they claimed would expect publications in that journal!). However, only 40 per cent of the *Transactions* papers listed were also starred, compared to ten of the 14 published in *Nature*: if you have what you think is a very good scientific paper, it seems, you place it in the country's leading general science journal, not in its leading geography journal.

In a recent book entitled *On Becoming a Professional Geographer* (Kenzer, 1989), two geographers offered advice to new recruits to the profession on how to achieve publication of material in journals. For physical geographers, Butler (1989, p. 91) states that:

> Your duty, as a new professional geographer, is to have a general idea which journals are highly ranked: (1) by the discipline as a whole; (2) by your peers in your specialized subfield of physical

geography; and (3) by your faculty colleagues who will evaluate you for eventual promotion and tenure.

He then notes, with regard to the first point, that:

we all know intuitively the reverence that most colleagues hold for the *Annals*, the *Professional Geographer*, and a few other major journals. To enhance your visibility in the field as a whole, you will wish to publish in this group (regardless of your own opinion about the quality of these journals compared with other geographic or more specialized journals). This visibility helps to establish the regional or national scholarly reputation that tenure and promotion committees look for.

But he then continues:

You also need to build your reputation among members of your particular subfield. . . . These individuals frequently have a different perception of journal quality and ranking than do geographers in general. . . . Physical geographers are, I think, a contrary bunch: we think that many nongeography and interdisciplinary journals are more appropriate for some of our most significant works. You will probably want to consider publishing some of your more narrowly focused, but very significant, research results in specialized, frequently nongeography, journals.

You also have to please your colleagues, who have control over your career advancement, however. Thus 'Do not assume that the high quality of your articles in specialized journals will be apaprent' (p. 92); 'Also remember that many of the so-called specialty journals . . . began publishing only ten or fifteen years ago. Your more sedate colleagues may not be familiar with them'. His advice is 'Learn where your faculty peers publish', and if they believe that the mark of a paper's quality is that it appeared in the *Annals*, then make sure you publish there.

Bourne's (1989) advice to human geographers is slightly less clear-cut, because of the wide range of outlets available and the absence of an 'annual consumer report on journals' (p. 105). He argues that there is an implicit ranking of journals, however:

based on a combination of the size of the audience (that is, the print-run), the latent demand for publication (the backlog or wait time), the awareness level of the readership (the citation indices), the reputations of the editors and previous contributors, the rejection rate (if known), and the apparent thoroughness of the review process.

You need to trade-off speed and ease of having something published against perceived quality and impact. He advises new academics to focus on the latter, on placing 'one or more of their early papers in a mainstream or "flagship" journal within the discipline, or to high quality journals in closely related field. . . . it is usually wise to select a high quality journal over a low quality one, even if it slows down the rate and volume of publication.'

LESSONS FROM OTHERS

Geographers are somewhat schizophrenic in their attitudes towards other academic disciplines. On the one hand, many have strong links with one or more – drawing on their literature, publishing in their journals, attending their conferences, and so on. On the other, they tend not to be involved in the 'academic politics' of those disciplines, and assume that, unlike geography, they are unified homogeneous communities of individuals with common goals and a strong sense of disciplinary solidarity, or academic tribes defending their unified territory, to use Becher's (1989) analogy. They see geography as lacking such communality, as an internally divided discipline which is rapidly falling apart. Recent American writing suggests that it is not alone in that respect, however, and as well as illuminating two other social sciences provides some interesting paradigm exemplars against which the widely-perceived situation in geography can be assessed.

Sociology divided?

Jonathan Turner gave his 1988 Presidential Address to the Pacific Sociological Association under the title 'The disintegration of American sociology' (Turner, 1989), a theme developed further in two recent books (Turner and Turner, forthcoming a and b). His definition of 'distintegration' sounds very much like some of the cases for a fragmenting geography summarized above.

> The term is used here in both an evaluative and a more technical sense. Its evaluative connotations are that American sociology is 'falling apart' and losing organizational as well as intellectual coherence; and most importantly, it has lost its vision as a science of human organization . . . we have lost our vision of what sociology is, what it should produce, and what its goals are.
> . . . more technically. In the context of an intellectual (including scientific) enterprise, what would we mean by 'integration'? . . . I

visualize integration as the situation where there is a high degree of mobilization and control over resources, particularly symbolic, material and organizational resources, while at the same time controlling and regulating how these resources are distributed and used. (pp. 419–20)

In his case, American sociology fails to meet the criteria for integration on technical grounds.

Turner defines the three types of resource in more detail. Symbolic resources 'refer to the capacity of a discipline to display stores of accumulated knowledge, to maintain common definitions of important problems, to agree upon relevant procedures, and to develop . . . theoretical principles about crucial processes' (p. 420). The members of a discipline must identify with its community, shared goals and modes of argument, and agreed standards. By material resources he means the ability to attract students, university facilities, and research moneys. Finally, organizational resources are defined as the 'success with which a discipline (a) can develop coherent patterns of structural interconnection and mutual dependence among its members; (b) create mechanisms of decision-making, administration, and control over its members; and (c) implement effective means for reproduction of members'.

American sociology fails on all counts, according to Turner; it is 'clearly disintegrating' because:

Symbolically, it has no accumulated body of knowledge that goes unchallenged; it reveals no real consensus over important problems; it can articulate few abstract laws, and even those that are articulated will be challenged; and its practitioners do not see each other as members of a consensual community, nor do they share goals, procedures, discursive forms, or standards of adequacy. Materially, sociology has lost students, research funds, and clients. And organizationally, sociology has lost members, while proliferating so many sections, specialty associations, journals, and subfields that structural connections, control, and administration are loose, ad hoc and haphazard. And even in the reproduction of its members, sociology produces such an eclectic mix that relatively few of them have anything in common; those who do share a commonality isolate themselves in network cliques and specialty associations. (p. 420)

This fragmentation is not welcomed as providing evidence of a 'healthy eclecticism and as encouraging exciting debate and discourse'. It will probably not lead to the demise of sociology but will ensure that it is 'not going to have a great impact on the world' (p. 421). Other, more unified, disciplines (he cites psychology, economics, and political science – though for an alternative view on the last, see below) are having this impact 'despite the fact that their knowledge is narrow and often wrong', so that 'Sociology has . . . deeded over areas to practitioners of other disciplines who are far less knowledgeable and qualified than we are'.

Turner's conclusion is that:

> Sociologists want recognition, prestige, money, students and influence, but we do not want to organize, symbolically unify, and materially endow ourselves in a manner that can make sociology a more potent force. . . . We tolerate just about any point of view, no matter how imprecise and noxious. We proliferate a new organization . . . or journal as a means for resolving our differences. And we are colossally smug about all this, even as we whine about our lack of recognition. . . . We can lobby, stamp our feet, and shout until the roof caves in, but few will take us seriously until we return to our original vision: to be a science that can be used to construct more humane patterns of social organization. (p. 421)

He reaches that conclusion through a brief history of the discipline, identifying fragmentation as parallelling growth, because of organizational unpreparedness, both institutional and intellectual. The main lack is a theoretical core to the discipline, and the weak links between theory and practice: 'Indeed, with a few notable exceptions there has now been a significant split between theory as a whole and research, with each going its own way' (p. 429). The answer, for him, is the reconstruction of sociology as 'a science which can accumulate knowledge through tests of theoretical ideas', rather than as a discipline which informs social policy through 'ideological commitments, guesswork, and extrapolation from past experiences' (p. 431). The nature of that science is not displayed, however.

'Separate tables': a view of American political science

Much of what Turner wrote has strong parallels with the views of a contemporary in American political science, Gabriel Almond, who used the Terence Rattigan play *Separate Tables* as an analogy for the fragmentation of his discipline, comparing the loneliness of solitary diners in a second-rate residential hotel to the condition of political science. Almond (1988) admitted that the metaphor may be a little far-fetched, but argued that:

in some sense the various schools and sects of political science now sit at separate tables, each with its own conception of proper political science, but each protecting some secret island of vulnerability. It was not always so. (p. 828)

The result is an uneasiness within political science, not in its body but in its soul.

Almond's analysis of the fragmentation of American political science was a little more formal than that of his sociologist contemporary, though it was impressionistic and not based on technical manipulation of data as in the geographical works discussed above. He identified two dimensions of separation within the discipline (figure 1.7) – ideological and methodological – and divided each into two to provide four quadrants, or different types of political science. These are the separate tables of the analogy.

The methodological dimension is divided into the 'soft' and the 'hard' components. The extremes of the former are characterized by studies described as 'thick description' (Geertz, 1973) – many with an 'almost complete lack of conceptualization, hypothesizing, efforts to prove propositions and the like' (p. 829) – whereas closer to the centre, but still in the 'soft' half, are studies of political philosophy 'more open to empirical evidence and logical analysis. ... A logical argument is advanced, often tested through the examination of evidence, and developed more or less

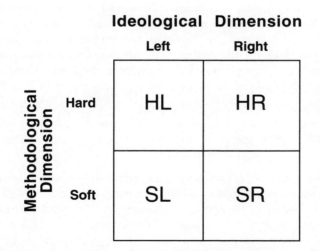

Figure 1.7 The four 'separate tables' of contemporary political science. *Source*: Almond, 1988, p. 829.

rigorously.' The 'hard' end comprises quantitative modelling and analysis.

Almond split the ideological dimension into 'left' and 'right'. The extreme of the former contains what he identifies as four separate groups working in the Marxian tradition – critical political theorists, dependency theorists, world-systems theorists, and 'Marxists properly speaking': all, he claims, 'deny the possibility of separating knowledge from action, and . . . subordinate political science to the struggle for socialism' (p. 829). They are countered, at the other extreme, by neo-conservatives whose preferences include a free economy and limits on the state. Together with the methodological division, this gives the four quadrants of figure 1.7 – soft left, hard left, soft right, and hard right – each of which is briefly characterized.

In Almond's analogy, these quadrants are equated with the separate tables of Rattigan's play. They dominate the discipline:

> The outlying tables in this disciplinary refectory are strongly lit and visible, while the large center lies in shade. It is unfortunate that the mood and reputation of political science is so heavily influenced by these extreme views. This is in part because the extremes make themselves highly audible and visible – the soft left providing a pervasive background noise, and the hard right providing virtuoso mathematical and statistical displays appearing in the pages of our learned journals. (p. 830)

But the noise is created by minorities, he claims, for 'Most political scientists would find themselves uncomfortable seated at these outlying tables' (p. 835). There is a silent majority in the discipline, characterized by 'methodologically-mixed and objectivity-aspiring scholarship' (p. 836), sitting in the shade of the centre, and awaiting its renewed illumination. The occupants of the extreme tables have their disciplinary history wrong.

> Mainstream political science is open to all methods that illuminate the world of politics and public policy. It will not turn its back on the illumination we get from our older methodologies just because it now can employ the powerful tools of statistics and mathematics. (p. 840)

Almond's paper stimulated responses, including a round-table discussion of the issues raised. Gibbons' (1990) response, for example, decried the straitjacket that Almond, and also Eckstein (1989), appeared to be placing on the discipline, and instead lauded 'The current potential for theoretical pluralism . . . [that] would undoubtedly open up new terrain, generate new issues, and recast old ones. Political science would be impoverished if this potential were unintentionally shortcircuited by the adherence to a vocabulary that inaccurately predefines the issues and falsely prejudices the alternatives' (p. 46). Most agreed with the general tenor of Almond's case, however.

The round-table discussion was more concerned with the poorly illuminated central table that Almond identified (Monroe et al., 1990). The convener identified five questions as the core to the discussion:

> Is there a core to contemporary political science? If so, what is it? If not, does its absence matter? Should there be a core? And how important is communication among the different branches of political science? (p. 34)

Her own answers were that a core is necessary, and that communication is vital. She also believed that a core presently exists but found it hard to define – 'I know it. I recognize it when I see it. I respond to it with great excitement and a feeling of being alive. And I'm prepared to follow it wherever it leads me intellectually': it is probably concerned with power and influence, with the authoritative allocation of values, and 'the proper and the actual relationship of the individual to the society in which he or she lives'.

Almond began his contribution by pointing out, as did Turner for sociology, that rapid disciplinary growth has been accompanied by intra-disciplinary fragmentation (though neither argued that the latter was a necessary consequence of the former). He identified individual (American) university political science departments as little more than 'a loose aggregation of special interests, held together by shared avarice in maintaining or increasing the departmental share of resources. . . . in allocating the resources within departments, typical log-rolling and coalition behavior are the order of the day' (p. 35). This comes about, he argues, because of the absence of a disciplinary core; departments comprise groups of workers whose main attachments are to other disciplines, so that they

> cannot decide professional issues on the basis of principle, since they have no principles on which they agree. They can only act jointly on the basis of a common interest in rewards and benefits.

Shapiro agrees, though contending that the situation is even more serious than Almond suggests. He claims that fragmentation is self-generating once established, and that in the case of contemporary political science this situation is exacerbated by both intellectual and institutional causes. Intellectually, there is the lack of a predominant paradigm and a shared agenda, the absence of which

> obviates the felt need to explain or justify the broader relevance of
> one's work. Indeed, in such circumstances inter-disciplinary ambition
> almost inevitably seems risky and grandiose. The more prudent path
> less fraught with the possibility of quixotic failure is toward smaller
> problems or parts of problems, and it cannot be surprising that many
> people opt for it. (p. 35)

And those intellectual reasons are bolstered by institutional ones; departments are at best only confederations, and once the fight for resources
between the parts is over most of the allocation procedures take place
within separate subfields.

The basic reason for the fragmentation, according to Almond, is the
absence of a disciplinary core. The core used to be, and still should be,
the study of political theory, which

> ought to codify the history of the discipline, the development of
> central ideas, concepts and theories. . . . It ought to face toward the
> discipline, interact closely with its various parts, and relate them to
> one another. (p. 35)

But it doesn't. At one stage, all PhD students 'had to know it all, a part
of it better than the rest, but you had to have more than passing familiarity
with it all. You could understand the discourse of all your colleagues, and
were able to judge their performance'. There was unity then, and its
recovery, via political theory, should be among the discipline's highest
priorities.

Others agreed with Almond's diagnosis and prognosis (Monroe et al.,
1990). Gunnell, for example, argued that the demise of political theory led
to the discipline losing much of its critical self-awareness. But some found
the problem's origins elsewhere, in the distancing of academic political
science from the study of 'real politics': as Barber put it, 'the tendency to
exclude the genuinely political from the study of political science – because
it is so often messy, ambiguous, controversial, and in tension with standard
paradigms – continues' (p. 40). To him, the creation of introverted specialist subfields has led to the discipline's marginalization in 'academic slums
and backwaters with names like Afro-American studies, or women's studies', which breeds complacency.

> Above all, what our discipline does not need is complacency. For
> complacency is the enemy of freedom and democracy, and those who
> study what they aspire to be, rather than what they are, quickly are
> transformed from political scientists into ideologists. And, much in

the same way, those who celebrate their liberty rather than practise it are the first to lose it.

Like some human geographers in recent years (for example, Bennett, 1989, Openshaw, 1989, Rhind, 1989), he is arguing for an applied discipline rather than a theoretically-based one, perhaps, following Taylor's (1985) argument, because the times demand it.

Although Almond identified the absence of a disciplinary core for political science, he did not also argue that the 'centre ground' was empty. Quite the reverse; he noted that a majority of the discipline's members are not associated with the visible and audible minorities at the separate tables but rather occupy the shaded central table. Illumination there would presumably draw the discipline together. This point is taken up by Shepsle (Monroe et al., 1990), who develops an alternative metaphor of an archipelago of islands joined by bridges, and surrounding a mainland (see also Johnston, 1983a). An open community would have a great deal of trade crossing all those bridges, and with mutual respect among the various groups. But that ideal is not met. Instead, 'For island intellectuals, off-islanders are either hostile tribes, located on other islands, or the great unwashed, located on the mainland' (p. 41). The various islanders are exporters only, wishing to convert the residents elsewhere but barring imports: their ideas can inform others, but not vice versa.

The problem at the central table, according to Shepsle (Monroe et al., 1990), is that the mainlanders are 'blithely indifferent to, if not ignorant of, the internecine quarrels, both among and within the various islands off their shores'. There is no core, because those at the centre don't seek to integrate the parts. Instead:

> They are mildly amused by the numerous attempts at converting them. They are content to sample the spices and other exotica exported from the island intellectual economies. On the whole, life goes on on the mainland, changing slowly but mostly staying the same. Mainlanders are content in their undisciplines. They share no common church; indeed, many don't go to church at all.

The consequence of this situation is that the island economies decline once their resources are exported, which is typical of export-dominated economies, whereas 'Those that neither import nor export [the mainlanders, or Almond's hidden central table] are quickly ignored in the world intellectual economy'. If multi-directional trade were to develop, however, then vitality would be restored. Comparative advantages would be established and:

The mainland draws sustenance from the islands. . . . The islands prosper at their respective tasks from having frequent intercourse with the mainland. As in so many other areas of life, specialization need not entail isolation, suspicion, or antipathy. Trade and exchange make us all richer.

There is no necessity for a core, therefore, as long as there is mutual respect. Shepsle would like a core, however, based on both political theory and comparative statics and dynamics, in a discipline whose major goal should be 'to determine what will or what should or what actually does happen when relevant parameters – history, culture, institutional practice, economic conditions – change' (p. 42). Its grounding would be in practice.

These analyses of political science, and to some extent Turner's of sociology also, have parallels with what many see as the contemporary situation within geography. There, too, there are functional, philosophical, methodological, and ideological divisions, in a discipline the majority of whose members probably would ally themselves with the shaded central table of Almond's metaphor. And, as a consequence, there are geographers who are actively seeking a focus around which the discipline can be united.

SUMMARY

The data presented in one part of this chapter are quantified indicators of an issue which at least some geographers see as presenting the discipline with a major problem. Membership of specialty/study groups and patterns of citations are evidence in support of the case, but not in themselves sufficient to create a problem. As suggested earlier, those who identify a problem do so on two grounds – political and intellectual – of which only the latter is of relevance here. Fragmentation is seen as a problem because it fails to acknowledge the integration necessary for a proper understanding of much of the subject matter of geography and, specifically for the present volume, of human geography. The argument to be presented below is not for some reintegration of physical and human geography (against which I have argued at length, on intellectual grounds, elsewhere: Johnston 1983a, 1989c) but for a much greater integration of specialisms within human geography than the data outlined above suggest.

It would be presumptuous and wrong to present the general case as entirely novel and one that only I am arguing at the present time. A number of other geographers have been advancing similar arguments in recent years (looking for a core to geography in the same way, it seems, that their contemporaries have been looking for a core in other social sciences). They have illustrated the directions that they believe geographers should take, and why. Stoddart (1987, p. 331), for example, advocates the need 'To build regional geography. To show the distinctiveness of places' and Palm (1986, p. 473) writes of 'the basic strength of geography as a field that seeks synthesis of human action and environmental structure in order to understand the complexity of place'. My case begins with their work and builds on it; the novelty of the present book lies not in its general case but in the details of its argument, in the framework it provides for an integrated human geography focusing on the nature of places. The next chapter reviews other 'integrationist' writings, to set the present work into context. The remainder takes the argument forward.

Note

1 By 1990 there were 39 Specialty Groups within the Association. The biggest (with 962 members: the second largest – Urban geography – had 759 members) was the Group concerned with Geographical Information Systems, a technology developed during the 1980s for the storage, integration, display and analysis of spatial data sets. Its membership increased by 12 per cent over the 1989 figure: only the Groups concerned with American Indians (17 per cent), Cultural Ecology (13 per cent), Cultural Geography (33 per cent), Energy and Environment (28 per cent) and Hazards (22 per cent) grew at a faster rate. Geographical Information Systems was also the largest 'topical proficiency' listed by AAG members on their annual dues form, with 784 (681 in 1989): Urban Geography was next with 822 (824), followed by Cultural Geography with 658 (613).

2

Attempts at Integration

Ever since regional geography was declared to be dead – most fervently by those who had never been much good at it anyway – geographers, to their credit, have kept trying to revive it in one form or another.

D. Gregory, *Ideology, Science and Human Geography*

The fragmentation of geography is not a recent phenomenon, although its extent may have increased in recent decades. Nor are attempts to integrate the various parts of the discipline recent. There have been many cases of geographers who have promoted not only an integrating focus within the discipline but also a centrality for such a focus; see, for example, the essays in Eyre and Jones (1966). To some, integration, or synthesis, has been the hallmark of geography, its true *raison d'être* within the disciplinary structure of academia. The reason for writing the present book is that those cases have largely failed, and that a new attempt to stimulate coherence is needed.

The goal of the present chapter is not to provide a detailed history of the 'integration/synthesis' theme within geography. A brief resume only is presented here, as a backdrop to a more detailed exploration of recent literature which has sought, in a variety of ways, to create a new integrating focus. Most attention is given to those recent works.

REGIONAL GEOGRAPHY: THE HIGHEST FORM OF THE GEOGRAPHER'S ART?

The classic presentation of geography as synthesis has been made, throughout the present century, through the promotion of regional geography, defended by John Fraser Hart (1982) in his Presidential Address to the Association of American Geographers in 1981 as 'The highest form of the geographer's art'. According to Hart (p. 1), and probably to many other defenders of what we might term 'traditional' regional geography (many of them probably sitting at the shaded central table referred to in Almond's metaphor – p. 32):

> Society has allocated responsibility for the study of areas to geography; this responsibility is the justification for our existence as a scholarly discipline. Most people are inherently curious, and they want to know more about the world in which they live – about their home area, about what's over the hill, about what's beyond the horizon, about what's across the sea – and it is our duty, as geographers, to satisfy their curiosity.

Thus geography is about what places are like, or about the variety on the earth's surface. Few academic geographers would disagree with this statement; many would agree with Hart on its centrality to the geographical enterprise. But there is little agreement about how the task is to be undertaken, what the nature of regional geography – the production of 'evocative descriptions that facilitate an understanding and an appreciation of places, areas and regions' (Hart, 1982, p. 2) – should involve.

The need for and importance of regional geography have been argued in the English-speaking world throughout the present century, with origins in the writings of Herbertson and Mackinder (see Johnston, 1984a). The basis of the argument was that the earth's surface comprises a complex mosaic of separate areas, or regions, each with its unique assemblage of phenomena, both 'natural' and created by humans. It is the task of the regional geographer to analyse and promote the appreciation of those unique assemblages, by taking the disparate material of the various sub-disciplines of geography (plus, where relevant, other academic disciplines) and synthesize it into a description and analysis of the whole. Thus to some, such as Hartshorne (1939), there was a close analogy to be drawn between the tasks of historians and geographers: the former synthesize material for 'temporal sections of reality' whereas the latter do the same for 'spatial sections of the earth's surface' (p. 460).

As it developed, regional geography took a particular form in the decades around the Second World War, with characteristics reminiscent of the by-then largely discredited notions of environmental determinism. Regional geography almost invariably synthesized material in a particular format, beginning with details of the physical environment, moving through descriptions of various aspects of the human occupance of the area concerned, and finishing with a definition of its constituent regions. In some cases, the result was exciting and evocative scholarship, particularly those who wrote about the evolution of a landscape, as in Darby (1973) and others with a detailed field appreciation of an area's characteristics, e.g.

James (1942). But in some hands, as clearly illustrated by many of the regional texts that appeared during those decades, the result was a rather tedious catalogue of factual material within an uninspiring framework, which offered no excitement to potential researchers. As such it was roundly criticized in the 1960s. According to Freeman, a relatively sympathetic critic and author of major regional texts (e.g. Freeman, 1960), the works of regional geographers generated only disappointment and 'led many to wonder if the regional approach can ever be academically satisfying' (Freeman, 1961, p. 141).

The result of such wondering about regional geography was that many geographers moved away from it in the 1960s, preferring to focus their interests on the systematic sub-disciplines into which geography is now firmly divided (see Johnston and Gregory, 1984). The general gist of their criticism was trenchantly expressed by Gould (1979) in his contribution to the seventy-fifth anniversary edition of the *Annals of the Association of American Geographers*. He characterized work in the previous decades as 'banal, factual boxes' (p. 139) and 'shabby, parochial, and unintelligent' (p. 140), and averred that 'With the exception of one or two works of scholarship in historical geography, it was practically impossible to find a book in the field that one could put in the hands of a scholar in another discipline without feeling ashamed' (pp. 140–1).

Contemporary defences of traditional approaches

Although many geographers in the English-speaking world paid no heed to the claims of regional geography, especially those socialized into the academic discipline during the 1960s and 1970s when the emphasis on the systematic subdisciplines was at its greatest, others have continued to advance its centrality to the discipline. Their goal has been to revive regional geography as traditionally understood, rather than to advance an alternative interpretation.

One such defence was presented by John Paterson, himself the author of a highly-commended regional geography text (Paterson, 1984), whose focus was 'Writing regional geography' (Paterson, 1974). His definition of regional geography was

> work in which the purpose of the study is to clarify a specific situation in a particular locality; in which, in other words, attention is focused upon the region for its own sake and that of its inhabitants. (p. 4)

He then noted that 'writing successful regional geography appears to be a very difficult task' (thereby agreeing with Freeman and Gould), leading him to argue that as a consequence either the task should be abandoned or its inherent difficulties should be appraised to provide a context for evaluations of what is done. Writing good regional geography faces six major problems, he contended.

1 The limitations of the verbal form for describing the coexistence in space of disparate phenomena (see also Darby, 1962, and, in a very different context, Soja, 1989). This has been tackled in two ways: either

(a) highlighting what are perceived as the salient features of the regional assemblage, and focusing on them; or
(b) prefacing description of an area's regions by a presentation of thematic material reflecting the various subdisciplines of geography.

The latter, he observes, is common to many textbooks, especially those produced in North America where knowledge of the systematic information cannot be assumed and so the regional geographer cannot move directly to a synthesis.

2 The limitations to innovation, if the writer is to convey the essentials of a region – 'to illuminate the landscape with analytical light' (p. 8). This constraint can lead to 'writing by formula', the use of a standard format, which can rapidly lead to uninteresting material.

3 The difficulties of defining regions. All regional geographers have faced this problem, because few regions have clearly-defined edges, which perhaps accounts for the popularity of islands with some of the strongest proponents of regional study (e.g. Clark, 1949, 1959). Clark (1954, p. 95) argued the case for historical-regional geography that 'through its study we may be able to find more complete and better answers to the problems of interpretation of the world both as it is now and as it has been at different times in the past'. It is a problem that can be circumvented by the good regional geographer, however, who can identify and portray the essential divisions of the landscape.

4 The problem of scale. Following resolution of the previous problem, the regional geographer has to determine the scale of analysis, 'picking a level of generalizaiton that will neither drown the reader in detail nor leave him feeling that he still has no clear image of the region' (p. 11). This is clearly a matter of judgement, and success at it indicates that the regional geographer has mastered the craft.

5 The growing shortage of 'subordinate materials'. Given the great expansion in geographical writing over recent decades this may seem a surprising problem; one could have anticipated that regional geographers would be embarrassed by the richness of the systematic studies on which they could draw. Paterson argues differently, however, claiming that the

altered emphasis of much geographical work means that the numerous small-scale local studies produced in the past (such as student dissertations) are no longer being written: regarding American cities, for example, 'Of Cleveland or St Louis we seem to know nothing at all – nothing recent of Pittsburgh or Houston and little, overall, even of Los Angeles. . . . All this means that the task of the regional geographer is becoming harder with the passage of time' (p. 14).

6 The submergence of regional distinctiveness. Regional geography is about local variation, but recent changes in the organization of societies are removing some of that variation, potentially making regional geography obsolete. (This point is also made, though in a very different context, by Peet, 1989.) Paterson believes that argument to be much overdone:

> There has certainly been a reduction in the distinctiveness of local conditions. . . . But it seems curious to recognise this and thereafter to argue that, with the overriding of local differences, all places have now in effect become the same place. . . . All places are manifestly *not* the same place. . . . What the argument appears, at least, to say is that since *some* regional distinctiveness has been lost, the remainder is not worth pursuing. But even if there are geographers who take this view . . . there is certainly no need to be driven into this kind of corner. . . . So long as there are contrasts between region and region, no matter to what they are attributable, there is work for the geographer to do. (p. 16)

Paterson believes that these six problems can be resolved. Regional studies can be developed which are

> less bound by old formulae; less obliged to tell all about the region; more experimental and, in a proper sense of the word, more imaginative than in the past, and covering a broader range of perceptions. (p. 23)

His case is clearly defensive, however, promoting the traditional values of regional geography rather than seeking to make an accommodation with developments elsewhere in the discipline and contributing to them. This is stressed in his argument that

> Its goals are general rather than specific; it is not primarily problem-orientated but concerned to provide balanced coverage, and its aims are popular and educational rather than practical or narrowly professional. Such relevance as it possesses it gains by its appeal, at the lowest educational level, to the two universal human responses of

wonder and concern – that is, wonder about the nature and range of earth phenomena and concern about the lives of those whose circumstances differ from our own. (p. 21)

This is very different from the argument to be developed here, which is not for a separate activity known as regional geography but rather for a geography that is regionally informed – 'we do not need regional geography, but we do need regions in geography' (Johnston, 1990b, p. 139). While recognizing geography's important role within the educational system of catering for the wonder and concern to which Paterson refers, I will be arguing here (as elsewhere: Johnston 1989a, 1989b) for incorporation of the study of place into all aspects of human geography, not the use of material from them to create an overall synthesis. Paterson's educational goals, which form his definition of relevance, can in my argument be achieved in other ways than a more imaginative revival of traditional regional geography.

Hart's (1982) Presidential Address was much more polemical in tone than Paterson's essay, but was oriented towards the same end – the promotion of regional geography as a unifying focus within a discipline performing a major educational function. The first part was a riposte to recent trends within the discipline, and in particular a counter to the attack on regional geography launched in the 1960s (viz Hart's characterization of Berry's (1964) 'reformulation' of regional geography in the terminology and procedures of the 'quantitative revolution' as knocking the whole discussion of the theory of regions into 'a cocked hat' – p. 12). He accepts the need for systematic as well as regional work, presenting the intellectually arrogant argument that

> The integrative nature of geography requires its practitioners to be able to wander blithely back and forth across the boundaries between disciplines. One of the great strengths of geographers, in fact, is their ability to cope with a wide range of variables. They cannot pretend to the status of specialist in more than one or two of the cognate disciplines in the physical sciences, the biological sciences, the social sciences, and the humanities, but any geographer worth the salt has long since lost his amateur standing in all of them. (p. 14)

(One of his predecessors as President argued very differently, bemoaning 'woeful deficiencies' among geographers (Zelinsky, 1975). It is doubtful if Zelinsky would have been optimistic about the changes in the following seven years!)

Hart was concerned about the fragmentation of geography – with 'geographers riding off in all directions with little sense of common purpose or mutual understanding' (p. 17) – and offered them the region as a unifying theme:

> I know of no other theme that is even remotely so satisfying as the idea of the region. All of the different strands of geography converge when we try to understand regions, and we need the concept of the region in order to understand why we need the diverse and variegated systematic subfields of geography. We need both systematic and regional geography, and we hobble along like a one-legged beggar if we try to make do with either. (p. 18)

For geographers themselves, according to Hart, the study of regions not only provides a uniting sense of purpose, it also offers an empirical testing ground for general theories being developed in the systematic subdisciplines.

In addition, Hart was concerned with geographers' societal responsibilities

> Ask whomever you will – the man in the street, the taxpayer, the educated layman, the enlightened citizen, your students, even your colleagues in other departments – what they expect of geography, and to the extent that they have any idea at all they will all tell you that one of the principal goals of geography has been to satisfy human curiosity about how much of what is where and why it's there, about the where and why of places and people, about the land and how people have used and abused it. (p. 19)

So geographers must make sure that they cater for that general audience.

> It is inconceivable that anyone could consider himself educated who does not have a basic knowledge of world patterns – the distribution and interrelationships of the major physical, biotic, political, social and economic lineaments of the contemporary world. Society expects geographers to provide this information in a systematically organised framework that will facilitate an understanding of our large and complex world. (p. 20)

Regional geography provides that framework.

Hart fails to provide a clear definition of a region, however. Instead, he argues that because regions are 'subjective artistic devices' (p. 21), created by the person using them, there can be 'no standard definition of a region, and . . . no universal rules for recognizing, delimiting and describing regions' (pp. 21–2). He quotes Fenneman and Spate to suggest (following Fenneman) that the best region is the one that permits the largest possible number of general statements before details and exceptions become necessary (p. 22)

which implies internal homogeneity with regard to both individual (salient) phenomena and inter-relationships between (salient) phenomena (with the definition of salience being part of the 'subjective artistic device').

The identification of the salient phenomena is clearly a vital task for the regional geographer, and Hart suggests the organization of any regional geography around 'the dominant theme of each region' (p. 23). This will vary between regions, but he believes that three key themes will recur in most, and should therefore receive particular attention:

1 the historical geography, since the present is inherited from the past;
2 the relevant scale for the theme and subject; and
3 the importance of the physical environment.

Appreciation of these three, and their inter-relationships in particular areas, requires detailed field experience, which in turn calls for a lifetime commitment to its study (see also Mead, 1980); from that commitment will also come an appreciation of the values of the people who live there, for 'the regional geographer must cultivate a sensitivity for the relationship between people and place, the attachment of people to place, and the causes of their activities in particular places, which often are highly personal' (p. 26).

This appreciation of regions must be transmitted:

The understanding, appreciation, and interpretation of any part of the world is completely worthless until the insights one has gained have been effectively communicated to others. Communication is the sole purpose of scholarship. (p. 27)

That communication will involve the weaving together of words, maps, pictures and numbers, but not the 'austere and mechanical symbols of mathematics' (p. 27). Good geographical writing about regions, with associated descriptive materials, is called for, because

the highest form of the geographer's art is writing evocative descriptions that facilitate an understanding and an appreciation of places, areas, and regions. Good regional geography should be written with imagination, flair, style, verve, dash, panache, enthusiasm, vivacity, animation, and perhaps even a bit of flamboyance. Above all, it should be fun to read. (pp. 27–8)

Regional geography is not the whole of geography, Hart admits in his final paragraph, but he challenges individuals to adopt a region, to immerse themselves in its culture, to acquire a specialist understanding of it, and to contribute to our store of knowledge about some small segment of this complex, surprising, exciting and utterly magnificent world we live in. (p. 29)

Cultural geography: an alternative approach?

Hart called for geographers to immerse themselves in a region's culture. There is a subdiscipline called cultural geography, which is particularly strong in North America. A brief consideration of cultural geography's potential contribution to the integrating synthesis called for by Hart, Paterson and others is thus provided here.

Cultural geographers receive scathing criticism from Hart (1982), who believes that they should have made 'a special contribution to our understanding and appreciation of the importance of non-economic values' (p. 26); they have not done so, because their work has been 'unscholarly'. Most cultural geographers' major concern has been landscape evolution, and in particular with using human artifacts (such as building styles and place names) as indicators of the cultural characteristics of an area's inhabitants. As recent reviewers put it, they have emphasized 'the relation between a particular landscape and the people who produced it' (Rowntree, Foote and Domosh, 1989, p. 212). The associated field of cultural ecology, according to Butzer (1989, p. 192),

focuses upon how people live, doing what, how well, for how long, and with what social and environmental constraints.

It is especially concerned with the inter-relationships among societies and their environments, with food production a particular theme, and

Cultural behavior is explicitly considered in its functional role, and with respect to material culture as well as the tangible reflections of nonmaterial culture. (p. 193)

Like much other work in cultural geography, it depends on a limited operational definition of culture. Williams (1976) calls it 'one of the two or three most complicated words in the English language' (p. 76), which leads to a focus on material elements in the landscape rather than the wider meaning as 'a particular way of life, whether of a people, a period or a group' (p. 80).

This view of cultural geography has recently been challenged, notably by British geographers (e.g. Cosgrove and Jackson, 1987) whose definition of culture is closer to Williams's cited above than the more narrowly-confined usage typical of American cultural geographers and cultural ecologists. A recent book by one of them (Jackson, 1989) is disappointing, however, in that although it avoids both the geographers' concentration on material artifacts (as in Zelinsky, 1973) and the ecologists' anthropological concentration on 'primitive' societies, nevertheless its own focus is not on what could be described as the 'mainstream' of contemporary urban culture. He draws inspiration from, *inter alia*, the work of the Centre for Contemporary Cultural Studies at the University of Birmingham, and quotes a definition of culture from their writings:

> [Culture is] the way the social relations of a group are structured and shaped: but it is also the way those shapes are experienced, understood and interpreted. (p. 2)

This is very much the argument of the present book (although culture is rarely used, because of its ambiguities and the danger that the preferred usage will differ from most readers' interpretations), including the commitment to Raymond Wiliams' version of cultural materialism. Jackson argues that

> A broader conception of culture is required than one which limits its attention to physical artefacts and landscape features. Breaking out from traditional views of culture and landscape involves an analysis of the nature of ideology and its significance for social relations of production and reproduction. It implies a thoroughly politicized concept of culture and turns attention to areas of social life that have rarely been treated by geographers. (p. 45)

I have no difficulty with Jackson's general argument, or his initial concentration on 'culture as ideology', because it is necessary to appreciate the world view with which people develop and transmit their understanding of their context. But I do criticize Jackson's choice of topics with which to illustrate the general theme: 'popular culture'; gender and sexuality; language and racism; and the politics of language. All are important topics, so the criticism is not of what is included but rather of what is excluded: if culture is to be defined as 'systems of meaning' (p. 2), then we also need detailed coverage of, for example, the world of production and the world of politics, but neither is considered in detail. Only in his final chapter, 'An agenda for cultural geography', does Jackson mention such issues, with regard to patterns of uneven development (pp. 181ff.). Thus while he goes a long way to breaking cultural geography away from what he terms its 'antiquarian phase' – 'limited to the interpretation of historical, rural, and relict landscapes, and to a static mapping of the distribution of cultural traits, from barns and cabins to field systems and graveyards' (p. 1) – he has not provided a clear statement of how cultural geography could integrate the discipline, in a way that regional geography has failed to do, and which the atheoretical descriptive goals of Hart and Paterson ignore.

Summary

The preceding paragraphs have considered only a relatively limited range of material, selected to represent the recently-made arguments for regional and cultural geography. (It could be argued that the selection is unrepresentative, and that I have not identified the salient elements in recent writings. But on Hart's criteria the selection process is central to portraying a region's culture. Those criteria can be modified only slightly to suggest that it is for authors to immerse themselves in the relevant literature and select the salient themes from it; this is what I have done.) With regard to regional geography, the case has been made as follows.

1 Regional geographers integrate the salient material of the systematic subdisciplines of geography, plus that of other relevant disciplines, into a coherent whole. They are thus able to appreciate and use a wide range of scholarly material.
2 Regional geographers use their particular synthetic skills and. their 'genius' for communication (Hart, 1982, p. 28) to evoke the nature of a region for a wide audience, which extends well beyond that of their professional geographer peers. This is geography's most important educational task.
3 There is no standard model to which regional geographers can turn for guidance.

While accepting the foundation of the case – that the world is divided into a complex cultural mosaic, whose understanding is crucial to living in and with that world – I cannot accept what follows. My argument in the rest of this book is not for an integrating regional geography that stands both outside and above the other elements of the discipline, but rather for an acceptance of the nature of the cultural mosaic and of the importance of appreciating local cultures in all geographical (indeed, all social scientific) scholarship. Thus, to repeat a point already made several times, I argue not for the study of regional geography but rather for the study of regions in geography.

With cultural geography, the case reviewed above is that much of what has been presented within that subdiscipline is limited because it seeks to 'read off' culture from material artefacts in the landscape and so is based on a restricted definition of culture itself. Again, I accept the foundation of the case, but argue that it has not been followed through. To appreciate the cultural mosaic in all its complexity, we need to attack the study of cultural geography on a much wider front.

The argument that I am advancing here is not mine alone, though I have developed it in a particular form. Thus the remainder of this chapter reviews, again selectively but representatively, the literature which some characterize as the 'new regional geography'.

A NEW REGIONAL GEOGRAPHY?

There has been an increased interest among human geographers over the last decade in what several have termed a 'new regional geography', which addresses some of the concerns raised by critics of the 'post-regional geography' developments within the discipline since the mid-1950s, but not in the ways promoted by Paterson and Hart. The foundation of this new approach is the recognition that spatial variations are fundamental to the organization of society, with the world comprising a complex mosaic of specific places within which general processes are enacted but whose features cannot be accounted for by those processes alone. Thus the nomothetic analyses of spatial structure which characterized much of the 1960s and 1970s are criticized for their emphasis on general laws which determine spatial patterns; so too are the idiographic alternatives proposed by some, which focus entirely on the specific characteristics of places and fail to acknowledge the existence of any general processes. As A. Gilbert (1988, p. 208) expressed it:

> Confronted with realities too complex to be subsumed under mere generic models, geographers are rediscovering the study of the specific. . . . Their renewed interest in the specific resurrects some of the traditional concerns of regional studies, and thus can be interpreted as a return to chorology. However . . . the regional geography practised since the 1970s is a new one.

That new regional geography has sought a philosophical middle road between, on the one hand, the generalizing excesses of the nomothetic tradition (the 'generalization trap', as I have defined it elsewhere: Johnston, 1985a, p. 335) and, on the other, the excessive concentration on uniqueness among proponents of idealism and associated philosophies (the 'singularity trap'). The literature on that search is large.

The importance of place

Why the renewed focus on the specific? The answer has been offered in a number of essays, with titles as provocative as 'geography matters!' (Massey, 1984b), 'places matter' (Johnston, 1985b), and 'place as histori-cally contingent process' (Pred, 1984). Fundamental to all these arguments is the role of the local milieu in structuring how people tackle problems, both the small and usually trivial problems of everyday life and the large, infrequently met, problems which call for major decisions. That milieu has been given a variety of names, including place, region, locality, and locale. Although the exact terminology is not unimportant, it is not a focus of concern here, and the various words will be used interdependently, though with a preference for 'place', which has neither the association with the 'old' which 'region' carries, the link to Giddens's (1984) structuration theory which exists for 'locale', nor the association with the British ESRC 'Changing Urban and Regional System' programme carried by the use of 'locality'.

The argument for the importance of milieu is provided (and, according to the brief discussion above, could be even more strongly provided) by the subdiscipline of cultural geography. Places differ culturally, in terms of what I will call here the 'collective memory'. For a variety of reasons, some associated with the local physical environment, people's responses to the problems of surviving collectively vary from place to place, at a whole range of scales. How they respond becomes part of the local culture, the store of knowledge on which they draw as they face the problems of survival. They add to that store as they tackle new problems and their success in some cases provides the resources with which to alter their mode of living. That store of knowledge then becomes the inheritance of those who succeed, being transmitted inter-generationally to· others who will modify it as they in turn tackle problems old and new. Thus cultures develop in places and are passed on in places. They are continually changing and have no existence independent of the people who use them (see Duncan, 1980).

Local cultures will also be influenced by wider changes and by practices introduced from without. Some may be expunged, because the introducers want to erase differences, but in most cases they will remain, at least in part, both modifying and being modified by the new; the result is a continuous process of hybridization, one which some (e.g. Peet, 1989) see as increasing in pace and threat as the result of the pursuit of cultural hegemony by economically and politically powerful groups within society.

The importance of culture as place-specific context was stressed in Thrift's (1983) seminal essay 'On the determination of social action in space and time'. Many developments in social theory have occupied one of the poles of the structure-agency dualism, he argued: at the structural end, people are seen as 'bearers of the structure', with their behaviour determined by forces over which they have little or no control (see Duncan and Ley, 1982); at the agency (or voluntarism) end, people are identified as operating unconstrained free will. Neither is convincing. As stressed in Marx's famous phrase, 'people make their own histories but not in conditions of their own choosing': people, individually and collectively, determine how they act, but drawing upon the knowledge and other resources made available to them by their context. That context, their cultural resource, is both enabling and yet constraining.

Thrift suggests that another dualism within social theory is that between the compositional and the contextual. According to the compositional view, people are categorized according to certain perceived salient characteristics, and it is then assumed that all members of a category will act similarly. In the contextual view, on the other hand, the salient characteristic for category-definition is co-residence in an area, and all people from a particular context are assumed to act in the same way. Neither is acceptable, according to Thrift, who argues that the nature of compositional categories is defined in local contexts – in locales in his use of the language of Giddens's structuration theory. People learn what they are (what categories they belong to) and what they should do (how members of their categories behave) at particular times and in particular places – 'Space and time are always and everywhere social. Society is always and everywhere spatial and temporal' (p. 49). Cultures are locally defined and acted upon.

The nature of the intermixture of the general and the locally specific is illustrated by McDowell and Massey's (1984) essay on 'A woman's place?'. The spread of the capitalist mode of production through Great Britain during the nineteenth century was uneven and differentiated in its impact, they argue, because of the economic differences between regions: 'different regions of Britain played different roles, and their economic and employment structures in consequence also developed along different paths' (p. 128). But it was not only in their economic roles that regions differed. A further consequence of the spread of capitalism was that

it disrupted the existing relations between women and men. The old patriarchal form of domestic production was torn apart, the established pattern of relations between the sexes was thrown into question. This, too, was a process which varied in its extent and in its nature between parts of the country. . . . In each of these different areas 'capitalism' and 'patriarch' were articulated together, accommodated themselves to each other in different ways.

Capitalism posed a challenge to the existing systems of patriarchy, according to McDowell and Massey, and the patterns of male dominance had to be reformulated to take account of that challenge.

McDowell and Massey illustrated their argument with four brief case studies of different types of economic milieu: pit villages in Durham; Lancashire mill towns; the 'rag trade' areas of Hackney in inner London; and the rural areas of the East Anglian Fens. Different systems of gender relations developed in each, and these have survived as parts of the local cultures of those areas, long after the reasons for those relationships have disappeared in some cases, such as the Durham pit villages. (For a further excellent case study, see Rose, 1987.) And the nature of those relationships influences later economic and social changes in the areas: as Allen (1984, p. 110) expresses it:

The structure of the gender relations of an area is conceived . . . as the product of a combination of historical layers, in which each layer represents a geographically specific articulation of economic and patriarchal relations. Changes in the wider economic organisation of society, the successive roles that an area has played within a wider national and international division of labour, are shown to structure and restructure the division of labour between men and women. . . . [Furthermore] changes within gender relations are not conceived as a simple effect of economic change – the relation is reciprocal. . . . Subsequent changes in the economic base of an area are, to a certain degree, also a reaction to the established pattern of gender relations laid down within previously articulated layers. The two complex layers combine to produce a qualitatively new pattern of gender relations which will vary in its form from area to area.

This notion of superimposed layers – not altogether different from the earlier concept of sequent occupance (Whittlesey, 1956) – is used by Massey in her seminal work on the spatial restructuring of the British economy (Massey, 1984a) and has been appropriated by Gregory (1989a) in his essay on areal differentiation and postmodernism (see also Soja, 1989).

A parallel case to McDowell and Massey's is Agnew's (1987a) work on political behaviour. Fundamental to his argument is the frequently observed existence of 'the persistence of place-specific and regional voting patterns'

(p. 1) which cannot be accounted for by nomothetic approaches to the study of voting behaviour. These specific features indicate that individual places are not 'mere *instances* of a general process' but rather illustrations of the '*distinctive* social and historical characteristics of places' (p. 2). Agnew's approach to electoral geography (one increasingly adopted by others: Johnston, Shelley and Taylor, 1990) involves focusing on what he terms the hypothesis that 'place-specific social structures and patterns of social interaction give rise to specific patterns of political behavior' (p. 44).

Underpinning Agnew's argument is the assumption that socialization is the mechanism whereby individuals develop their political attitudes. To the extent that such socialization occurs in particular places – which Agnew and others argue that it does, very substantially (see also, for example, Johnston, 1986a, 1986b and Taylor and Johnston, 1979) – then if places differ in their cultural matrices so they may also vary in their residents' political attitudes and behaviour. There may be 'types of places' with similar social structures and, hence, similar political behaviour, but never-theless it is the local milieu, and its cultural content, that is the crucial influence on how people learn to interpret and react to politically-relevant information. In other words, whereas political parties and other organiza-tions (including the mass media) may carry certain politically-relevant information into a large number of places, people in those places may not react to it in the same way, depending on their local culture and the meaning which it places on that information. A party may seek to mobilize voters around class issues, for example, but if subjective interpretations of what it means to be a member of a particular 'objective' class vary between places, then the party's electoral success will vary accordingly.

Agnew sustains this contention with a large number of illustrations, including his own detailed studies of the geography of support for the Scottish National Party. More generally, he identifies seven separate themes which make the argument convincing. First, he illustrates how many histori-cal studies have demonstrated the role of local socialization in a particular context for the development of attitudes within a population; the growth of particular political norms among the working-classes of Lancashire mill towns, reflecting the attitudes of employers there, provides an example (Savage, 1989). Secondly, he draws on the literature regarding the neigh-bourhood effect, which argues that the wider the support for an attitude in an area the greater the likelihood that others there, whatever their backgrounds, will be influenced by the dominant flow of information and adopt the same attitude; this is a process which he terms 'behavioral contagion' (for a critique, see Johnston, 1986a). His third theme builds on the work of French political sociologists who identify types of area with similar patterns of political (usually electoral) behaviour, and from that classification seek explanations of the behaviour in terms of other shared characteristics. This approach was pioneered by Siegfried (1913) and continued by, *inter alia*, Derivery and Dogan (1986). The mode of analysis used is often termed ecological and is frequently based on large-scale statistical correlations; it faces the traditional problem with such aggregate approaches of equating correlation with cause.

Agnew's fourth theme focuses on the local base for changes in political behaviour, as exemplified by the development of a new cleavage in the southern states of the United States after the Civil War (Archer and Taylor, 1981); as Agnew describes it, the events associated with the emergence of massive support for the Democrats reflected 'interests and sentiments that were place-specific' (p. 52). Fifthly, and developing from the previous theme, he argues that 'Most popular political movements and parties, even those wanting to operate at a national level, have their origins in specific places and regions' (p. 53): the rise of nationalist parties in the peripheries of several western European states in recent years provides an excellent illustration of this (as in Scotland and Wales), as does the growth of the German National Socialist Party in the 1920s and 1930s. The sixth theme ties these spatial variations in behaviour to policy outputs: different political cultures lead to different political actions, as illustrated by variations among British local governments in their attitudes to both levels and types of public spending in the 1960s (Sharpe and Newton, 1984). Finally, he points out how local campaigning and other strategies are important in the mobilization of electorates. Quoting the work of Lancelot (1968) on abstention within the French electorate, he notes that spatial variations in turnout rates reflect the combined influences of such factors as local social homogeneity, political integration, conformity of place of work and place of residence and high levels of participation in trades unions. Thus:

> Political mobilization . . . is place-specific, reflecting the history of integration into a national political system, local organizational capacity, and other facets of group formation. (p. 59)

Certain milieux provide much easier environments than others in which to canvass and win political support.

Agnew argues that, despite this wealth of empirical material indicating the importance of place as the local cultural medium within which political socialization and mobilization occur, with spatial variations in political behaviour as the consequence, place is nevertheless substantially devalued in contemporary political sociology (within which he places contemporary electoral geography). Thus:

Contemporary political sociology has inherited from its parent disciplines, political science and sociology, a set of biases against the
possibility that place can be of any significance in modern societies.
It may be of importance in traditional ones, but not ultimately since
they too are fated to modernize. Place, it seems, has no present or
future, only a past. (p. 62)

Geography is also a discipline in which, for a short period in the recent
past at least, place has been devalued. But geography has had little in the
way of close contact with political science and sociology in recent years,
and so the place-perspective which its practitioners have revived has had
little impact on those other social sciences. (As Laponce's (1980) work
cited in chapter 1 shows, geographers have 'imported' ideas and methods
from those disciplines in large volume, but have 'exported' little in return.)
Hence Agnew's desire to pull together his seven themes into a coherent
theory of political behaviour which puts place in a central position. He
claims that 'It is quite remarkable how much empirical political sociology
has suggested the importance of place without its authors making the
connection' (p. 62), and having offered an account for that (see also Agnew,
1989) he then promotes a revaluation of place through case studies of
Scottish nationalism and United States politics. His goal is to develop

> a social theory that provides a linkage between, on the one hand,
> locally structured microsociological arrangements within which
> agency is realized (work, home, school, church etc.), and on the other
> hand, the 'structurally determined' limits set by the macro-order
> through restricting, directing and obscuring agency. (p. 230)

He claims to have provided such a theory

> in terms of the three 'faces' or dimensions of place: locale, location,
> and sense of place. Locale and sense of place describe, respectively,
> the objective and subjective dimensions of local social arrangements.
> Location refers to the impact of the macro-order, to the fact that a
> single place is one among many and subject to influence from these
> others, and that the social life of a place is also part of the life of a
> state and the world-economy. Taken together they constitute the
> defining elements of a place as a historically constituted social context
> for political and other forms of social behavior. (pp. 230–1)

The nature of a new regional geography

The arguments rehearsed above about the importance of place in the constitution of society make many claims which are similar to those advanced by Hart, Paterson and others regarding traditional regional geography. But, as Pudup (1988) argues, the case is much more than that; as she puts it, 'traditional regional geography has not provided conceptual bases of description and, as recent statements [e.g. Hart, 1982] indicate, is unlikely to do so presently' (p. 385). A restructured regional geography must therefore identity its differences from that failure, by emphasizing the strength of its theoretical base and the relevance of its methodological programmes.

The arguments for a 'new regional geography' and its role within the structuring of knowledge do not form a single, coherent whole. A. Gilbert (1988) has identified three separate versions of the case for studying regional specificity in the contemporary English- and French-language literature.

The first version presents *the region as the result of local responses to capitalist processes*. Following the arguments of Massey (reviewed above), Harvey (1982) and others, the theory of capitalism as a mode of production has been substantially extended in recent years by the incorporation of space as an integral element in its dynamic processes. This spatial element is usually represented by the concept of combined and uneven development which operates in three ways (A. Gilbert, 1988, p. 209):

> the process of capital accumulation organized as a net of interwoven partial accumulation processes that have defined territorial bases; the regionalization of the reproduction of the labour force, whose logic relates the region of labour markets to the spatial organization of population; and the regionalization of the political and ideological possesses of domination used to maintain the social relations of production.

Regional differentiation is created, recreated and transformed by the operation of capitalist processes. Investment in fixed capital and in human resources occurs in places, as those with capital seek substantial returns: the pattern of investment creates regional differentiation as, to continue Massey's metaphor, new layers of investment are superimposed on an existing map of regional variation. Over time, that investment becomes less valuable, in turns of the return on capital relative to other potential investments, and change occurs. A new regional pattern is created as capital is shifted to new activities and, in many cases, to new places. Regions, then, are the contexts within which capital is invested, the outcomes of particular patterns of investment, and the contexts within which further rounds of investment are distributed.

The second version of the 'new regional geography', according to Gilbert, portrays the region as a focus of identification. In it

> the region is defined as a specific set of cultural relationships between a group and particular places. It is based on a certain awareness among its inhabitants of their common culture and of their differences from other groups . . . The region is a symbolic appropriation of a portion of space by such a group . . . and is a constituting element of its identity. (p. 210)

The particular concern of this version is the cultural specificity of places, with the residents of regions being tied together through locally-focused communication channels which 'enhance their collective way of thinking about places and space' (p. 211). Culture is interpreted broadly, as discussed above, and involves much more than the artifacts in the landscape that have been the traditional focus of attention for cultural geographers.

The third version identifies the region as a medium for social interaction, the context within which people are integrated, through locally-based social interaction, into collectivities with shared cultures. Many of those who promote this version are strongly influenced by Marxian theory, which concentrates on the general processes that are fundamental to the operation of the capitalist mode of production. To them the region is the arena within which those processes are interpreted and played out. The necessities of capitalism (such as wealth accumulation through the creation of surplus value) are interpreted in regions through the lens of local cultures, with resulting regional variations in the creation of infrastructures within which capitalism can operate and in the various social relationships (at the workplace, in the home, in politics etc.) established to sustain the capitalist operations. There is therefore in each region a combination of what Gilbert (p. 213) terms 'general and region-specific processes'.

These three versions are not independent, and are combined in various versions of the 'new regional geography'. Regions are presented as media of social interaction, through which culture is transmitted and transformed, with which individuals and groups develop a sense of identity, and into which investments are made in the endless capitalist search for profit. Change in any one can induce change in the others in a continuous dialectic process. This leads Gilbert to suggest a 'theory of regional process', which is summarized as regions are not the fortuitous result of any sequence of independent events in a portion of the earth. They are formed through an historically determined sequence which both stems from the social relations specific to the region and allows them to be reproduced. . . . Regions develop from regional social interaction while being both the condition and the outcome of social relations between individuals, groups and institutions in regional space. They are structured in the process of being transformed through these relations of which they are the medium. This dialectical process – the regional conditioning of society and the effects of society on region – creates the internally homogeneous mode of thought and action which distinguishes one region from another. (pp. 216–17)

The outcome is a theoretical approach to region formation 'whereby the region is explained as a structure in constant evolution'.

Theory and method: realism and structuration

The literature just reviewed provides a series of strong arguments for the revival of work by social scientists, and especially by geographers (see the essays in Agnew and Duncan, 1989), which focuses on local variability but doesn't fall into the singularity trap of traditional regional geography with its strong empiricist foundation. A theoretical base is required for such work. As already noted, some see Marxism as providing this: the base argued for in the present book also draws on Marxian traditions and writers, and sets their work in a wider framework provided by the philosophy of transcendental realism and the theory of structuration.

Transcendental realism was developed by Bhaskar (1975, 1979) as a philosophy relevant to both the natural and the social sciences, where its case has been advanced by Sayer (1984, 1985). Fundamental to the philosophy is the recognition of three levels, or domains: the real, the actual, and the empirical. The domain of the real comprises the structures which underpin a society's operations, and which are necessary to it: in a capitalist society these comprise the continued accumulation of wealth through the creation of surplus value gained through selling commodities (goods and services) at prices exceeding their cost of production. If these structures are not operated successfully, then the society will collapse, as hinted by the frequent capitalist 'crises' when the processes of wealth accumulation falter.

The basic processes of a capitalist mode of production are its general laws, therefore, just as the law of gravity is one of the general laws of the solar system. Neither set of laws can be observed directly (you cannot see the law of gravity, only infer it from events that are consistent with its presence), and thus the domain of the real can only be apprehended theoretically, in the abstract. There is a major difference between the general laws of the physical world and those of the social world, however. In the physical world, the laws operate independently of people, who can only manipulate situations in order either to reduce or to accentuate the law's operations. The laws of the social sciences are not independent of people: they are human creations and they can be changed by human action (capitalism could be removed and replaced, for example). Thus the actualization of the laws – putting capitalist processes into operation – is the consequence of deliberate human action, of decisions to do things consistent with those necessities. (Decisions may be made that are inconsistent with the necessities expressed in the laws; these will presumably harm capitalist operations.) Those actions occur within the domain of the actual, and involve people interpreting what they should do in order to keep the system in operation. And the outcomes of those actions are the empirical worlds which people experience day-by-day, such as the built environments created in order for lives to be lived and society to be reproduced.

This basic difference between the operation of laws in the physical and social world is the foundation of what realists see as the fundamental philosophical difference between physical and social science. In both, if the conditions within which the laws operate are held constant, then the same results should occur. In physical science, it is possible to assume that similar conditions can be reproduced, so that repeated experiments can be conducted and conclusions drawn about how nature operates on the basis of large volumes of data. The assumption is not valid in the social sciences, however, because implementation of the laws involves deliberate human action, and that never recurs in exactly the same conditions – if for no other reason than that people learn from the earlier events. (For a development of this case, see Johnston, 1989e.) Whereas physical scientists work with, or can validly simulate, closed systems, therefore, social scientists deal with open systems. For the latter, the philosophy and methods of positivist science are thus irrelevant (as Sayer 1984, 1985) argues, although some extend that argument to methods that are widely used within that philosophy but are not peculiar to it (see Johnston, 1986c).

According to the realist position, therefore, there are *necessary relations*, the basic structures that must be operated, and *contingent circumstances*, the particular situations within which people operate; Kennedy (1979) uses different terminology for the same concepts. As I have set out in more detail elsewhere (Johnston, 1986c, ch. 4), this puts human agents in a central position within a society. They are concurrently interpreting both the necessary relations, the abstract world of the real, and the contingent circumstances, the empirical worlds of the outcomes of actions. (The latter are both concrete – the environment – and abstract – the world of ideas, or 'World Three' according to Bird (1989) after Popper: see also Johnston (1984b), which uses that concept to interpret my own learning within geography.) The operation of a society involves knowing agents both interpreting and creating both necessary relations and contingent circumstances.

But how do they do that? As Walker (1989) points out, transcendental realism provides a framework within which societies can be studied but provides no theory of a society operating within that framework. Marxism provides such a theory, he contends: it articulates ideas regarding the necessary relations of the capitalist mode of production. With that articulation, produced through abstract thinking informed by empirical analysis (Harvey, 1989c), it is possible to appreciate the contexts within which people have created the particular (time- and space-restricted) societies that form the contingent circumstances which are the milieux for learning and action.

How does one study those milieux, not just in the empiricist sense of describing what is there but also in the scientific context of wishing to understand why it is there and how it operates? In pursuing an answer, several geographers have recently been attracted to the theory of structuration developed by Anthony Giddens (1984), in which he draws on Hagerstrand's time-geography concepts (on which see Gregory, 1985; Gregson, 1986). As a theory, structuration seeks to appreciate the roles of individuals as agents operating within both the contexts of local social systems – locales – and the wider social structures of which they are part. Those social structures, encompassing the necessary relations of the realist approach, are human creations: so too are social systems, the local representations of the structures.

Capitalism is an example of a structure, a series of human-created rules for the promotion of human survival. Within the contemporary capitalist world a very large number of overlapping social systems provides examples of how those rules have been put into operation to create the milieux within which people learn about the rules. The differences between the separate social systems result from locally-varying interpretations of the rules, which provide the contexts for the recreation of those differences: as people obey the locally-constituted variants of the rules, so they reproduce them. The rules are both constraining and enabling, therefore: they are constraining because they limit the range of actions open to people – we learn a particular set of interpretations and are not presented with others; but they are also enabling, because people's actions are not determined by the rules, which are only resources on which they draw in exercising their free will to act within the constraints set. Over time, as people act so they probably alter the local social system somewhat (by changing the physical environment, for example, or by altering the dominant set of ideas), thereby changing the milieux – the constraining and enabling situations – within which people are subsequently socialized. Thus systems and structures are always changing, as people are created in milieux, act, and change milieux.

Although the theory of structuration provides a framework for appreciating how contingent circumstances are created and recreated non-deterministically within a mode of production (with most attention focused on contemporary capitalism), relatively few authors have seen it as providing a research methodology (see Gregson, 1986, 1987a). Indeed, Giddens (1990, p. 299) himself, in responding to Stinchcombe's (1990, p. 47) claim that structuration theory is obscure and empirically empty, argues that it is 'relatively autonomous from research'; he has 'never thought of structuration theory as providing a concrete research programme within the social sciences', and it provides 'sensitizing devices' for research rather than empirically applicable concepts (pp. 310–11).

Adherents use structuration theory as an organizing framework within which empirical work can be set. Locales are presented as comprising social systems that provide the contexts within which individuals become 'knowledgeable actors': Sarre et al. (1989, p. 43) define 'knowledgeability' as:

> individuals' ability to infer from the complex and contradictory situations and processes of society both the prevailing rules and the most advantageous strategies and tactics.

The ability to apply that knowledge reflects people's 'capability' to act in the ways that they wish. Their locale is both enabling and constraining, therefore: it is enabling in that it provides them with resources – knowledge – on which they can base action, and it is constraining in that it limits how they can act (both in the knowledge provided and the milieux in which it can be used). As people act, so they reproduce that knowledge, and thus ensure that the social system remains to constrain and enable further actions (their's and others'). But as they act by making choices, so they also may change the local knowledge somewhat, creating an altered set of enabling and constraining conditions for future action. In this way, 'The course of history is therefore neither determined nor open, but a

process in which rules and resources are both reproduced and to some
degree changed' (p. 45).

Can such a theoretical framework be made empirically operational?
Sarre et al. (1989, p. 46) claim that:

> Giddens offers few prescriptions about methods, though he stresses
> that the task is essentially hermeneutic, indeed it is doubly her-
> meneutic: the social scientist must interpret a social reality which
> crucially involves the actor's own interpretations. The way-in to study
> is an immersion in a particular area of society which allows the
> observer to 'get to know' 'how to be able' to act in it. However, this
> must not result in assimilation – the observer must be more aware
> than the actors of the nature of the rules and resources involved and
> of the way particular situations relate to wider structures.

Researchers interested in actions in a particular locale must both appreciate
its social system and understand how it is interpreted by its residents: their
work must both set the empirical domain in its wider context and study
how the actors do the same. This, they argue, involves adopting the realist
approach promoted by Sayer (1984). However, 'the practicalities of what
it means to do realist research are still emerging' (Sarre, 1987, p. 10), so:

> Our response was to utilise familiar methods of data gathering and
> analysis but to seek to interpret the data we collected in the light of
> emerging realist and structurationist views. (Sarre et al., 1989, p. 53)

This type of argument has led some to equate realist research with empiricism (e.g. Bennett and Thornes, 1988), and has stimulated substantial
arguments among those who accept the realist-structurationist case. Those
arguments are clearly illustrated by one major research programme.

Localities

A recent large research enterprise formulated within the context of these
theoretical positions was the 'Localities' – or 'Changing Urban and
Regional System' (CURS) – research programme which originated in Massey's (1984a) work on the changing geography of economic activity in the
United Kingdom. Central to that work was an argument that understanding
the changing locational patterns of industries requires appreciation of the
links between economic and social change. The social structures of local
areas vary in terms of how the labour process is organized, she argued, so
that a comparison of two case study regions showed that

although both . . . are now being drawn into a similar place in an emerging wider division of labour, their roles in previous spatial divisions of labour have been very different; they have different histories. They bring with them different class structures and social characteristics, and, as a result, the changes which they undergo . . . are also different. (p. 194)

(This argument parallels that of structuration theory, without the terminology.) Thus we get a changing industrial geography linked to a changing social geography as new 'layers of investment' are superimposed on those of earlier eras.

The outcome of these processes is areal differentiation, a regional mosaic of unique areas reflecting the interpretations of the actors involved in creating the United Kingdom's changing industrial geography. Massey later generalized this in her essay 'Geography matters!' (Massey, 1984b) in terms of each of the discipline's three traditional concerns – space, environment and place. Regarding space, for example, she argues that

aspects of 'the spatial' are important in the construction, functioning, reproduction and change of societies as a whole and of elements of society. *Distance* and separation are regularly used by companies to establish degrees of monopoly control. (p. 5)

On the environment, she contends that conceptions of the 'natural' are socially produced, and so might vary between areas as a reflection of separate social systems there, whereas with regard to place she contends, in exactly the same way that Giddens does, that general processes can have particular outcomes in unique areas. Thus the study of geography involves unravelling the unique and the general (p. 9):

the fact of uneven development and of interdependent systems of dominance and subordination between regions on the one hand, and the specificity of place on the other

is thus a central concern for the discipline.

Massey illustrated her general contention through a number of case studies in *Spatial Divisions of Labour* (1984a), and provided others in the essay on women in the labour force referred to earlier (p. 51). Arising out of this work, she was instrumental in the development of the major 'Localities', or CURS, research initiative, financed by the British Economic and Social Research Council. This was introduced by the coordinator (Cooke, 1986) and summarized by him in a volume which reported on the programme's seven case studies (Cooke, 1989a). The substantive focus of the research was the spatially varying processes of economic restructuring taking place in Britain during the 1980s. Thus (Cooke, 1989a, p. ix):

> The overall objectives of the programme were to explore the impact of economic restructuring at national and local levels, and to assess the role of central and local government policies in enabling or constraining localities, through their various social and political organizations, to deal with processes of restructuring.

(The terminology is direct from Giddens.) In addition

> an important dimension of the research involved seeking to establish the conceptual status of the idea of 'locality' by taking account of a wide range of social scientific theory and research.

The term 'locality' was chosen after both the traditionally-used community and Giddens's preference for locale were rejected. As Cooke expressed it (1989a, p. 10):

> There is a gap in the social science literature when it comes to a concept dealing with the sphere of social activity that is focused upon place, that is not only reactive or inward-looking with regard to place, and that is not limited in its scope by a primary stress on stability and continuity.

'Locale' was rejected because its spatial scope is vague; it suggests a passive rather than an active context for action, it was claimed, and lacks any specific social meaning. A locality, on the other hand, is

> the space within which the larger part of most citizens' daily working and consuming lives is lived (p. 12)

and in which their citizenship rights are defined.

At the end of the summary volume, Cooke argues that the seven case studies sustain his earlier contention regarding the crucial role of localities in the restructuring process and in the creation and recreation of uneven development. They illustrate, he contends:

> the argument that the relationship between the different scales is not simply a one-way street with localities the mere recipients of fortune or fate from above. Rather localities are actively involved in their own transformation, though not necessarily as masters of their own destiny. Localities are not simply places or even communities: they are the sum of social energy and agency resulting from the clustering of diverse individuals, groups and social interests in space. They are

not passive or residual but, in varying ways and degrees, centres of collective consciousness. They are bases for intervention in the internal workings of not only individual and collective daily lives but also events on a broader canvas affecting local interests. (p. 296)

This conclusion, and the path towards it, has been the subject of considerable debate, much of it unfavourable on conceptual grounds.

An initial critique by Neil Smith (1987) argued that the CURS programme as formulated was likely to be submerged in a morass of statistical information and contained within it the potential for being no more than a repeat of the earlier empiricist studies of particular places 'which deliberately examined individual places for their own sake, and [did] not attempt to draw out theoretical or historical conclusions' (p. 62). He was also concerned about the vagueness of the spatial scale in defining localities. Nevertheless, he applauded the attempt to blend theoretical analysis with local understanding, which Cooke (1987) welcomed; the empiricism charge was refuted by Cooke, who argued that the objective of the CURS initiative was 'theorised interrogation' (p. 75) of available data.

Cochrane's (1987) critique wondered whether CURS was 'just a cover for structural Marxism with a human face, or . . . the cover for a return to empiricism with a theoretically sophisticated face' (p. 355). He concluded that the programme contained within it the danger that as a guide to political action it could suggest that local struggle might suffice (what he terms 'micro-structuralism') rather than the realization that parts cannot readily be isolated from wholes. Gregson (1987b) was perhaps even less sanguine, arguing that the theoretical purpose of undertaking the seven case studies was far from clear, thus making the likelihood of falling into the empiricist trap high: without a properly-articulated theoretical core 'CURS simply replicates the mistakes of previous local studies; with such a core it could be so much more' (p. 370). Beauregard's (1988) criticism is that the programme lacks any clear directions for practice, for using the radical theory to achieve social change, whilst Jonas (1988) sustains the 'drift into empiricism' argument.

One of the fullest critiques is Duncan's (1989), who accepts that the concept refers to something important – spatial variability and specificity – but concludes that 'the locality concept is misleading and unsupported' (p. 247). Elsewhere, in Duncan and Savage (1989, pp. 202–4), he concludes that it is 'confused, unsatisfactory, and largely redundant . . . a mystification'. He agrees that 'space makes a difference', in three ways. Firstly, social processes are constituted in places, which may differ because of previous 'layers of investment' (to use Massey's term). Secondly, actions take place locally and so can vary spatially. And, finally, spatially-varying actions can create spatially-varying contexts. But for him, the concept of locality implies 'social autonomy and spatial determinism' (p. 247), both of which he rejects. And he is unconvinced by the implicit claim that local differences are particularly important, relative to more general processes. Thus (p. 248):

> Locality is . . . only important if and when locality effects are part of the causal group explaining any event. And locality may well not be important

which implies a verdict of 'not proven'. Cooke's (1989b, p. 272) response (to the Duncan and Savage paper in particular) was trenchant.

> Local social processes are clearly an abiding feature of contemporary social life. Duncan and Savage's injunction to ignore them and settle on the structural level, supra-local, supra-national or whatever, in order to describe spatial variation in terms which deny agency to the social groups comprising localities, is both dated and redundant

And he concludes,

> 'Locality' can be seen to be a fascinating, complex concept of considerable value to geographical theory and empirical research.

Cooke (1990) continued arguing his case in a later book which set the localities material within the debates concerning postmodernism, a literature that has interested a growing number of geographers in recent years, e.g. Dear (1988), Gregory (1989b), Harvey (1989b), and Soja (1989). A basic tenet for postmodernists is a belief that the preceding 'modernist' project, with its emphasis on the search for 'grand theory' (or 'totalising discourses') is fundamentally flawed: the alternative, as Cooke (1990, p. 94) expresses it, comprises 'local narratives ungoverned by general rules, critical of the grand institutions and structures of thought which are expressive of modern society'. If there is no general theory through which we can appreciate the empirical world, but only a large number of local theories – because thought and action are locally determined – then, Cooke argues, the Localities programme and the view of society that it represents can justifiably be located within this emerging strand of social thought. Modernism – within which the positivist spatial science of 1960s and 1970s human geography can be located – neglected the local dimension; postmodernism 'shifts the pivot of creativity from top down to bottom up' (p. 115). This is illustrated, he argues, by the different ways in which restructuring has occurred in the seven case study areas of the CURS research programme. In Swindon, for example, the attitudes of local politicians (characteristic of the benevolent paternalism found in many working-class Labour-led local authorities) and senior local government officers were crucial to two phases of restructuring as the former railway town was converted first into a 'Fordist' manufacturing centre and then, three decades later, into a financial services complex. (See also Bassett, 1990 and, for a comparison, Seyd, 1990 on Sheffield.) These decision-makers were able to benefit from local advantages, such as the transport system, but it was their interpretations of the situation, drawing on the local milieu, that led them to act in that way; others, in other contexts, acted differently.

A WAY FORWARD?

So how might human geography be reorientated (I hesitate to propose something as grand as a restructuring) in order to overcome the problems of fragmentation discussed in the first chapter? Do the approaches outlined in this chapter offer a way forward? There are three possibilities according to the authors discussed here:

1 a return to 'traditional regional geography';
2 the creation of a 'new regional geography'; and
3 a focus on 'locality'.

My clear preference is for the third, but not in the form presented by Cooke and others. I argue instead for a regional perspective that informs all geography, for an approach in which we do not give privilege to one subdiscipline (presumably called regional geography) but rather insist on the study of regions in all geography: we do not need regional geography, but we do need regions in geography.

This conclusion was reached after an analysis of what the study of regions in geography should demonstrate, set out in six points, presentation of which follows the earlier presentation in Johnston (1990b, pp. 130–2).

1 The creation of regions is a social act; regions differ because people have made them so. The differences may be underpinned by differences in the physical environment, but similar physical environments can be associated with very different human responses and similar patterns of human organization can be found in very different physical milieux.
2 Regions are self-reproducing entities, because they are the contexts in which people learn. They provide role models for socialization and

they nurture particular belief sets and attitudes, if not values – on the difference between attitudes and values, see Scarborough (1984). People are made in places; if places differ, so will people.

3 The self-reproducing features of a region are not deterministic, and no regional culture exists separately from the people who remake it as they live it: regional culture should not be reified (Duncan, 1980). Change can be brought about by one or more of the need for people to respond to new stimuli (physical and/or human), contact with people from other regions, and the determined actions of individuals who wish to promote change. Changing regions are also human creations.

4 Within a capitalist world-economy, regions are not autonomous units whose residents have independent control over their destinies. People in places, acting in what Taylor (1982) calls their 'scale of experience', are subject to the demands of an essentially placeless economic system, which Taylor calls the 'scale of reality', the source of many of the stimuli to which they must respond.

5 Regions are not simply the unintended outcomes of economic, social and political processes but are often the deliberate product of actions by those with power in society, who use space and create places in the pursuit of their goals. Thus regions are resources to be manipulated in the creation, recreation and restructuring of the contexts in which people are made.

6 Regions are not only containers for existence but also potential sources of conflict.

The remainder of this book develops the argument laid out in those six points. Chapter 3 looks at ways in which places can be characterized, providing the framework for analysis which is sadly lacking from so much of the work on localities. Chapters 4 and 5 exemplify that framework, with case studies of the National Union of Mineworkers' 1984–5 strike in Great Britain and of the southern states of the USA. In chapter 6, the argument of points 5 and 6 is taken up, with a discussion of territoriality, bounded places, and geopolitical conflict. Finally, by way of an epilogue, chapter 7 illustrates the restructuring of a place, and the attempted destruction of places within it, in the recent political history of the United Kingdom.

3

Approaches to the Study of Place

> We all know in very broad terms that locality is somehow bound up with social relations and social change. The more difficult question, however, is precisely *how* locality 'matters' in social, economic and political terms.
>
> P. Dickens, *One Nation? Social Change and the Politics of Locality*

The previous chapters have established that human geography is fragmented and lacks a core, like several other contemporary social science disciplines, and that some human geographers are promoting the recreation of a form of regional geography to provide a needed integrating core. The remainder of this book explores what the nature of that core might be. As stressed earlier, I am not arguing for a revived regional geography *per se*, but rather for 'a regional perspective that informs all geographical activity' (Johnston, 1990b, p. 135). Hence my preference for the term 'place', which has not been promoted by any of the other writers.

In this and the next two chapters I develop, largely through case study material, a framework that can be used which employs place as a central concept in geographical analysis. In doing so, I offer no rigid model to be used whatever the context. Rather, my concern is to identify the salient characteristics of a place that might be called upon, singly or together, in any analyses which seek – like those in chapters 4 and 5 – to understand the nature of spatial variability and spatial change. One of the major difficulties with much of the literature on regional geography – both the 'traditional' and the so-called 'new' – is not only that no methodology is provided but also that the main differentiating characteristics of places are not identified. The intention here is to essay such an identification and therefore move beyond the empiricism with which the Localities programme has been charged.

The task being undertaken here is similar in many ways to Paasi's (1986) exploration of the parameters of a region. He contends that geographers have undertaken no profound analysis of two of their central concepts – region and place – between which he considers there are important differences. A place is an individual construct, he claims, whereas a region is a collective one – thus:

> A region is mediated in our everyday life in the form of various symbols, which are the same for all individuals in the one region, though the meanings associated with them will always be construed personally on the basis of the individual's life situation and biography ... though the regions of a society obtain their ultimate personal meanings in the practices of everyday life, these meanings cannot be totally reduced to experiences that constitute everyday life, since a region bears with it institutionally mediated practices and relations, the most significant being the history of the region as a part of the spatial structure of the society in question. (p. 114)

The nature of a region is interpreted individually, therefore, but as an historically-created entity it is more than just one person's interpretation. Paasi separates the two concepts in the following way:

> it is the *place* where an individual reproduces his material and intellectual existence. This is structured through participation in social actions and in interaction with other people and institutions, and through the meanings given to these. One's place ceases to exist when one dies. The *region*, on the other hand, is an institutional sphere of *longue duree* representing one specific dimension of the spatial structure of the society. Although a region is a contingent historical process within the society, just as is a place for an individual, the former, because of its institutional role in the society, manifests itself in a more permanent structure.

(See also Entrikin (1991), who distinguishes between the terms place and region on the scale criterion: the region is the larger unit.)

Paasi then investigates what he terms the 'institutionalization of regions', the process by which they are created, which involves four stages in the formation of 'structures of expectations' that embrace both the physical and the cultural characteristics of a region. These

> collective, institutionally mediated roles expressed in the structures of expectations are essential as for the transformation of regions into places [i.e. collective concepts into individual 'action spaces'], centres of feeling of belonging to time-space specific, more or less abstract reference groups or communities. (p. 123)

Following Pred, e.g. Pred (1984), he argues that one of the most important of those collective qualities is language – 'the medium through which speakers and hearers realize certain fundamental demarcations'. Structures of expectations also legitimate the sense of belonging to a region, often ideologically, and 'are essential for establishing the past (and also the future) as a common frame of reference'. Such a creation of regional consciousness 'can take shape *only* after there are institutions capable of reproducing and maintaining them'.

The first of the four stages in the creation of regional consciousness is *the assumption of territorial awareness and shape*. Fundamental to this, Paasi argues, is the identification of regional boundaries which provide 'the foundation upon which the conceptual shapes (the manifestations of symbolic orders) and institutions that commence the process of maintaining and reproducing the existence of the region will be constituted' (pp. 124–5). A clear spatial identity is necessary to a region's existence.

Within the defined regional territory occurs *the development of conceptual (symbolic) shape*, which promotes the inhabitants' regional consciousness. Social institutions associated with the territory are crucial to this, as are other consciousness-creating acts such as the coining of a regional name. Symbols are very important in this stage, and names can provide a strong link with a perceived regional past.

The third stage involves *the development of the sphere of institutions*, which Paasi sees as simultaneous with the second – 'the emergence of institutions is naturally linked with the increasing employment of the name and other territorial symbols and signs of the region' (p. 126). Both formal (e.g. the mass media and educational systems) and informal institutions are central to this stage, creating a sense of regional membership for the inhabitants:

> The sphere of institutions undertake to maintain the process which aims at reproducing the idea of a common consciousness among the people. The reproduction of symbolic dimensions of space consists of the *production* and *consumption* of space, which manifest themselves as being interwoven institutional practices in the field of *communication*. (p. 126)

Nation-states are thus very important, especially in the education system which they provide (or require to be provided) and its role in the creation and reproduction of an ideology.

The final stage involves *achievement of the region as an established part of a regional system and regional consciousness*, when it has 'an established, although not necessarily administrative, status in the spatial structure of the society and its social consciousness' (p. 130). From then on, its structure of expectations ensures continued reproduction of the region's identity,

although both external and, less likely, internal forces may conspire to
destroy it.

According to Paasi, therefore, a region is an institutionalized division of
space, and is more than the myriad individual places which come and go
in the lives of their creators. A place is structured 'on the basis of one's
lifeworld and its meanings' (p. 131) but a region

> comes to individuals through institutional practices, though the role
> of region is not inevitably manifested in the lifeworlds of all individ-
> uals. Hence the essence and history of a region is connected with
> the biographies of individuals through the agency of the sphere of
> institutions, which again is reproduced in the everyday practices of
> individuals.
>
> Regional identity is a theoretical category which as such is not of
> much obvious importance for one's everyday life. The concept weaves
> together elements that are significant in the institutionalization of a
> region and which are represented in its structures of expectations,
> while the latter, for their part, operate as a framework for social
> classification among the inhabitants and those living outside the
> region.

Of course, the identity of the region and the regional identity of its
inhabitants may not coincide: what outsiders identify as a particular region
may not have the same contours as the insiders – on the outsider's and
the insider's view, see Johnston (1988a, 1988b). But the identity which a
region gives – through collective institutions such as its legal, educational
and political systems – cannot be provided by individuals alone, through
the meanings which they attribute to their lifeworlds: 'In this respect
the regions contain an explicit collective dimension which has relative
independence, being continually reproduced by institutionally embedded
power relations that influence the socialization of individuals' (p. 139).

In many ways, the framework developed in this and the following
chapters is consistent with Paasi's definition of a region rather than his
usage of place. However, region has a history as a concept within geography
and it is better to use a new term than to try and alter the definition of a
long-established one. Hence my preference for place (though region is
occasionally used as a synonym!) because of its relative neutrality in the
history of geography. To me a place is a set of institutionalized relationships
of the type described by Paasi.

THE BASES FOR DIFFERENTIATION BETWEEN PLACES

A long-standing contention among geographers has been the importance – if not uniqueness – of their discipline as a bridge between the natural and the social sciences; to some, its *raison d'être* has been its integrating function. I have argued against that elsewhere – Johnston (1983a, 1986d, 1989c) – on the grounds that the two types of science are incommensurable, and thus cannot be integrated. This does not deny the importance of studying both human use of and interference with (if the two are different) physical systems, nor of investigating the role of nature in social systems: quite the contrary. But the good work that is done in those two areas does not integrate the two very different types of science: the claim that geography is an integrating discipline is both unsustainable and diversionary. What is important in the present context is to build an appreciation of environmental variations into our understanding of why places differ.

Environmental variations are fundamental to the creation of the complex cultural mosaic that comprises human occupance of the earth, but their existence is insufficient to account for that mosaic. To continue with the use of terminology from structuration theory, the environment is both enabling and constraining: it presents humans, individually and collectively, with opportunities, and it also faces them with constraints. Crucial to an understanding of the human mosaic, therefore, is appreciation of how the opportunities have been identified and acted upon, and how the barriers posed by the constraints have been tackled.

Although the physical environment is important to individuals and communities in a variety of ways – as prospect and refuge, for example (Appleton, 1975) as well as an aesthetic resource – its main function by far is as the foundation for human survival. The environment is the source of all ingredients for human subsistence – food, water, and shelter; how it is perceived, and how its potential as a resource base is realized, are the foundations of the contemporary human occupance of the earth, even if those foundations have been substantially reworked many times, in many places. If we accept Massey's (1984a) argument regarding 'layers of investment' as the mechanism through which places are constantly being remade, then we are similarly accepting the longer-lived view of the landscape as a palimpsest, a parchment on which several (perhaps many) layers of human occupance have been laid, with the nature of each layer influencing that of the next.

The earth is the resource base for human life; its nature is fixed by physical processes – which can be altered both endogenously (within the physical system) and exogenously (by human action) – but identification of aspects of the environment as a resource is a human creation. With foodstuffs, for example, there has been a great deal of trial and error over many millennia to determine whether a given animal or plant provides desirable food. In addition there has been considerable cultural experimentation, with the result that what is considered desirable in some places is not in others, where its consumption may indeed be taboo. Different cultures have their own interpretations of the natural environment and its utility for them in the processes of survival and reproduction.

Human cultures are produced and reproduced during the creation, recreation and alteration of these interpretations. They are communal answers to the problem of human survival, a problem which requires collective solutions because, in the final resort, individuals cannot ensure the reproduction of the species even if they can, for a finite period, ensure their own. Each culture has its own 'agreed' way of surviving, which involves a social organization constructed to ensure that sufficient food, drink and shelter is obtained to allow reproduction for as many members of the cultural group as possible. Not all aspects of the organization may be directly related to the process of subsisting, but together they form a collective memory which provides both opportunities and constraints on which members of the culture draw as they live their daily lives. For much of the time, the culture may be unaltered, as well-tried routines are reproduced, but when new problems face the community – after a bad harvest, perhaps – then the collective resources have to be drawn upon to provide a response to the new situation.

Over the millennia, cultures have changed very substantially as they have learned to cope with environmental vicissitudes. More importantly, through good fortune and good management – as they played out their 'games against nature': Gould (1963) – some cultures were able to control their environments sufficiently that their level of living far surpassed that needed for simple subsistence – even though not all survived. The so-called 'hydraulic civilizations' depicted by Wittfogel (1957) provide early examples of such 'successful' cultures, which nevertheless eventually failed. With the development of strong, authoritarian, state-like bodies, human control over arid and semi-arid areas was extended through irrigation works, whose construction and maintenance called for an organization which Wittfogel (1957, p. 136) characterized as 'benevolent in form and oppressive in content.' Where the control failed – largely, he argued, because the autocrats lost control of the bureaucrats who carried out the day-to-day organization – the cultures collapsed.

Successful cultures needed room to expand, because their success usually led to population growth which eventually was too great for the local environment to sustain. Expansion could take a number of forms, as exemplified not only in the differences between, for example, Spanish and English colonization of the 'New World' but also between different English colonies. Contrast, for example, not only the settler colonies of Australia and New Zealand with the 'temporary intruder' colonies of the Indian subcontinent, but also the plantation colonies of the southern states of the USA with the communal colonies of New England. Thus over time, and at a variety of scales, cultures were mixed and accommodations were reached (often between groups with unequal power), producing hybrid forms. Such mixing restructured the complex mosaic of world cultures.

CREATING A STRUCTURE FOR ORGANIZING SUBSISTENCE

The material in the preceding section will be seen by some as both uncontroversial and trivial, but it forms a basic backcloth for the argument being developed in this book. Places differ not simply because their physical environments differ but also because, for a variety of reasons, people have responded differently to the opportunities and constraints that those environments offer. The nature of their responses is important, because they provide the cultural resources within which societies 'develop'. (Note, for example, Hechter and Brustein's (1980) argument as to the importance of the feudal mode of production in parts of western Europe – as against the sedentary pastoral and petty commodity modes elsewhere – to the transition to capitalism appearing there first.) In appreciating the contemporary cultural mosaic, therefore, we must appreciate its foundations in the accommodations between communities and their environments in the creation of social structures as 'machines for living'. Such material was part of most introductory courses in British geography degree programmes a few decades ago – using texts such as Forde (1934) – but today the topic is much less studied, though there are notable exceptions such as Brookfield's collaborative work with anthropologists in Melanesia (Brookfield and Brown, 1963) and Watts's (1983) detailed study of northern Nigeria.

Those 'machines for living' were many and varied, differing to large and small degree over distances long and short. There was little homogeneity over even relatively small areas such as the island of Great Britain where the developing agricultural practices required systems for allocating land between uses and/or users. Baker and Butlin (1973, p. 619) concluded from their major edited survey of those field systems that 'As the number of local studies has increased, so to some extent has the difficulty of attempting generalizations and it becomes increasingly clear that no single interpretation will exactly fit all the known facts'. They quote Postan's (1966, p. 571) conclusion that:

> It is even more dangerous to generalise about the organisation of medieval agriculture than about its physical and demographic background. The rules and institutions which regulated medieval agriculture and ordered rural society differed in almost every particular from place to place and from generation to generation. So great were the variations that no student of medieval agriculture would nowadays dare to assemble all the medieval agrarian institutions into a portmanteau model capable of accommodating the whole of England during the whole of the Middle Ages.

(Baker and Butlin wryly note that, paradoxically, this statement itself is a generalization.) The same resources were drawn upon in a myriad slightly different ways, producing a complex cultural mosaic. At the larger scale, this involved substantial differences in the basic organization of land use, with the open field system predominant in the 'Midlands' only; at the smaller, local scale, there were substantial variations, as illustrated by Thirsk's (1973) survey of the East Midlands in the same volume.

The importance of variations in the physical environment as a foundation for those differences is stressed, at both scales. Locally, for example, Thirsk (1973, p. 262) notes that 'The nature of the farming economy in each agricultural region gave a certain bias to its bylaws; communities inhabiting the same kinds of countryside upheld some regulations with great fidelity, while others did not'. Thus:

> In short, we may recognise three sources for the similarities in bylaws of common field farming in the East Midlands: first, a pattern of intermingled parcels of land involving all classes of tenants and lords; second, some commonly accepted principles governing social life, which may fairly be regarded as the necessary outcome of the first proposition; third, a similar physical environment which influenced the choice of farming objectives; and last, similar economic pressures arising from the basic human need for food, and developing along similar lines, as the market in agricultural produce expanded and communities were driven to pursue change in the same general direction. (p. 263)

The last point indicates the importance of the expanding market system and the transition from feudalism to capitalism as homogenizing forces in the later reduction of local differences. As she notes, 'economic rationality led in neighbouring villages to the creation of rules of cultivation which sufficiently resembled one another for us to classify them as a system' (p. 273). Such standardization and rationalization of diverse local practices was promoted by lawyers who were the agents of change.

At the wider scale, Baker and Butlin point to two important influences which the physical environment had on the developing cultural mosaic based on farming patterns: its influence on the pace and timing of settlement and colonization, and its influence on the amount of wasteland available, which acted as a safety valve and meant that no provision for grazing need be made within the settlement itself (1973, pp. 630–1). Nevertheless, they counter that the physical environment should not be considered a constant, even over the relatively short period of agricultural settlement in Great Britain, in part because of climatic change and its consequences, in part because of changes wrought by land use practices, and in part because of changed perceptions of the environment; see also Prince (1971), and Blaikie and Brookfield (1987).

One of the crucial differences between areas in the organization of land use, and hence in the recreation of social systems through the processes of structuration, according to Baker and Butlin (1973, p. 631), has been 'the procedure whereby land in all its forms – parcels and fields, farms and estates – passed from one generation to the next.' These practices, they further note, 'varied not only from region to region and from time to time but also from social class to social class, so that their impact on field systems and rural settlement patterns is complex and not easy to determine.' Changes in these practices were stimulated, in many if not all cases, by the need to respond to population pressure; once again, the same problem may have invoked a different response in different cultural milieux.

Changing land ownership

The creation of a pattern of land ownership, through field systems, whereby some if not all land was held individually rather than collectively, was a 'solution' to the problem of how to organize the production of the means of reproduction. Yet at the same time it created a potential new 'problem' with regard to how ownership of land was to be transferred. The development of different methods of handling land transfer, especially inter-generational land transfer, introduced further variations within the cultural mosaic.

This cultural variation is well-illustrated by the land tenure systems established in the islands of the South Pacific. As Crocombe (1972) points out, agricultural practices across this widely-scattered area of small islands were in many ways comparable at the time of the European invasions. There were no metal tools – only stone, wood and bone were used; there was no written language and thus recording of land rights and rules for their disposal; there were no cereal crops, and limited means only of storing foodstuffs; and so on. But within this apparently uniform pattern of land use were a number of local variations, including those pertaining to land transfer.

Inheritance was the normal form in which individual rights over land (or other resources, such as water) were obtained: sale of land was unknown in both Polynesia and Micronesia, and in most parts of Melanesia too. Similarly, gifts of land were rare. The main method of obtaining rights was through inheritance, but the operation of inheritance systems varied: in Polynesia and mainland New Guinea it was predominantly patrilineal; in Micronesia it was predominantly matrilineal; and in Melanesia outside New Guinea there were both matrilineal and patrilineal systems, as well as others that were either ambilineal or bilineal.

> But nowhere was any one principle of inheritance applied exclusively, and nowhere was inheritance the only means of transferring land rights. Such terms as patrilineal and matrilineal refer to ideal patterns which apply in the majority of instances. But a man may have no son, or he may have too many among whom to share his limited lands and principles had to be modified continually to meet particular circumstances. As Nayacakalou (1961, p. 125) has said, 'the people in a village cannot be bothered with neat pigeonholes – what they are concerned about are the exigencies of their daily lives'. (p. 227)

In other words, the small island communities modified their rules as conditions required, and such modifications became part of the collective cultural inheritance, to be called upon when new situations arose. Because those rules were not written, memory was crucial – and with the passage of time the rules were likely to be further modified, reflecting imperfect recollections of what had been done before. Thus even if separate communities had begun with similar ways, it is likely that the processes of structuration would lead to divergence over time.

Contact with alien, European, societies initiated changes in these land tenure and inheritance arrangements. The introduction of Christianity, and its widespread adoption by the islanders, brought a predominantly patrilineal system into conflict with the matrilineal systems of Micronesia, for example: 'all colonial powers in the Pacific regard matrilineal inheritance as an aberration which should, immediately or eventually, be adapted to the "proper" patrilineal or bilineal form' (Crocombe, 1972, p. 231). New agricultural practices also created tensions within the land-owning systems. For example, whereas land rights were inherited through the mother in the matrilineal systems a father could leave economic trees to his sons, thereby providing them with a small independent base. But as tree crops (coconuts, coffee, cocoa, rubber) became increasingly important in the mercantile economy into which the islanders were drawn, so conflicts developed between the men who planted the trees, their sons who inherited them, and the matrilineal inheritors of the land on which they stood. Resolution of those conflicts involved the creation of new cultural arrangements.

Land tenure systems, and the arrangements for land transfer, are thus cultural creations, which enable life to continue (providing opportunities) and yet constrain changes. The constraints must be modified occasionally, to enable changes which otherwise could not occur. Such modifications may be determined endogenously, as a society itself modifies its cultural form in order to cope with circumstances, such as population pressure, or they may be influenced exogenously, as with the impact of the colonial powers in the Pacific. Such changes are 'required' with alterations in the power base within a society and its influence on the means of organizing societal reproduction. The new powerful groups may perceive the existing arrangements as limiting their abilities to achieve their desired ends, and lead them to demand change. In the context of the present discussion, such demands are frequently characterized as 'land reform', changes to land-ownership and to rights to use land. In Great Britain, and especially midlands England, the enclosure movement involved the use of Parliamentary Acts to alter the pattern of land ownership (forcibly in many cases), thereby allowing the creation of a new pattern of farms and fields within which more productive (and less labour intensive) agricultural methods could be employed.

As King (1977) shows in his major study of land reform in most parts of the world, altering the patterns of land ownership, inheritance and use has been seen by many as a necessary part of the search for more productive use of land, and hence as a solution to the endemic pov... terizes so much of the world:

> Poverty is one of the world's greatest p...
> it involves raising the living standards ...
> population. The great majority are rur...
> denied access to their most basic need a...

Land reform can involve one or both of the re...

and alterations in the conditions whereby people occupy land. In many parts of the world, as King's survey stresses, the redistribution process involves the splitting-up of large estates, where land is farmed to produce a satisfactory return for the owners but not as intensively as could be the case; insufficient land productivity is thus a contributory cause of the widespread poverty. But such division of land is not the only reform considered necessary in certain situations, as exemplified by the enclosure movement in England and the *remembrement rurale* programmes in France.

This brief discussion of land tenure, occupancy and inheritance systems has illustrated the general argument that how people have collectively organized their survival and reproduction has varied very substantially over space and time. Different arrangements reflect cultural responses to perceptions of environmental constraints and opportunities, perceptions which may alter as the environmental context changes, thereby provoking changes in the cultural system too. The environment does not determine the nature of the world of production; it provides a context within which people develop and redevelop their own rules for survival.

In outlining these differences and their bases, the goal has been not just to present some geographical details but rather to exemplify a more general point with regard to the collective organization of survival. Complex societies have evolved in which production is organized in massively detailed systems of interdependency. Most – if not all – of those which have survived to the present are capitalist, and operate with wealth accumulation as their driving force. But within capitalism there are many variations – at all spatial scales – in the detailed arrangements for its operation. The 'world of work' varies substantially, through a complex of cultural arrangements for employing, rewarding, and disciplining people. Contrast, for example, Japanese and British factories, and also the differences between the latter and those recently opened in the UK by Japanese companies.

LIFE BEYOND WORK

The previous section has concentrated on cultural, and hence spatial, variations in what for shorthand can be called the 'world of work', that part of life which is concerned with creating and sustaining the means of subsistence. It has argued that the physical environment is the foundation which this creation is based, but in a non-deterministic fashion: the environment provides opportunities and constraints, which are resources be realized in different ways by different social groups in different places. The ways in which those resources are appraised and their potential realized become part of a culture, a collective system for the organization of survival which provides the rules within which societies seek to ensure their reproduction. Over time, those rules will be altered: in many cases slowly as responses to gradual changes in both the society and the environment that it occupies; in some cases rapidly, as a reaction to a sudden crisis; and occasionally as a consequence of contact with other cultures, when changes may be either voluntarily adopted, because the impacted group has observed the benefits from doing something differently, or imposed by powerful external groups.

In societies close to subsistence levels, there may be relatively little outside the 'world of work', which occupies most of their individuals' time and energy. But in many, and certainly in all those which have achieved relatively high average levels of living, not all time and energy need be devoted to work and the creation of the means of subsistence. In such situations, cultures will then develop rules for organizing their 'non-work' time and for using their 'spare energy'. This introduces further elements to a society's culture, and so to the potential bases for inter-cultural, and hence spatial, variations.

The two worlds of 'work' and 'non-work' are separate but far from independent, and the rules established for one impact on the other. And even in societies where 'work' predominates in its demands on time and energy, rules will need to be established to order aspects of life which are not directly concerned with the production of subsistence, i.e. with its consumption, as in the organization of the fundamental units within the society.

Family forms

Todd's (1985) work on spatial variations in family structures provides a stimulating examination of variations in this aspect of the organization of life. Families are the major socialization contexts for individuals in most societies, being the milieux in which most obtain their basic values. According to Todd (p. 196) the family is:

> the infrastructure: it determines the temperament and the ideological system of the statistical masses which make up sedentary human societies. But the family, varied in its forms, is not itself determined by any necessity, logic or rationale. It simply exists, in its diversity, and lasts for centuries or millennia. A unit of biological and social reproduction, the family needs no sense of history or of life in order to perpetuate its structures. It reproduces itself identically from

generation to generation; the unconscious imitation of parents by their children is enough to ensure the perpetuation of anthropological systems.

Variations in such basic anthropological elements, creating a further element of differentiation within the complex cultural mosaic, need to be appreciated.

Todd identifies seven basic family types. These are initially defined through the use of two axes of discrimination drawn from the work of le Play, e.g. le Play (1875).

1 The *liberty–authority axis*: authoritarian family structures are those in which children remain within an extended group with their parents after marriage, whereas liberal structures have adolescents leaving to form independent households on marriage.

2 The *equality–inequality axis*: an egalitarian structure involves the division of parental property equally among all of their children (or all of their male children in some cases), whereas the unequal structure sees the parental property unevenly divided.

A binary division on each of these axes produces four family types, as shown in figure 3.1, which also indicates the parts of northern Europe that Todd associates with each.

Todd deems le Play's schema incomplete, however, because it ignores a further crucial discriminating variable – whether marriage is endogamous or exogamous with regard to the family. The concept of incest has been the focus of much anthropological study, and by introducing this third variable Todd is able to identify seven family types, which are listed in table 3.1 Within families where the spouses are determined by custom there are two sub-types: in the endogamous community family, there is equality between brothers in matters of inheritance, married sons cohabit with their parents, and there is frequently marriage between the children of brothers; whereas in asymmetrical community families the first two conditions also hold but marriages between the children of brothers are prohibited, although there may be a preference for marriage between the children of brothers and sisters. (Approximately 10 per cent of the world's population live in cultures characterized by the former sub-types, whereas 7 per cent live under the latter.)

In families where spouse selection is parentally determined, the first sub-type – the exogamous community family – covers 41 per cent of the world's population. It is characterized by equal inheritance among brothers, married sons cohabiting with their parents, but no marriage between the children of siblings. The authoritarian family, on the other hand, is

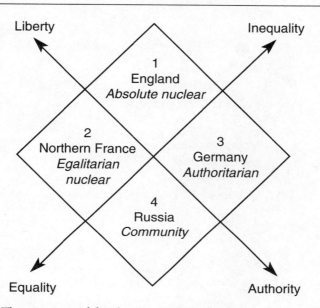

Figure 3.1 The two axes of family types and the four 'regions' that they define, with examples. *Source*: Todd, 1985, p. 16.

Table 3.1 Six family types according to method of spouse selection

Method of spouse selection	*Family type*
Determined by custom	Endogamous community
	Asymmetrical community
Determined by parents	Exogamous community
	Authoritarian
Determined by the individual with a strong exogamous obligation	Egalitarian nuclear
	Absolute nuclear
Determined by the individual with a weak exogamous obligation	Anomic

Source: Todd, 1985, p. 30

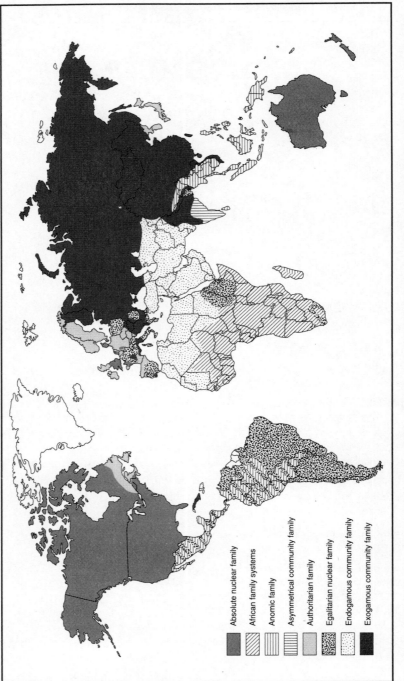

Figure 3.2 The world distribution of family types. *Source:* Todd, 1985, p. ii.

Absolute nuclear family

African family systems

Anomic family

Asymmetrical community family

Authoritarian family

Egalitarian nuclear family

Endogamous community family

Exogamous community family

characterized by unequal inheritance and unbroken patrimony to just one son, by only the married heir cohabiting with his parents, and by little or no marriage between the children of two brothers.

Where spouse choice is determined by the individual, but with a strong exogamous obligation, there are two sub-types of nuclear family. In the egalitarian, brothers have equal inheritance rights, do not live with their parents after marriage, and allow no marriage among their children. In the absolute nuclear sub-type, on the other hand, whereas the last two conditions hold inheritance rights are different; there are no precise rules, and frequent use of wills as a consequence. These two cover 11 and 8 per cent of the world's population respectively.

A further 8 per cent of the world's population live in cultures dominated by anomic families, in which individuals select their spouses, but with weak exogamous obligations. In these, inheritance rules are uncertain, being egalitarian in theory but flexible in practice; cohabitation of parents and married children is similarly rejected in theory but accepted in practice. Consanguine marriage is permissible, and frequent in some situations. Todd argues that social anthropology – 'a Western science' (p. 171) – has trouble accepting the existence of consanguinous marriages, because of its Christian roots, but he claims the existence of anomic structures in two geographical blocks – southeast Asia (plus Madagascar) and South American Indian cultures.

Todd adds an eighth type – the African.

> In Europe, in South and North America, in Asia and in Islamic countries, mutual relations between individuals – between parents and children, husband and wife, brothers and sisters – are relatively stable. The household, the domestic unit, is a basis for analysis. This is not true of the African systems where the relationships between individuals are in a constant state of flux. . . . In the innumerable African models, men, women and children are forever on the move, making and remaking, in a single lifetime, domestic forms which cannot logically be called households. . . . marriage . . . in Africa is an extremely fragile bond. (p. 25)

This does not imply an absence of norms, nor does it incorporate an implicit racism: rather, polygamy and divorce are the norms, leading to a wide range of local, unstable types.

Todd's maps (figures 3.2 and 3.3) show the general distribution of these types through the world and, in more detail, within Europe. He stresses that they are generalizations, using the term 'main anthropological regions only' in the subtitles. The distributions displayed could be determined by

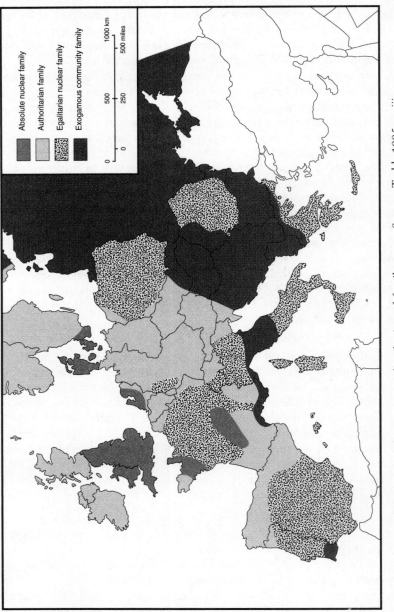

Figure 3.3 The European distribution of family types. *Source*: Todd, 1985, p. iii.

Absolute nuclear family

Authoritarian family

Egalitarian nuclear family

Exogamous community family

0   250   500   1000 km

0   250   500 miles

other factors – such as the physical environment or the rules in the infrastructure that govern the 'world of work', but Todd (pp. 196–7) argues otherwise:

> it [the family structure] is completely independent of its economic and ecological environments. Most family systems exist simultaneously in areas whose climate, relief, geology and economy are completely different. It is impossible to perceive any global coincidence at all between ecological or economic factors and family types.

The geography of family types is incoherent, he claims, reflecting the operation of no factors other than chance and what we term here structuration.

> Affective rather than rational, originating by chance hundreds of years ago and according to individual choices made in small communities, later expanding through the demographic growth of tribes and peoples, family systems perpetuate themselves by inertia. . . . this combination of anthropological types, coming down to us from an indeterminate past, has in the twentieth century played a trick on the ideal of modernity. It has seized and deformed it, in each region twisting it into a latent value-system which, put into an abstract, depersonalized form, has in one place produced the French revolutionary ideal, in another Anglo-Saxon liberalism, elsewhere communism, Muslim fundamentalism, social democracy, Buddhist socialism, and many other secondary forms. (p. 198)

And so, according to Todd, not only is variation in family types an interesting further element of the cultural mosaic, it is also linked to other aspects of that mosaic; as such, it requires understanding, as a part of the whole and not just as a thing in its own right.

Todd's interest in family structures was part of his search for an explanation of 'the distribution of political ideologies, systems and forces on our planet' (p. 1), which political science had significantly failed to provide. He suggested that each family type is linked to particular ideology. As an example, he contends that 'communism is a transference to the party state of the moral traits and the regulatory mechanisms of the exogamous community family' (p. 33), so that the electoral success of communist parties had occurred only in areas dominated by that family type, whereas in France 'Socialism . . . follows on quite naturally from Catholicism' (p. 86).

In a later work, Todd (1987) linked aspects of family structure to another

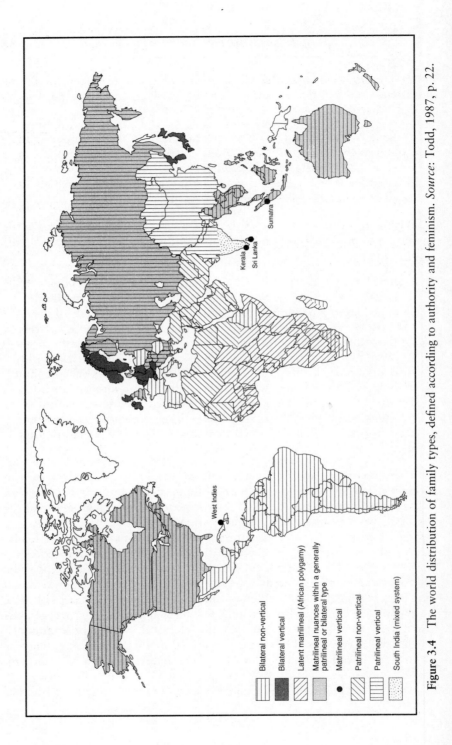

Figure 3.4 The world distribution of family types, defined according to authority and feminism. *Source:* Todd, 1987, p. 22.

variable – literacy – which is closely associated with economic and social development: the more literate societies are the more developed. He noted a high correlation between the literacy rate of young people in a country and the age of women at marriage there – 'The regions of the world where most of the people can read and write are those where women are not getting married too young' (p. 14). The correlation is much higher than that with male age at marriage, leading him to hypothesize that 'the educational power of a family system may well be determined by the strength of maternal authority' (p. 17). The reason for this, he argues, is that the older the average age of women at marriage the greater the equality between the sexes, the greater the commitment to feminism, and the smaller the age-difference between husband and wife: 'Cultural take-off brings about the disappearance of the child-woman and thus of the child-wife' (p. 17). The stronger authority of the wife over the children is reflected in their literacy, and hence in the society's general level of development.

On the basis of these observations and hypotheses, Todd develops another classification of family types based on two variables, parental authority and status of women. The former produces a binary division into authoritarian (where one finds parents and their adult children cohabiting in three-generational households) and non-authoritarian. Authoritarian households are termed *vertical* whereas non-authoritarian households are *non-vertical*. For the second variable – feminism – a trichotomy is used, dividing family types into *patrilineal*, *bilineal* and *trilineal* according to the relative importance of the two parents in the household. Together, these give six family types, whose distribution across the world he maps (figure 3.4). The matrilineal types are rare, but he argues that the development potential (via literacy) of the bilineal is as strong.

Todd's detailed analyses relate the distribution of these family types to cultural development processes, leading to the conclusion that development involves two processes: the first is 'self-generated take-off' (p. 176) and there is 'a geographical coincidence between the distribution of these family types and that of the literacy take-off'; the second is the outward diffusion of development from the initial poles, which 'occurs all the faster, the more receptive to it is the anthropological terrain'. This leads him to a much wider generalization that the course of history, over space as well as time, is closely linked to the anthropological map. As a consequence, the role of social and political factors in the processes of development are substantially downplayed, and the key sequence is (p. 168) 'authoritarian family → literacy → fall in mortality rate → fall in fertility rate → (at last) rise in the standard of living'. But Todd also comes to a more pessimistic conclusion:

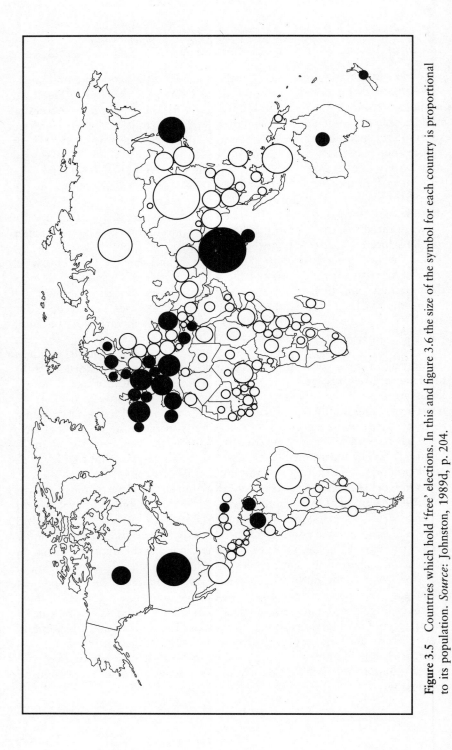

Figure 3.5 Countries which hold 'free' elections. In this and figure 3.6 the size of the symbol for each country is proportional to its population. *Source:* Johnston, 1989d, p. 204.

Those family systems that possess high potential for cultural development have as one of their necessary components a certain authoritarianism within the parent-child relationship which – on the ideological plane – rules out their close adherence to liberal values. From this, it appears that cultural efficiency and political freedom do not go hand in hand. . . . Germany and Japan are highly efficient countries. But, unlike Britain, France and the United States, they are not the traditional homes of liberal thought. (p. 177)

This is somewhat similar to Olson's (1982) argument that the rise and then decline of countries can be linked to their degree of pluralism – an argument which has found little substantial empirical support.

This discussion of family types based on Todd's stimulating, if somewhat controversial and iconoclastic, writings provides just one example of the variations between places in social organization of inter-personal relationships outside the 'world of work'. Many others could have been cited, relating to religious practices, relationships between age groups, gender groups, racial groups, and so on. All would illustrate the basic point that the cultural mosaic comprises a very wide range of rules of behaviour which differentiate places on virtually every conceivable criterion.

POLITICS AND STATES

Todd's work was not introduced here to present his conclusions as uncontestable 'facts' – for there is much to debate regarding the nature of his sweeping generalizations – but rather to illustrate the importance of aspects of diversity which are not directly linked to either or both of the physical environment and the world of work. Todd linked family structures to other aspects of society – political and economic – and indeed suggests that the anthropological differences between places are the crucial determinants of other aspects of activity there. Others disagree, and find the determinant factors in the economic sphere. Urry (1986, p. 234), for example, writes that

this one set of social relations, of production, accounts for the relations in other spheres of social life within each locality or region, that politics and ideology are essentially explicable in terms of economic change and restructuring.

The argument in the present book identifies no one set of factors as determining the others, but rather focuses on the separate but interlinked

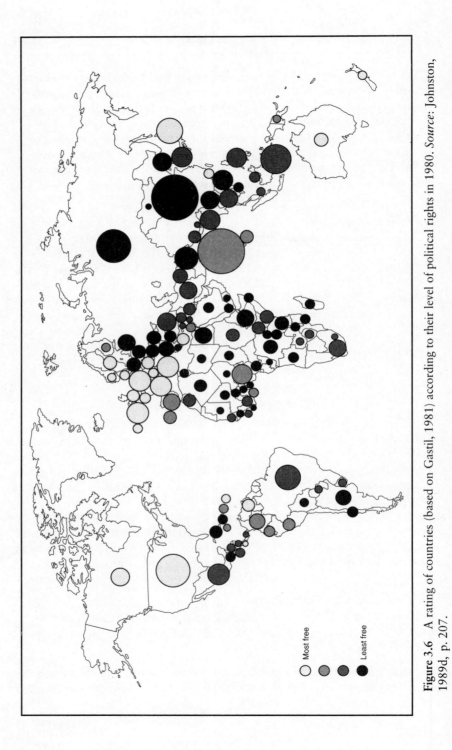

Most free

Least free

Figure 3.6 A rating of countries (based on Gastil, 1981) according to their level of political rights in 1980. *Source*: Johnston, 1989d, p. 207.

dimensions of society whose appreciation is necessary to understanding. So far, two such dimensions have been identified – and defined as the 'world of work' and the 'world outside work'. The present section introduces a third.

Todd linked family structure to ideology and politics, and indeed sought to account both for types of regime and for the electoral support given to particular types of party by an area's dominant family structure. His anthropological attempt to account for spatial variations in the nature of politics is countered by others who associate the origins of political variations across the earth's surface with variations within the sphere of production (notably with the core-periphery structure of the capitalist world-economy: Johnston, 1984d, 1989d; Taylor, 1989). For example, they associate liberal democracy with the core countries, arguing that such a system is only sustainable over substantial periods in countries which are exploiting the entire world-system, and can 'buy-off' popular demands from their own residents because of the wealth that is being appropriated from other countries. Experience has shown that the latter cannot sustain liberal democracy in the context of their weak economic situations.

Liberal democracy describes the political system in a number of countries that meet certain criteria, such as the freedoms to form and join organizations, to express opinions, to vote and to compete for votes and to stand for public office, plus the holding of free and fair elections and the existence of institutions which ensure that government policies reflect popularly expressed preferences (Johnston, 1989d, after Dahl, 1978). Only a small number of countries meet those criteria (figure 3.5), and on a scale of political rights (Gastil, 1981) very many of those lacking liberal democracy rate among the 'least free' (figure 3.6).

Even among the relatively small number of countries characterized as liberal democracies there are considerable differences in how their political systems are structured, however. This is illustrated by Lijphart's (1984, 1989) analyses of types of democratic political systems, which was initially based on two dimensions reflecting different aspects of majoritarian and consensual rule.

Fitting different political systems into this schema empirically involved defining the dimensions on the following variables. For the first dimension, five used were: whether executive power is concentrated (as in the British Cabinet) or shared (as in the Swiss Federal Council, in which all parties are represented); whether the executive dominates (as in the UK), or shares power with the legislature (as in the United States); whether there is a two- or a multi-party system; whether parties are divided on one political dimension (e.g. the typical left-right division in Great Britain) or several (as in The Netherlands); and whether elections use plurality or proportional representation procedures. Together these measured the *majoritarian-consensual dimension*. The second dimension used three variables: whether the state is unitary and centralized or federal and dispersed; whether the legislature has one or two (strong) chambers; and whether there is an unwritten or a written, rigid constitution. This Lijphart termed the *federal-unitary dimension*.

Using factor analysis of data for twenty-one liberal democracies (with two data sets for France, representing the Fourth and Fifth Republics), Lijphart identified three groups on each dimension, giving nine in all: there was at least one liberal democracy in each of the cells (figure 3.7), indicating the very substantial differences between countries in their detailed operation of this basic political system. At one extreme were the countries characterized as majoritarian on both dimensions: in both the United Kingdom and New Zealand, for example, power is concentrated into the majority party in a two-party (or virtually so) system, where rule occurs without a written constitution and with no dispersal of power to subsidiary governments. At the other extreme is Switzerland, characterized as consensual on both dimensions; a strongly federal state with power shared centrally among several parties. Such consensus arrangements are typical of what Lijphart (1977) earlier termed consociational democracies, characterized by 'four essential practices: grand coalition, segmental autonomy, proportionality, and mutual veto' (Lijphart, 1989, p. 39). The majoritarian liberal democracies are basically those with a strong Anglo-American heritage; the consensual liberal democracies on the federal-unitary dimension are largely those with plural (i.e. strongly multi-cultural) societies.

Political parties mobilize bias within the populations of liberal democracies, identifying potential cleavages and presenting themselves as representing the interests of one group more than those of any other (while recognizing that, for the state to retain its legitimacy, it is necessary to respect the interests of other groups, and thereby present a 'one nation' perspective in certain situations). The nature of the cleavages identified and capitalized upon by the parties reflects the structure of the society – although if certain cleavages are ignored by parties (thereby 'organizing out' certain biases) the party system need not faithfully represent all the divisions within a society. In a classic study of the various cleavage systems mobilized by parties in western Europe, Lipset and Rokkan (1967) identified four that dominate. Two are related to the *national* revolution and to the growth of the nation-state: the first reflected differences between subject and dominant cultures within a multi-cultural society (such as Switzerland and, in a recent development mobilizing a bias that was

Dimension I \ Dimension II	Majoritarian	Intermediate	Consensual
Majoritarian	New Zealand (5) United Kingdom (4)	Ireland (4)	Australia (5) *Austria* (5) *Canada* (5) *Germany* (5) *United States* (3)
Intermediate	Iceland (3) *Luxembourg* (1)	*France V* (6) Norway (1) Sweden (1)	*Italy* (4) Japan (5)
Consensual	Denmark (1) *Israel* (3)	*Belgium* (1) *Finland* (1) *France IV* *Netherlands* (1)	*Switzerland* (1)

Figure 3.7 A classification of 22 democratic regimes according to two dimensions of majoritarian vs. consensus democracy. Notes: a) The plural and semi-plural societies are italicized. b) The intermediate category encompasses countries with factor scores between −.50 and +.50. c) The figures in parentheses are Dahl's (1971, p. 232) democratic scale types. *Source*: Lijphart, 1989, p. 35.

previously only potential, Belgium: Murphy, 1988); the second reflected differences between religious and secular authority, representing the 'old' and the 'new' in views about the location of power (again, as in Switzerland, and also in The Netherlands). The second pair of cleavages was associated with the *industrial* revolution: one was linked to the division between town and country (or agricultural and manufacturing interests); the other concerned the growing division between employers and workers (the class divide).

According to Lipset and Rokkan, the current pattern of cleavages mobilized by parties reflects a three-stage development of 'alliance-opposition structures': the post-Reformation stage, in which the state was allied either to a national church (as in England) or to the supra-national Roman Catholic church; a 'democratic revolution' stage, in which the established church retained much greater secular power in some countries than others; and the industrial stage, with the division between landed and urban interests. One or more of these stages may have had greater impact in some countries than others, creating separate democratic inheritances onto which the extension of the franchise was superimposed. Thus subject vs. dominant culture, church vs. state, and town vs. country cleavages were present to a greater or lesser extent before the gradual acceptance of universal suffrage, into which the class cleavage was placed. The outcome was variations between states in the relative importance of the class cleavage, which commentators found to be dominant in Great Britain (e.g. Alford, 1963) but much weaker elsewhere (Rose, 1974; Rose and Urwin, 1975; McAllister and Rose, 1984).

The wider relevance of the cleavage model is the subject of considerable debate (Johnston, 1990c), and later authors have suggested the addition of further basic divisions (Harrop and Miller, 1987). For the present purposes, however, the model's general validity for European societies pre-1980 illustrates that although a state is necessary in a capitalist economic system its particular form can vary substantially to reflect local circumstances: form and function should not be confused.

Even in a system dominated by the class cleavage, there is no necessity for people on the same side of the cleavage living in different places to favour the same political party. This is illustrated by Cox's (1970) work on Wales, which identified two separate milieux ('places') – 'agricultural, Welsh-speaking, Nonconformist areas on the one hand and mining, English-speaking, non-Nonconformist areas on the other hand' (p. 127). Each developed a separate cleavage structure. In the former area, what he terms 'traditional Wales', the interests of the tenant population against their English landlords were mobilized by the Liberal party, which has remained relatively strong in the area throughout the present century. In urban, 'modern' Wales, on the other hand, the social class cleavage among the mining and industrial communities was vigorously exploited by the Labour party, which retains its predominance there today. Thus the different socio-political contexts were mobilized by the political parties of protest in different ways, producing a more complex electoral geography than would have been the case if Wales had a uniform political culture.

SYNTHESIS

I have argued elsewhere that there are three components to the definition of a place – the physical environment, the built environment, and the people (Johnston, 1989a). Study of a place's people will be set within the context of both their physical and their built environment (with the latter encompassing the entire human-created landscape and not just the pattern of buildings and settlements) – with neither being determinate of the others, of course, but with all three inter-linked. Study of the people, according to the discussion in this chapter, involves their characterization according to how the world of work is organized, how social life outside work is structured in its manifold ways, and how politics are constructed (Johnston, 1990b). A full exploration of the nature of a place would explore all three components and the three sub-components of the third: my focus here is on the latter only.

This schema has much in common with those developed by two others, whose writings have influenced this presentation. Leeds (1984), for example, argues that whereas all nucleated settlements (or places in the present context) have the same functions – 'facilitation of all forms of exchange, transfer, and communications while linking the nucleation or locality both with other localities and with society at large (p. 295) – there is also a threefold specialization between places. First, places tend to take on specialized functions, in addition to the universal ones, thereby creating a spatial division of labour, at a variety of scales. Secondly, there is variation in that specialization in terms of technology and its application, with differences in the tools used, the tasks undertaken, the knowledge available, and so on. Finally, there is institutional specialization, what Leeds calls the 'more-or-less autonomously ordered and chartered ways of doing things, ranging from large-scale orders such as government, church and education, to small-scale institutions such as roles'. These produce what he terms locality specialization, technological specialization, and institutional specialization which interact and 'once they start interacting, the degree and rate of differentiation increase' (p. 297). The result is a complex cultural mosaic reflecting differences between places in what is done where, how it is done, and how the society is organized.

Urry's (1981) discussion of *The Anatomy of Capitalist Societies* similarly uses a threefold schema – of economy, civil society and state: economy covers the sphere of production, wherein material needs are met; civil society 'is that site where individual subjects reproduce their material conditions of life' (p. 6); and the state is that apparatus which, as Clark and Dear (1984) argue, concurrently sustains the sphere of production, by promoting accumulation strategies in a capitalist society, regulates the sphere of consumption in civil society, and, through the propagation of an ideology, welds the two in a social consensus. Variations in all three areas between societies means that they are far from homogeneous; rather they 'consist of patterned yet heterogeneous social practices' (Urry, 1981, p. 9). In identifying these three, Urry is concerned to argue against both the Marxist concept of base and superstructure and the 'autonomist' approach that the three spheres are autonomous are both inadequate, because they fail to

> grasp the forms and effects of struggle . . . the multitude of different efforts by which both individuals and groups of individuals struggle to maintain and expand their material conditions of life. I take it that these are essential to capitalist society and that what has to be explained are their precise bases, their degree of effectivity and their often largely unintended consequences. (p. 5)

Urry's model of how capitalist society operates explores the interdependence among the three spheres in which individuals struggle. This involves him charting 'the social space in which individual subjectivities are constituted and reproduced, the differing forms and effectivity of social struggle, and the character of the state' (p. 8). It follows from that objective that the nature of social space can vary, and hence that such variation must occur between places. Urry's model can thus be seen as representing the constituents of a place.

Urry sets out his model of a capitalist social formation in a diagram (figure 3.8) which shows three interacting components: a sphere of capitalist production; a state; and a sphere of struggle (civil society), which comprises the linked spheres of circulation and reproduction. With regard to the last of these, the sphere of circulation is that part of the social formation in which exchange takes place, through the buying and selling of all commodities (including labour power). Thus money obtained in the sphere of production is circulated through exchange processes, which are separate from those of production and which are also regulated by the state. Linked to the sphere of circulation is the sphere of reproduction, within which society is reproduced both biologically and culturally; the commodities that are bought with the money earned in the sphere of production are used for subsistence and for meeting the created 'needs' and 'wants' of individuals.

As Urry's diagram indicates, there is struggle within civil society, involving both its constituent spheres. Many models of society see the main nidus

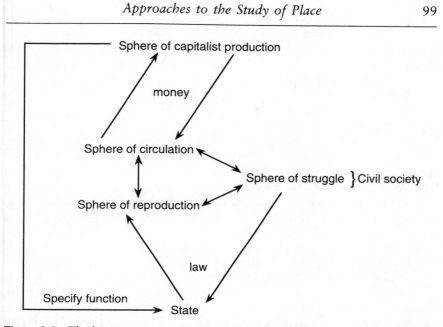

Figure 3.8 The basic structure of capitalist social formations. *Source*: Urry, 1981, p. 116.

of struggle residing in the sphere of production, between the capitalists and workers – the classic class struggle of Marxian writings. Urry terms this 'class-struggle', which he differentiates from 'classes-in-struggle' within civil society. The latter may not involve the two antagonistic classes of the sphere of production, but can involve struggle within such economic classes, reflecting the particular divisions of the social formation, such as generation, gender, race, religion, region, nation and so forth. These are not divisions which are necessary to the capitalist mode of production, whereas those divisions within the sphere of production are. There is a class-struggle in every capitalist society over the appropriation of surplus value, and this is reflected in the social relations at the workplace. There are also classes-in-struggle in every society, but the nature of these varies according to local circumstances and history: thus in one place there may be struggle within civil society between religious groups, for example, whereas in others such struggle may be absent, despite a lack of religious homogeneity. (See, for example, Katznelson's (1982) suggestions why city politics in the USA are organized around racial groups rather than occupational classes, and Smith's (1988) discussion of the differences between American and British cities in the degree of local political mobilization.) Many of those struggles are linked to the sphere of circulation; groups are contesting access to the commodities produced within the society. Such struggle may involve spatial structuring of the society, as with the construction of residential segregation in urban areas to promote the interests of some groups and retard those of others (as with racial groups in the United States: Johnson, 1984c, and chapter 5 below).

The struggles involving civil society are not contained within it, but are implicated in both the sphere of production and the state. With regard to the former, power in the sphere of circulation is linked to power in the sphere of production: the greater a group's access to rewards in the latter, the greater its strength in the exchange processes. Hence the classes-in-struggle seek to influence the social relations in the workplace by, for example, creating differential access to jobs and incomes – as with the reservation of certain types of employment for white persons only under the South African apartheid regime in the 1950–80s. Similarly, the classes-in-struggle contest control of the state and its apparatus, thereby seeking to promote their own interests. The state, as argued by many theorists, is necessary to the capitalist mode of production, and it must ensure the conditions for capitalist success. But there is no single way in which that can be done, and so people contest within the state apparatus to promote their self-interest – both individually and collectively. (The Labour Party in Great Britain was created to promote the interests of the working class against those of the capitalist class, for example; before that, much of the contesting within the nineteenth century British state involved different capitalist interest groups – manufacturing vs. agriculture vs. trade, etc. – seeking advantage over the others.) And beyond that, many groups seek power within the state apparatus to promote interests that are only indirectly, and in some cases very slightly, related to the spheres of production and circulation – as, for example, in the promotion of particular art forms and sports. These Urry terms the popular democratic forces.

Urry argues that it is the varying inter-relationships among these various spheres of capitalist society which determine its local form – or, in the terminology of this book, create the nature of each place. Civil society is at the centre of this web of inter-relationships, comprising: the sphere of circulation, in which people and groups contest in the 'market place'; the sphere of reproduction, in which social groups – classes-in-struggle – compete to promote their economic, biological and political reproduction; and the popular democratic forces, through which much of the struggle within civil society is organized. (Parenthetically we may note, too, that Urry argues that it is these struggles within civil society that dominate in capitalist societies rather than those in the sphere of production, hence the fragmentation of the working class in national politics, because classes-in-struggle are much more important to them than class-struggle. Work on voting behaviour in Great Britain in the 1980s illustrates this, with the class divide much distorted according to power in the market place, which in turn has become increasingly spatially variable: Johnston and Pattie, 1988, 1990.) The state is linked to all three components, through a set of institutions which: regulates the sphere of circulation, in order to ensure continued accumulation of surplus value in the sphere of production, but in doing so may promote the interests of certain intra-class groups over others; oversees the processes of economic, biological and cultural reproduction; and acts as the arena within which the popular democratic forces struggle over the other two. It does this through its monopoly of physical coercion. And, of course, the state is linked directly to the sphere of production, for which it performs necessary functions, being also an arena within which the class-struggles are fought out. Further, as Harvey (1978) makes clear, the resolutions of those struggles in any one place and time are represented in the built environment (illustrated in his work on Paris: Harvey, 1985a), which in turn constrains and yet enables further developments in the reproduction of society, as illustrated by his work on American suburbia: see Harvey (1975) and also Walker (1981).

Full appreciation of place will involve exploration of the inter-relationships among the physical environment, the built environment, and the people. Here, the focus is only upon the people, however, and the three sub-components identified in this chapter – social relations in the workplace; social relations in civil society; and political institutions in each. The next two chapters use case studies to expand the framework that they provide for an appreciation of the variety among places, without explicit recognition of the interactions with the physical and built environments (although both are implicit, especially in the first). The goal is a straightforward and modest one: to build a structure within which it is possible to appreciate differences between places which is not empiricist (as the CURS initiative largely is) but is set within an appreciation of the nature of capitalist society. The construction task will not end with this book, which does little more than lay the foundation for an approach that will celebrate geography as focusing on the 'question of place' within contemporary society.

4

Pit and Place:
The Dukeries in the National
Union of Mineworkers' Strike of
1984–1985*

*This chapter draws extensively on a paper jointly written with Michael Griffiths – Griffiths and Johnston (1991) – and his substantial contribution to development of the ideas in it is fully and gratefully acknowledged.

> Differences in strike commitment are liable to be more effectively explained in terms of such variables as the culture of each coalfield, traditional loyalties to the area or national levels of the union and the type of lead given by branch and area officials at the outset of the dispute.
>
> D. Waddington, M. Wykes and C. Critcher, *Split at the Seams? Community, Continuity and Change after the 1984–5 Coal Dispute.*

An excellent example of the role of a place as a focus of collective identity is provided by one of the major events in British industrial relations in recent decades – the National Union of Mineworkers' strike of March 1984 to March 1985. Furthermore, one aspect of that strike – and in particular of its geography – provides clear evidence of the importance of the three elements of a place identified in chapter 3. The present chapter, which draws heavily upon, and develops, arguments first presented in Griffiths and Johnston (1991), illustrates these points, and advances the arguments presented throughout the book.

THE NATURE OF THE STRIKE

The National Union of Mineworkers' (NUM) strike of 1984–5 had several peculiar characteristics. First, it was not a strike over wages – although a wage claim was later added to the terms on which the Union was prepared to return to work; it was about the future of the coalmining industry in

Great Britain, and in particular was a protest against a plan for extensive pit closures with consequences for both miners' jobs and the future of their communities. Secondly, there was no settlement agreed by the parties involved – the Union and the National Coal Board (NCB); the strikers simply decided to return to work in March 1985. Thirdly, and with particular interest for the present work, the strike was uneven in its geographical impact; whereas in some areas support for the union was virtually 100 per cent throughout the year-long dispute, in others there was very little backing and coal was mined throughout the period. Before turning to that geographical variability, however, and what we can learn from it about the nature of a place, a brief outline of the strike's context is provided.

The coalmining industry has been a major symbol of the differences between the two main political parties of post-war Great Britain: the Labour party, with its firm commitment – especially in the first decades of the period – to public ownership of the 'commanding heights of the economy', and the Conservative party and its much greater (and increasing from the mid-1970s on) commitment to free market operations with minimal state interference, let alone ownership. The coalmining industry was one of the first to be nationalized. In addition, the coalminers, through their trades unions, have long been major actors in the political arena – those of both the workplace (notably the Trades Union Congress) and the state (the Labour party). Strike action on the coalfields was the major catalyst for the 1926 General Strike, and the miners have been widely perceived for several decades as at the forefront of trade union militancy in the United Kingdom.

The strike itself has been the subject of a great deal of analysis: by participants, e.g. Barnsley WAPC (1984), MacGregor (1986), People of Thurcroft (1986); by journalists and other commentators, e.g. Adeney and Lloyd (1986), Crick (1985), Goodman (1985); and by academics, e.g. Beynon (1985), Fine and Millar (1985), Samuel, Bloomfield and Boanas (1986), Winterton and Winterton (1989). To most of them, it was important because 'in the breadth of the issues involved, and in the drama of its actions, it stands out – even to the casual observer – as a major social and political event' (Beynon, 1985, p. 17). Five years later, its repercussions were still being widely aired in the media, with conflicts over the sources and use of money available to the NUM's elected officers during the strike period (Lightman, 1990).

Many people saw the strike as a conflict arising out of antagonisms between the NUM's president, Arthur Scargill, and the Prime Minister, Margaret Thatcher. On the former's side, there was a clear, oft-stated belief that the union movement represented the best chance of overthrowing the government, given both the electoral weakness and the apparent shift from 'left wing principles' of the Labour party (see Crick 1985, p. 140). Thus the strike was portrayed by Scargill as both industrial and political, as a means of destroying Thatcherism as well as advancing the miners' job interests.

For Mrs Thatcher and her government, antagonism towards the miners in part reflected a desire for revenge against the union which was widely perceived as precipitating the political crisis which led to the downfall of a previous Conservative government, led by Edward Heath, in 1974. Plans had been put in hand as early as 1978 (the so-called 'Ridley plan': Young, 1990, pp. 358–60) to tackle the miners in a later confrontation on terms favourable to the government; indeed, because the conditions were not felt to be ripe, the government pulled back from an earlier potential confrontation in 1981, and allowed a large pay settlement for the NUM (Young, 1990). But revenge, while it would be sweet, was only part of the government's reason for 'taking on' the miners. Its case for wholesale economic, social and political restructuring of the United Kingdom included arguing against the substantial power that the unions had obtained during the corporatist decades of the postwar period, especially within the monopoly nationalized industries. This was perceived as a source of inefficiency and uncompetitiveness through overmanning and other policies, which the government was determined to remove in its quest to create an 'enterprise economy'.

Reducing the power of the unions was thus central to the goals of Thatcherism (see also chapter 7). Although it has been claimed that the Conservative Party under Margaret Thatcher had no carefully thought-through strategy to deal with the unions when it came into office, but rather proceeded pragmatically (Roberts, 1989), nevertheless (Young, 1990, p. 353):

> Mrs Thatcher had always said, when asked to crystallize the essence of the British disease, that the nationalized industries were the seat of it: where monopoly unions conspired with monopoly suppliers, to produce an inadequate service to the consumer at massive cost to the taxpayer. . . . The unions, who were the beneficiaries of these monopolies, were accomplices to the most scandalous inefficiencies, and had to be stripped of their power.

Thus while there was no intent to 'pick a fight' with the NUM, there was also no doubt that one would eventually come, because the trade union legislation passed and planned by the Conservative governments of the

1980s was designed to reduce the NUM's power very substantially. When a dispute did arise, and the government was confident of the outcome, then no quarter would be given: as with earlier strikes, such as that involving the steel industry, the government's resolve to weaken the unions, thereby aiding in the regeneration of British industry, would be displayed – as a 'demonstration effect pour encourager les autres'. (That the government was ready for a strike was a widespread interpretation of its appointment of Ian MacGregor to chair the NCB from September 1983 on; MacGregor chaired British Steel in 1980–1, a period encompassing its major dispute, and was believed responsible for the major cuts in job levels; it was assumed that he was expected to achieve the same in the coal industry.)

The NUM's strike action in 1984 was thus a conflict between the perceived 'irresistible force' of the union and the 'immovable object' of the government. Both had much to win and to lose through the action. For the government, not only was it a further opportunity to display its resolve in the face of a union challenge but it also provided the chance of defeating, if not publicly humiliating, one of the country's most powerful trade unions. For the union, it was an opportunity not only to protect its long-held privileges – such as consultation over pit closures and the cutting of coal on five days a week only – but also to demonstrate the power of extra-parliamentary opposition to the 'elected dictatorship' in Whitehall.

The strike's rationale

Arthur Scargill was in no doubt that the government intended to reduce the size of the coalmining industry substantially, through a major programme of pit closures: many tens of thousands of miners' jobs would be at risk as more and more pits were declared uneconomic, not necessarily because the coal reserves had been worked out but rather because of the perceived costs of mining them, relative to the costs of imports. (Hence Scargill was strong in his opposition to the extension of nuclear power, explicitly on safety grounds, but implicitly because of its impact on his members' jobs.) This belief was widespread in the NUM, and was demonstrated by the overwhelming support for Scargill in his 1981 campaign for the presidency, in which fighting pit closures – and thus the jobs and communities of the miners – was the central theme (Taylor, 1984). Scargill argued for national unity within the (federal) union, against the growing call for local wage and conditions bargaining – which he believed would favour some fields but be the harbinger of closure for others. For him, the main issue was job security, to be sustained by keeping pits open and working hours restrained (the latter policy being advanced on the argument that longer working hours and working weeks threatened safety standards).

Despite this general situation and the latent support for Scargill's aggressive stance against the NCB (and hence the government), nevertheless there were several 'false starts' to the eventual conflict of 1984–5. According to the rules then extant, a national strike could only be called by the NUM if it had the support of at least 55 per cent of the members voting in a secret ballot: the union prided itself on its democracy in this context. Three previous attempts by Scargill to get a strike declared (in 1981, 1982 and 1983) failed because of splits within the union. It was uncertain whether a ballot in 1984 would obtain the needed support, and so Scargill developed an alternative strategy to achieve a national strike without calling one. This was within the union's rules, but nevertheless was seen by many, including a substantial number of NUM members, as an indication of his weakness. The relevant rule – 41 – is published by Crick, 1985 (p. 149). It states that any industrial action or strike called in any area of the union – the NUM is a federation of independent Branches, most of them geographically defined – must be sanctioned by the National Executive, or by 'a Committee . . . to whom the National Executive Committee may have delegated the power of giving such sanction . . .'. Thus if Scargill was satisfied that (a) Branch members would accede to a call for a strike by their local officials, (b) that those officials would call a strike, and (c) that the National Executive (over which he had a strong influence) would sanction such strikes, then he could achieve the equivalent of a national strike without submitting it to the membership at large for their endorsement. Furthermore, if some Branches struck and called on others to back them, that support could be ensured by picketing the workplaces of those who were to be persuaded: Scargill was strong in his insistence that miners do not cross picket lines formed by other miners, but he was eventually defeated by both the unwillingness of an increasingly large body of miners (especially those working in Nottinghamshire, see below) to disregard this advice in the absence of a national ballot on strike action, and the government's preparedness to counter the pickets by mass policing and other tactics which limited the freedom of movement of perceived would-be pickets (Fine and Millar, 1985).

The strike began in the Yorkshire Area of the NUM (the NUM and the NCB use different spatial divisions of the country), on 12 March 1984. The ability to call a strike without a ballot was provided by the result of a 1981 ballot on the principle of fighting pit closures (where the grounds were economic; the NUM was prepared to accept closures if they agreed that the pits were 'worked out'). The ballot asked 'Are you in favour of giving the Yorkshire Area NUM authority to take various forms of industrial action (including strike action, if necessary) to stop the closure of any pit, unless on the grounds of exhaustion?' (Crick, 1985, p. 86); it was endorsed by 86 per cent of those voting. Scargill was still the Yorkshire Area President at the time of the ballot. The Area was one of the NUM's most militant, after decades of a much less aggressive stance (Taylor, 1984). In October 1982, when the NUM as a whole rejected Scargill's first strike call as national President, by 61 to 39 per cent, the Yorkshire Area voted 56 per cent in favour. In 1983, when the South Wales Branch voted to strike on the issue of closure, the Yorkshire Area Council voted by 73 to 27 in favour of a strike in support, in line with the 1981 agreement, but the issue went to a national ballot for a strike, which was once again lost. Thus Scargill was reluctant to go for a third national ballot under his leadership, and the fourth in four years. But he was able to win support at a National Delegate Conference in 1983 for an overtime ban, linked to both the believed closure programme and an outstanding pay claim. The proposed closure at Cortonwood, Rotherham, in the heart of the militant Yorkshire Area, then provided him with the opportunity to launch a strike, under Rule 41 and the 1981 Yorkshire ballot, without, as he perceived it, any need for the potentially damaging national ballot which Rule 43 demanded. (Rule 43 specifies that 'In the event of national action being proposed by the Union in pursuance of any of the objects of the Union, the following provision shall apply: that a national strike shall only be entered upon as the result of a ballot vote of the members taken in pursuance of a resolution of Conference, and a strike shall not be declared unless 55 per cent [changed in April 1984 to 'a simple majority'] of those voting in the ballot vote in favour of such a strike': Crick, 1985, pp. 149–50.) Scargill hoped for a 'domino effect', to be promoted if necessary by the type of mass picketing which had been perfected a decade earlier, and the National Executive supported him; only three members voted for a proposal that the demand for a national strike be put to a national ballot.

The 'domino effect' was only partly successful, however, and this was very substantially responsible for both the course of the dispute and the lack of any final outcome, other than the return to work in March, 1985. In particular, for reasons that will be taken up below, the Nottinghamshire miners decided to remain at work. Their intransigence, plus the unwillingness of other unions (notably on the railways and in the steel industry) to provide supportive action, was sufficient to ensure the strike's defeat. Enough coal was mined and transported to the power stations and coke works to ensure that the impact beyond the mining industry was minimal.

The miners were eventually forced back to work – some might claim they were virtually 'starved back' by the operation of the social security benefit rules – because there was no apparent chance of success. Within months, Scargill's warnings of substantial pit closures were transformed into reality: the NUM was unable to resist – with most of its members at the affected pits rapidly opting for the generous redundancy terms – and with the privatization of the electricity-generating industry at the end of the 1980s the ability of many British mines to compete was in question; closures were instituted even in the more productive fields.

COMMUNITIES AND THE STRIKE

Most British coal mines are outside the main industrial conurbations, and their employees live in isolated settlements – 'pit villages' – which offer no alternative work and are not very accessible to other employment opportunities. In addition, most of those relatively close to other industrial settlements are in areas where the alternative sources of employment, such as the iron and steel and heavy engineering industries, are also in decline. They are thus relatively closed communities. Furthermore, the strength of the bonds of workplace, residence and social life, all focused on the pit and the trade union, has made these closed communities very cohesive. This provided what was perceived as a very secure milieu: as Chaplin (1978, p. 82) describes it: 'You were known, you were named, you had your place, you could make your mark in life'. And as he and Bulmer (1978) describe it, in that place the solidarity provided what amounted to 'a sort of complete welfare system' (p. 81).

Bulmer (1975), following Kerr and Siegel (1954), has characterized mining communities as isolated and homogeneous, and with a much weaker 'exit' option for the dissatisfied than is typical of other industrial settlements. ('Exit' was advanced by Hirschmann, 1970, as one of the three options for dissatisfied consumers: the other two were 'voice' and 'loyalty'.) Thus, according to Bulmer, (1978, p. 68):

> Occupational, geographical or social mobility rarely offer avenues out of the mass. The skills of miners . . . are not easily transferable to other industries; protest is less likely to take the form of moving to another industry. The miner . . . lives in communities detached from the society at large and often from the absentee employer as well. . . . Though geographical mobility is possible, to move means severing all the social ties which the miner has built up. *Social* mobility

is even more problematic. Apart from some very limited opportunities for mobility within the industry, to what higher occupational strata can the miner . . . rise in the natural course of events?

This sense of 'apartness' reinforces the internal reliance of the mining community – or 'cohesive mass segregation' (p. 69) – and also promotes a greater level of strike-proneness than is the case in more heterogeneous industrial settlements.

Bulmer concludes that this is probably an 'oversimplified view' (p. 71), focusing too strongly on the functional characteristics of the places and ignoring (relatively, at least) the nature of the local culture and its institutional structuring (as, for example, with the nature and role of trades unions).

> The role of individuals is important because industrial behaviour is very strongly influenced by organized trade unions, and trade unions are led (at all levels . . .) by groups of individuals with considerable power, influence and discretion over the industrial relations strategies which they pursue. . . . [Thus] the sociological factors [the isolated mass] are mediated through particular individuals and groups in a quite distinctive way (p. 75)

which is a point stressed below in the analysis of the Dukeries field. Further, some at least of the influential individuals in a community may operate outside the field of industrial relations: drawing on the work of Blauner (1960), Bulmer suggests that the strong occupational communities characteristic of mining settlements occur because the social relations forged in the workplace are carried over into the arenas of non-work activity, creating overlapping primary group affiliations in which

> people who work together tend to spend their non-work time with persons from the same industry. In doing so, they tend to 'talk shop'. (p. 79)

Further, such occupational communities 'tend to be relatively self-enclosed, and to be the reference group for those who belong, setting standards of behaviour and providing its own system of internal differentiation'. Such communities are characterized as wholes, in which (pp. 87–8)

> The social ties of work, leisure, family, neighbourhood and friendship overlap to form close-knit and interlocking locally based collectivities of actors. The solidarity of the community is strengthened . . . by a shared history of living and working in one place over a long period of time. . . . Meaningful interaction is confined almost exclusively to the locality

which creates a very contained and powerful vessel for the transmission of a local culture.

The nature of the mining industry with its shiftwork, its tradition of generation following generation 'down the pit', and the isolation of most of the pit villages (the majority of them built by the pit-owners: Bacon, 1986), meant that according to Chaplin (1978, p. 77)

> the very nature of pit work made most women slaves, wives and daughters all. Shifts split up the family so that men would be coming in at all hours of the day, waiting for the bath-tin and the water and a woman to wash their backs. Then clean the boots and wash and/or dry the duds. 'Service' was the only escape and amelioration of that black tragedy of the mining family – too many daughters. (Lads not only brought in money but added to status.)

Thus a proposed pit closure threatened the economic base of the entire community; an absence of work for the male adults meant the destruction of every family's economic foundation, for very few women (save a few who worked in village shops etc.) had either jobs or the local opportunities of jobs.

One of the major features of Scargill's campaign to mobilize support for the strike was his emphasis on the centrality of the pit to a community's economic and social health. By fighting for pits to be kept open, the NUM was fighting not only for miners' jobs but also for the survival of miners' communities. He used this argument not just to win the passive support of the miners' wives and other dependants but also to mobilize their active participation. The Miners' Welfare had long been the central social institution, and it became the focus of activity during the strike too.

> The Miners' Welfare was at the heart of this communal bonding. It was the nerve centre of the strike operations. . . . It combined the functions of a union office with that of a warehouse. . . . It was the daily port-of-call for the more active supporters of the strike . . . and an early morning starting point for the pickets. At lunch-time it was a gigantic communal restaurant. At the same time, the Miners' Welfare functioned as a more or less continuous social club. (Samuel, 1986, p. 10)

Into this focus, in many of the pit villages, came new groups, formed by the local women.

Most of the many Women's Action/Support Groups were founded spontaneously by residents of the communities, though in many cases they were stimulated to act by either or both of Scargill's rhetoric and the example of other communities – often perceived through the voluminous television coverage achieved. (The groups were linked informally both locally and regionally, and also through the national Women Against Pit Closures movement.) The scale of the mobilization was substantial: South Wales had 106 such groups, North Yorkshire had 34, and – despite the area being the weakest link in the NUM's operations – Nottinghamshire had 30 (Stead, 1987; Witham, 1986; North Yorkshire WAPC, 1985). The tenacity, ingenuity and resourcefulness of the women involved in these Groups' activities was remarkable for the sheer depth of social and material capacities which it uncovered. They operated food kitchens and community counselling services, raised funds and organized their own picket lines. Some Women's Action Groups were at the forefront of strike activity, sustaining its momentum; indeed, many of the women involved were opposed to the final return to work, which they perceived as a capitulation by the men, after great hardship which had achieved little in tangible terms (Young, 1985; Witham, 1986; Bloomfield, 1986). The hardships that they faced and shared brought both family stresses and personal dilemmas, but their activities undoubtedly prolonged the strike in many places.

The creation of the Women's Action Groups illustrates the nature of the communities involved in the strike, and the strong sense of belonging to a place, and of commitment to its future, which Scargill and the NUM were able to realize. It also illustrates how new institutions can change the nature of a place, as a milieu in which new patterns of behaviour will be formed. The title of Stead's (1987) book on women and the strike – *Never the Same Again* – encapsulates this. As she described the situation at Polmaise colliery, in Stirlingshire:

> Despite all the troubles, I never heard a woman say she regretted having supported the long strike. On the contrary, the miners' wives seemed desperate to keep the spirit that had seen them through the long months, the solidarity and friendship and, above all, the feeling that together they could do something to change the world and make it a better place, not only for themselves, but for all those suffering injustice. (pp. 164–5)

After the strike, however, they were called on to return to their 'service role' for the miners, and they faced difficulties sustaining both their solidarity and their ability to build on their new-found strength (see also Waddington et al., 1990). In Thurcroft, South Yorkshire, the same issues arose; women had found their feet but needed to identify a route that they could now follow (People of Thurcroft, 1986). Thus, not only did the strike draw new resources from the mining villages, it also recreated them as different places, with altered cultural forms.

SPATIAL VARIABILITY IN SUPPORT FOR THE STRIKE

The strike was never solid, supported by all NUM members, and as it progressed so the number of miners still holding out diminished. The claims and counter-claims of the NUM and the NCB regarding the number of strikers were the focus of much debate, but in general if not specific terms there is little doubt that MacGregor's (1986, p. 341) claims for January 1985 were accurate:

> we had 70,026 of his members back at work – representing 37 per cent of the NUM workforce. We were producing coal at 71 of our 174 pits – 47 of which were working normally. At only 32 pits was Scargill's strike still solid.

After the New Year, as the hardship faced by the miners, their families and their communities grew greater, so the drift back to work gathered pace. By the end of February 1985, the NCB claimed that 50.2 per cent of its estimate of the NUM membership was working, though the union itself claimed that 60 per cent were still on strike (Jones, 1986, p. 185). More important for the present discussion, however, was the spatial variability in both support for the strike over the full period and the rate of the drift back to work.

Figure 4.1 (reproduced from Duncan and Goodwin, 1988) gives a clear impression of that spatial variability at one date; approximately half way through the strike's duration, whereas support was almost complete in some areas (notably South Wales, Kent, Yorkshire and Scotland) in others, notably in the East Midlands (focused on Nottinghamshire), the great majority of NUM members were at work. This picture is enhanced by figure 4.2, which shows NCB estimates of the number of NUM members who were working in each field both during an early month of the conflict and on four dates in the middle of the strike period. From these data, it is possible to suggest a fivefold classification of the fields.

1 The *solid-for-the strike*, comprising five fields – Yorkshire, Northeast, Scotland, Kent and South Wales. These had all NUM members out at the start of the strike, and the great majority were still out six months later.

2 The *non-strikers*, at the other extreme, comprising the two fields

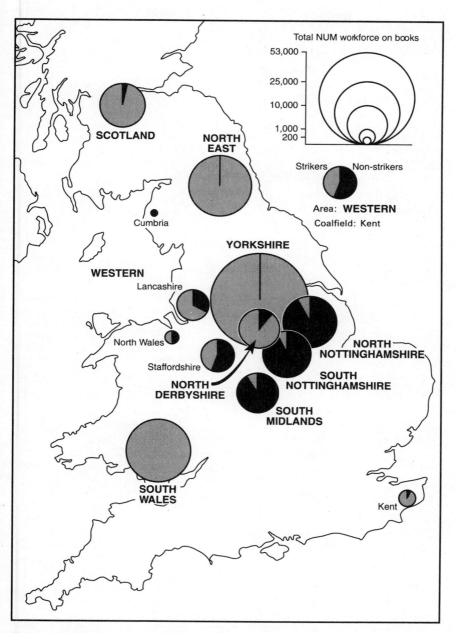

Figure 4.1 The distribution of support for the NUM strike in September 1984.
Source: Duncan and Goodwin, 1988, p. 50.

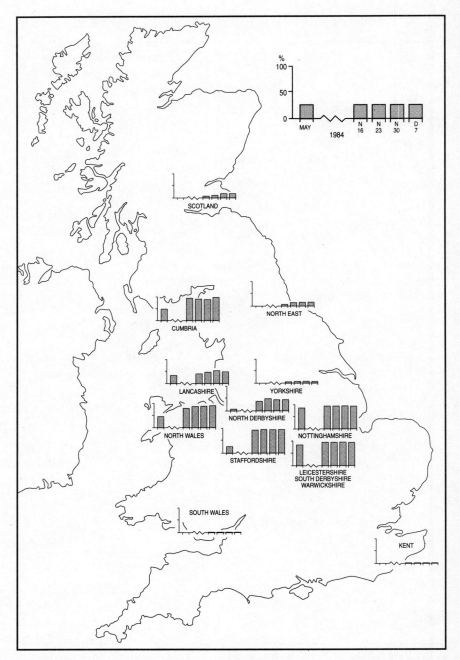

Figure 4.2 The distribution of support for the NUM strike at five dates in 1984. *Source*: Griffiths and Johnston, 1991, p. 191.

(Nottinghamshire and Leicestershire–South Derbyshire–Warwickshire) which had less than 15 per cent on strike in the early weeks of the dispute, and less than 5 per cent when it was six months old.

3 The *half-and-halfs*, comprising the two smallest fields (North Wales and Cumbria) where approximately half the miners joined the strike initially but most had returned to work by mid-December.

4 The *rapid returners*, where three-quarters struck at the outset, but by mid-November only 10 per cent had not returned to work. (Only the small Staffordshire field is in this category.)

5 The *undecided* (Leicestershire and North Derbyshire) where a majority were early supporters for the strike but within six months about half had returned to work.

A major purpose of the remainder of this chapter is to appreciate the reasons for at least some of that variability.

The implications of the arguments about the nature of regions and places reviewed in the previous chapter are that the pattern just described should reflect long-established cultural differences between the places concerned. To inquire whether this was indeed so, the militancy record of the various fields was investigated, using NUM voting returns relating to ballots for strike action. (Because, as noted above, the NCB and the NUM use different regional divisions of Great Britain the correspondence between the data discussed above and those presented here is approximate only.)

Between 1971 and 1983, the national executive of the NUM called six separate national ballots on strike action. Under its extant rules, support from 55 per cent of those voting was required for a strike to be called, and this was achieved on the first two occasions only: in December 1971, 59 per cent voted in favour, whereas in February 1974 support was an overwhelming 81 per cent. Figure 4.3 shows the trend in voting across the six ballots in all the NUM's Areas (i.e. excluding the Cokemen, and Colliery Officials and Staff, both of which vote 'nationally', plus the Durham and Northumberland Mechanics and the Scottish Craftsmen). With a small number of minor exceptions, the trend was the same in every Area, and February 1974 had the peak support for strike action in all cases. Nevertheless, although the trend was the same its amplitude varied, and the gap between Areas widened over time. This allows the identification of three separate groups of fields.

1 The *militant*, comprising four fields (Kent, Scotland, South Wales and Yorkshire) which consistently gave the strongest support to the strike call, although none gave it a majority at every ballot.

2 The *non-militant*, where support for strike action was consistently

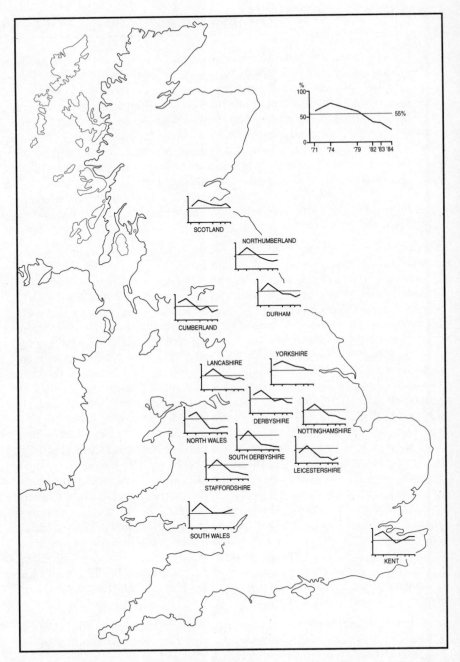

Figure 4.3 Variations among coalfields in support for NUM strike ballots, 1971–83. *Source*: Griffiths and Johnston, 1991, p. 193.

below average. All five fields (Leicestershire, Nottinghamshire, South
Derbyshire and Staffordshire in the Midlands, plus North Wales)
provided the 55 per cent majority in February 1974, but only one,
North Wales in December 1971, provided that level of support on
another ballot.

3 The *in-betweens*, a group of five fields (Cumberland, Durham, Derbyshire, Lancashire – or Northwest – and Northumberland) which
provided the 55 per cent vote at each of the first two ballots but on
average produced only 42 per cent support for the strike call across
the other four.

These three groups also behaved differently at the onset of the 1984
dispute. A local ballot was held in March 1984 in four of the five 'non-
militant' fields (Leicestershire was the exception) to decide whether to
follow Scargill's strike call under Rule 43; the results were 32 per cent in
favour in North Wales, 28 per cent in Staffordshire, 26.5 per cent in
Nottinghamshire, and 17 per cent in South Derbyshire. (The data were
published in *The Sunday Times*, 19 March 1984.) Similarly, four of the
five in the 'in-between' group held a ballot, with 52 per cent support in
Northumberland, 50 per cent in Derbyshire, 41 per cent in Lancashire,
and just 8 per cent in Cumberland; there was no ballot in Durham. None
of the four fields in the 'militant' group held a ballot; in all four, the
miners were prepared to strike following their local Executive's call, and
to remain on strike, in the great majority of cases, until the return to work
a year later.

During the 1970s and 1980s, therefore, Britain's coalfields differed
significantly in the degree of militancy of the NUM members, and those
differences carried through into the conduct of the 1984–5 dispute. In the
militant fields, members responded immediately to the call for strike action,
without waiting for a ballot, and then remained the strike's strongest
supporters throughout its course. In most of the non-militant fields, on the
other hand, ballots were held, support for the strike was low, and the
majority of miners worked through the entire period of the dispute. Finally,
although support for the strike call was not very strong across the four
local ballots held in the 'in-between' group, solidarity was high in the
early months, and remained so in Durham and Northumberland until the
dispute's end; in the other three fields, however, support waned, with most
Cumberland miners back at work by the end of 1984, alongside about
half of their contemporaries in North Derbyshire and Lancashire.

Exploring reasons for the variability

If we accept the 'cohesive mass segregation' argument derived from the work of Kerr and Siegel (see above, p. 108), then we would expect all isolated mining communities to be equally strike-prone. But they were not in Great Britain in 1984, and adjacent areas with similar relatively isolated mining communities (notably Nottinghamshire and South Yorkshire) differed very substantially not only in their support for the strike call but also in their level of industrial militancy over a substantial period of time. Knowles (1952) and Newton (1969) also illustrate differences between mining areas in both their strike-proneness and their support for the Communist Party.

An alternative explanation focuses on self-interest, arguing that miners in areas most under threat by the policies over which there is conflict would be much more likely to strike than would those in areas little, if at all, affected. In the context of a dispute over the future of pits and communities, the main difference is thus likely to be between those areas with good prospects (because of high productivity capabilities and substantial quantities of accessible, easily-worked coal) and those with much less secure futures. The NUM's accurate interpretation of the NCB's strategy was that the latter intended to concentrate production on a relatively small number of 'superpits' in the most productive fields, which it would achieve by changes in work practices and pay schemes and by closing those pits which it defined as 'uneconomic'. Within the union, therefore, Scargill's call was for solidarity, for those with more readily-guaranteed futures to support other miners' prospects which were less bright, especially so if the NCB could capitalize on splits and other weaknesses within the NUM, thereby enabling it to isolate vulnerable areas.

The most productive coalfields in Great Britain in the 1980s were on the eastern flanks of the Pennines. Mining in those areas occurred initially on the exposed fields in the area between Leeds and Derby, and it gradually shifted eastwards, as improvements in technology allowed deeper pits to be sunk, onto the concealed deposits. By the early twentieth century the focus of activity was just west of the River Trent, especially in the area between Doncaster and Nottingham (Griffin, 1977). The large pits sunk then continued to attract substantial investment through the 1970s (North and Spooner, 1982), by which time plans were well advanced to exploit the even deeper deposits further east (notably in the Selby area just south of the city of York and in the Vale of Belvoir northwest of Grantham), as well as further south in the Coventry area of Warwickshire and in Oxford-shire. The perceived good prospects in these areas (somewhat contradicted by closures in the late 1980s in parts of Nottinghamshire and Yorkshire), with much of the coal being sent to the string of power stations along the River Trent, contrast strongly with the bleak futures for many other areas. This is demonstrated by NCB operating returns for the period 1976–7 to 1981–2: North Nottinghamshire, North Derbyshire and South Yorkshire all recorded net surpluses, whereas South Wales, Scotland and Northeast England accounted for 90 per cent of all operating losses (Monopolies and Mergers Commission, 1983, p. 30).

A 'self-interest' explanation would suggest that whereas solidarity for the strike call to defend jobs and the future of pits would obtain strong support in the peripheral areas with relatively bleak futures, it would be harder to sustain in the central profitable coalfields of Nottinghamshire and Yorkshire. It fails, however, because although support was weakest in much of Nottinghamshire it was very strong in Yorkshire. A partial answer for the failure of that explanation is provided here, by looking at the characteristics of the Nottinghamshire mining communities which apparently set them apart from those of their neighbours further north. Doing this allows a development of the ideas set out in the previous chapter regarding the salient institutional features which characterize a place.

THE DUKERIES COALFIELD

Early mining of the concealed coal measures in Nottinghamshire occurred to the northeast of the county town, with later expansion at the end of the nineteenth century in the Mansfield area (Waller, 1983). The major developments in the twentieth century involved an eastward shift and the opening up of a number of large, highly productive pits in what became known as the Dukeries field. By the late twentieth century, this area was the focus of mining activity in the county.

The Dukeries was, and largely remains, a rural area of two contrasting types of land use – rich agricultural land, typical of lowland England, and the extensive woodlands of Sherwood Forest (figure 4.4). Much of it was part of large estates owned by members of the landed aristocracy, who became aware of the potential wealth beneath their holdings. (The aristocrats included the Dukes of Newcastle and Portland, Earl Manvers, Viscount Galway, and Lord Savile. Several of their stately homes remain, such as Thoresby Hall, the home of Earl Manvers, and Welbeck Abbey, which was the Duke of Portland's seat. Others have been destroyed, but Clumber Park, owned by the Duke of Newcastle, became a public park.)

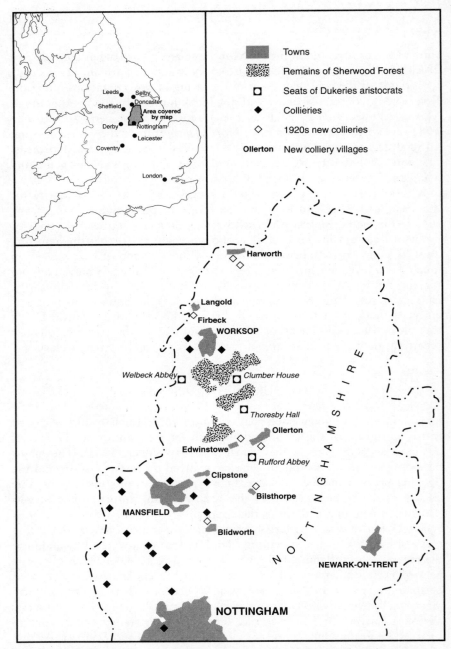

Figure 4.4 The location of the Dukeries area in North Nottinghamshire. *Source*: Griffiths and Johnston, 1991, p. 193 (after Waller, 1983).

Technological improvements allowed them to capitalize on that wealth in the 1920s.

The aristocratic landowners invited companies to tender for the development rights. This involved substantial investment to clear the sites, provide rail lines to move the coal, sink shafts (which took three years, on average), provide housing, and recruit miners (Waller, 1983, p. 17ff.). All the costs were met by the coal companies, who then paid royalties to the landowners on the tonnage produced. The investments were extremely profitable, however, and the companies were among the most successful in the country when they were nationalized into the NCB in 1947. Their intrusions wrought significant changes in the landscape, but stimulated the following lyrical description in the *New Statesman* (quoted in Beckett, 1988, p. 337) of the village of Bilsthorpe, which was represented as

> the latest, but far from the last, of the long lines of pits which have transformed the glades and villages of Sherwood Forest, and the Dukeries, into one of the greatest coalfields in the whole of Great Britain. Steadily, quietly, till we stumble on their existence with shocked surprise, pit after pit has been sunk and worked in the beautiful stretch of country which covers the eastern half of the county of Nottingham. It is one of the romances and revolutions of modern industrialism.

The nature of those developments, and the institutional structure of the villages, was peculiar to the Dukeries, as discussed here under the three separate headings introduced to characterize a place in the previous chapter.

The organization of work

The coal companies that won the contracts to operate in the Dukeries were experienced in the organization of large workforces which operated in difficult conditions and were potentially prone to industrial unrest. Most had obtained that experience by operating in the older parts of the Nottinghamshire field further east, where the workforce was relatively quiescent, as illustrated for Hucknall (D. Gilbert, 1988).

A characteristic working practice which the companies brought with them covered the organization of the underground process of coal-winning. This was known as the 'butty system', which has a long history in the area (Griffin, 1977, p. 26). 'Butties' – the local term for subcontractors or chargemen – were employed on a contract basis to run much of the day-to-day operations of each pit. Griffin (1971, p. 29) describes their role thus:

the company would sink a shaft, then invite tenders from the butties. The butty who quoted the lowest price per ton for getting and raising the coal was given the contract. The butty would then engage his men ... [and he] supervised and paid the men, and provided the working capital. Sometimes they were responsible only for work directly connected with production, but in some cases they were responsible also for development work, drainage and ventilation.

At the coal face, the butties were responsible for the actual mining processes, overseen by colliery company officials; the butties were in charge of organizing and paying for the winning of coal, though not in all cases for its transport to the pithead.

Under the butty system, miners' wages were not determined by the colliery company but by the individual butties: an individual's earnings depended on his butty's contract with the company, on the productivity of his gang, and on the wage rate offered by the butty. Some miners would have regular places in the gang assured, whereas others were employed on a casual basis only, being recruited at the colliery gates at the start of a shift if more labour was required to meet the contract (Krieger, 1983, p. 92). In these ways, the pit workforces were divided into many small, relatively independent units, each with its own wage rate: there was no miner solidarity. Within a gang, each member's wage depended on the overall productivity rate, so that low-productivity members were not popular. As Krieger (1983, p. 93) describes it:

> The butty (or the chargeman) had at his command, as people in the industry put it: the stick – complete discipline; the carrot – piecerate pay administered for individual production through the chargemen; and the extra threat – dismissal or relegation back to 'the market' [i.e. the casual labour system].

This created a workplace culture very different from that characteristic of many other fields, where collective attitudes were stronger, solidarity across the entire workforce was the norm, and standard rates of pay applied throughout a pit.

There were attempts to abolish the butty system in Nottinghamshire around the end of the First World War (i.e. before the opening-up of the Dukeries field), as part of a programme to improve working conditions (Griffin, 1962, p. 39). In 1918, a majority of the county's miners voted for its replacement by a day-rate system, but there were differences within the workforce over its implementation and the colliery companies were reluctant to change away from the butty system (Griffin, 1962, pp. 53–4). As a compromise, the Nottinghamshire Miners' Association and the owners agreed to a modified piece-rate system for each coalface, but nevertheless many owners retained the butty system, and it was revived when the Dukeries field was opened. In those new pits, the butty, according to Waller (1983, p. 126)

> became just a kind of foreman, or perhaps a member of lower managerial supervisory staff . . . the employers appear to have been determined to take the important decisions themselves rather than leave the butty with a significant degree of independence, as the modernity and high level of mechanization of the new pits perhaps dictated.

Thus the butty system slowly declined in importance through the 1920s and 1930s in Nottinghamshire, with Waller reporting from his interviews that 'few miners can now remember exactly when or how it disappeared' (p. 126).

For the present purpose, the existence of the butty system when the pits were opened, and the new coalfield's culture was established, is the crucial point. As a system for payment and the organization of underground practice, it was undoubtedly in decline during the decades prior to the Second World War, but the historical legacy of the butty and its ramifications permeated the lives of the miners. A work ethos was established that was individualistic, acquisitive and incentive-oriented, but which had little sense of solidarity or mutuality that might supersede this narrowly-conceived achievement ethic. Thus, reporting on his interviews in the Dukeries in the mid-1970s, Krieger (1983, p. 94) concludes that

> There was no . . . marra relationship [the Durham term for collective labour bonds] and, what is more important, miners in Nottinghamshire do not in any way feel the absence of these traditions. However severe the victimization or inequality of potential pay, they give no thought to having a lottery to determine positions on the coal face [the Durham tradition – of cavilling]; however their labor may be divided, they have little impulse to regulate production collectively or coordinate themselves in work groups to forestall management initiative. They have no tradition of sharing pay-notes as do miners who work under, or are influenced by rules for work relations generated under, the cavilling/marra system.

Compared with Durham, therefore (and to many other fields as well), Nottinghamshire in general and the Dukeries in particular had a particular set of social relations at the workplace established through the early use of the butty system. This was accepted within, and its acceptance was transmitted through, the collective culture established in the new pit villages opened to house the miners at these isolated establishments.

Home and social life

Most British coalfields were developed away from established population centres and required the provision of housing for miners recruited from elsewhere. In general terms, the Dukeries was a paradigm example of this situation: the companies built villages to house the majority of their workers, and recruited widely (and selectively), though notably from adjacent fields in Nottinghamshire, Derbyshire, and Yorkshire (79 per cent of the migrants to Langold, close to the Yorkshire border, came from these three sources between 1924 and 1932, for example: Waller, 1983, p. 40). But within this general process, there were particular developments that characterized the provision of village housing by the Dukeries' companies.

The condition of miners' housing was customarily poor in the early twentieth century, and there was considerable agitation for its improvement (Bacon, 1986). The housing constructed in the Dukeries was a marked improvement on that provided elsewhere in previous decades – as illustrated by Waller's (1983) detailed reporting of the work of the Butterley Company, which developed the village of Ollerton. In the design and layout of the housing, the new villages like Blidworth, Harworth and Ollerton bore the imprint of the ideas about planned communities (such as garden villages) extant at the time, and the companies claimed to be establishing model communities (Griffin, 1971, pp. 168–70; Waller, 1983, pp. 254ff.).

The companies' main concerns, however, were with social control of their workforces outside the pits. They were less bothered with the ideals of planned, balanced communities than with social control. According to Waller (1983, p. 103):

> It is clear that one of the reasons why the companies were prepared to invest so much in the provision of housing for their workmen was because they could influence employees living in company houses at the pit gates far more effectively than those living in a more mixed community several miles from their place of work.

(In this way the solidarity of the isolated culture – see p. 109 – was enhanced by the coal companies, who clearly then needed to manipulate the nature of that culture to their own ends.) Thus the miners became the tenants of 'tied cottages', albeit well-designed ones (rather than the serried brick terraces characteristic of other fields) in what, for industrial England, were attractive milieux, but the security of their tenancy depended entirely on their continued employment at their company's pit.

The situations within the villages were crucial. Within them, the companies either owned or effectively controlled the services, so that the miners and their families shopped at company shops, drank at company pubs, and played sports at colliery clubs. There were very few other sources of employment, so most miners' wives were confined to domestic labour (a confinement enhanced by the 'slave' relationship described earlier – p. 110), and were as tied to the colliery as their husbands. (Not all companies enforced these ties in the same way, however. The Butterley Company found that men whose wives could not find work were less likely to stay at Ollerton, and so planned the building of factories in the village which would ensure both that men were not lost and that family incomes could be supplemented. One proposal – which eventually fell through – involved the Butterley Company protecting the employer by agreeing to sell no land within five miles of the villages, thereby preventing any other sources of work being established, while the factory-owner would guarantee to take at least 65 per cent of his workforce from Ollerton. Eventually, a hosiery factory was opened there in 1937 – Waller, 1983, pp. 91–3.)

The companies also strongly influenced the social and cultural life of the villages. They were very concerned to encourage religious observance among their employees, for example, and not only provided the churches and chapels but also influenced the selection of the clergy: they 'insisted that they [the clergy] were solely concerned with the spiritual guidance of the miners, [but] their concern with religion fits in with their policy of making every aspect of life in the colliery villages a matter for their scrutiny' (Waller, 1983, p. 91). Sport was another activity in which the companies were active, not only encouraging local clubs (especially in cricket and soccer) but also being prepared to give preference in employment to good players. (Active sportmen – and active bandsmen too, for the companies encouraged the colliery bands – were felt to be less likely to engage in 'subversive' union and other activity, and inter-village rivalries were encouraged: Waller, 1983, p. 197, p. 208.)

Alongside the positive aspects of the social control of the villages were the negative. The villages were patrolled by company uniformed 'policemen' whose 'duties were primarily concerned with the maintenance of the appearance of the village, keeping the lawns tidy and litter off the streets, for example' (Waller, 1983, p. 98), but Waller's respondents also reported company 'policemen' who watched over children's play, recorded untidy properties ('It seems clear that the threat of dismissal was thought to hang over men who did not keep their gardens tidy in several villages' – p. 100), and ensured that dogs were not kept as pets (thus preventing the men from engaging in the popular contemporary sport among miners of training and racing greyhounds and whippets). To one resident, at least, the atmosphere was that of a 'prison camp' (p. 103), and this was enhanced by the fear of eviction if the miner lost his job. The colliery villages were clearly places in which control of the workforce was strong, beyond the normal social relationships between employers and employee which were established at the pit itself.

Village politics

Political activity is often divided between the two other spheres of civil society. With regard to the *politics of the workplace* – or the politics of production – trades unions are central to the mobilization of collective solidarity among the workforce, whereas in the wider sphere of non-work life – the politics of consumption – political parties are the focal organizations. The latter operate solely through the state apparatus; the former are active both in the individual workplaces and in the wider arena represented by the state. As with all other aspects of capitalist society, however, local variations in the interpretation of these two roles and the institutional framework within which they can be operated are normal. This was certainly the case in the Dukeries, where, as Waller (1983, p. 291) describes it:

> in the Dukeries colliery villages the mediation of this social control can be perceived in the painstaking policies of the employers. Determined to maintain these isolated villages as functional units separate from contaminating ideologies such as those purveyed by the Labour party and the Nottinghamshire Miners' Association, the companies stressed the unity of the model villages.

He believes that this policy was easier to pursue in smaller than larger units, and where the colliery manager and senior staff (i.e. those at the head of the local socio-economic hierarchy) also lived in the village, albeit in superior, segregated accommodation.

Regarding workplace politics, much has been written about the trades unions in the Dukeries, because of the dramatic events that occurred in Nottinghamshire in the aftermath of the 1926 General Strike. These reverberated throughout the labour movement at the time, and were reawakened in the 1984–5 dispute. In 1984, Griffin wrote that 'It appears that once again, as in 1926, the Nottinghamshire miners are the weakest link in the chain of national policy' (p. i), and they are represented as:

more interested in the pursuit of narrow self-interest than in displaying solidarity with less fortunate brethren working in coalfields or collieries earmarked for closure. . . . The . . . Notts. miners are working in the same, or similar, highly productive, profitable pits whose management decided to keep working if possible with the use of compliant labour. Moreover, the NUM decision not to hold a national strike ballot, but opt for the 'domino-effect' instead, was based on a belief that the former was too risky because the self-interested attitude of groups such as the Notts. miners would result in the rejection of the national strike call. Instead, a stiff dose of mass picketing from miners on strike would soon persuade the 'spineless gits' or 'jellybabies' to join the struggle.

Long after nationalization of the pits, the end of the butty system, and the handing-over of the colliery company villages to the NCB, it seems, there was a coalfield culture in Nottinghamshire (especially the Dukeries) which differed substantially in its politics – Waller (1983, p. 130) refers to 'the lack of conventional industrial and political organization in the new mines [which] provides one more example of the challenge the coalfield of the Dukeries offers to the established view of mining life and community. (See also Sunley (1990), and note that Griffin does not accept the above interpretation, but rather prefers one which sees the Nottinghamshire miners as determined to avoid splits within the union, which would have been the case if the rule-book, specifically Rule 43 – p. 107 – had been adhered to in 1984.)

The NUM's predecessor (like the NUM itself) was a federation of local miners' unions – The Miners' Federation of Great Britain (MFGB) – with which the Nottinghamshire Miners' Association (NMA) had been federated since 1888. By the 1920s there were clear strains within this federation, notably between the socialist majority on its executive and the 'lib-lab' element represented prominently by George Spencer and Frank Varley of Nottinghamshire (Griffin, 1977, p. 98). The NMA leadership and many rank-and-file members became increasingly disenchanted with MFGB strategy during the 1920 national miners' strike and the 1921 lockout, and less than a third of Nottinghamshire miners bothered to vote in a 1921 ballot on whether to accept the offered settlement or continue the dispute (Griffin, 1962, p. 91, p. 102).

These rifts, and the increasingly separate position taken in Nottinghamshire, reached their acme in 1926. The MFGB conference on 9 April endorsed a resolution insisting upon no increase in the length of the working day, no wage reductions, and firm adherence to a national minimum percentage principle agreed in 1924 (Griffin, 1962, p. 152). The coal-owners' response in most areas was to give notice that their workers' contracts were terminated from the end of the month: Nottinghamshire colliery companies did not follow this path, but the NMA felt bound to call a strike in solidarity with the MFGB. The national strike started on 3 May, with less support in Nottinghamshire than many other fields (Sunley, 1988); work continued unbroken at Blidworth and Clipstone, two of the newly-opened Dukeries pits, and by September some 70 per cent of the county's miners were back at work (Griffin, 1962, p. 183). The NMA argued from the outset for a negotiated settlement, in part because of a fear that intransigence might lead to total defeat and in part because it had little money with which to fight the strike following the run-down of its funds during the 1921 lockout. Spencer was the leading advocate of this view on the MFGB executive, persistently advocating greater district autonomy and full membership balloting.

Tensions between the MFGB and the NMA grew, and by mid-November Spencer was negotiating with the Nottinghamshire owners for a separate settlement; this was concluded on 20 November. Two days later, the separate Nottinghamshire and District Miners' Industrial Union (NMIU) was formed, with Spencer as its leader. This had overt employer support (Griffin, 1971, p. 247):

> The colliery owners undertook to support the new Union by giving it sole negotiating rights; by agreeing to deduct the Union contribution from wages; by contributing £12,500 to the Union's pension fund and by harrying known members of the NMA.

The NMIU did not join the MFGB, and competed with the NMA for members in Nottinghamshire and adjacent pits. Its success was greatest in the Dukeries field, where none of the pits had as many as 10 per cent of their miners in the NMA; the figure was less than 1 per cent at Harworth and Thoresby in 1934 (Waller, 1983, p. 118).

The NMIU, often referred to as the 'Spencer Union', led to the Dukeries being characterized as a 'blackleg district' (in that same *New Statesman* article which was lyrical about the conditions there – p. 121). It was a clear manifestation of the industrial and cultural ethos which the coal companies were fostering: it believed that trades unions should be concerned with industrial issues only, and not wider political goals; it gave privilege to local autonomy rather than general solidarity; it favoured compromise with employers; and it eschewed strike action. Griffin (1984) suggests that on a number of issues, such as its concern with safety matters, the NMIU cannot be associated with the American 'bosses' unions', but its basic policies were repugnant to many other trade unionists, including the majority in the MFGB.

The NMIU affiliated to the MFGB in 1937, following a campaign by the NMA to recruit more members at the Dukeries pits, notably at Harworth on the Yorkshire border (and some distance from the rest of the Dukeries field: figure 4.4) where there was substantial conflict (see Griffin and Griffin, 1977; Krieger, 1983). But the coalfield culture lived on, created, according to Waller (1983, p. 130) in the following way:

> The isolation and social dislocation of the company villages of the new Dukeries coalfield reinforced the traditional moderation of naturally prosperous Nottinghamshire to make possible the most serious incidence of non-political trade unionism in twentieth-century Britain.

This was apparently repeated in 1984–5, when the aftermath of the strike was the formation in Nottinghamshire of the Union of Democratic Miners (UDM), which was not federated with the NUM and was denied membership of both the Trades Union Congress and the Labour party.

Turning to the *politics of the community* the Dukeries again stands out as atypical among British coalfields. In general terms, these provided the main heartlands for the growth of the country's Labour party, providing its earliest successes in both local government and the winning of Parliamentary seats. But none of the Dukeries villages had a Labour party branch until the 1940s, and the area returned only one Labour County Councillor before then (in 1937). Furthermore, there was no Labour representation from the mining villages on the Rural District Council which served the area (Waller, 1983, p. 132). Prior to nationalization in 1947, the Dukeries was a vacuum as far as the Labour party was concerned.

The reason for this vacuum, and the consequent Conservative dominance of Dukeries' politics, was the colliery companies' hegemony, according to Waller, especially with respect to local government elections. At British general elections, vote counts are reported at constituency level only, so that where a party gets its votes is largely unknown (though party workers have efficient ways of estimating the geography of their support when acting as scrutineers at the count). Thus according to Waller (1983, p. 136):

> There is a great difference between, on the one hand, voting Labour in a constituency which spread beyond the boundaries of the colliery village, and, on the other hand, being seen to organize a local Labour party or even to stand against the colliery manager and the old elite.

Waller's informants illustrated the residents' reluctance to oppose the companies, for fear of losing their jobs and homes. As a result, the Labour party was organizationally weak in the Dukeries before the 1950s, and had no base on which to mobilize electoral support through grass roots activity. By contrast, the Conservative party was very active in the villages, establishing Associations for both men and women and thereby consolidating the party's general hold over the area despite the changed socio-economic context. (Interestingly, Waddington et al. (1990) report that whereas in a Yorkshire mining community the pro-Labour *Daily Mirror* was the most widely-read daily newspaper, both before and after the strike, in the Nottinghamshire community which they surveyed the pro-Conservative *The Sun* was the most popular before the strike, and equally popular with the *Daily Mirror* after it. *The Sun* had virtually no readers in the Yorkshire community in 1988. Similarly, whereas 65 per cent of those interviewed in the Yorkshire community voted Labour in 1987 and 66 per cent indicated that they would vote Labour again at the next general election, in the Nottinghamshire community the respective percentages were 51 and 48.)

Synthesis: a Dukeries coalfield culture?

The three elements of the Dukeries culture outlined above are interdependent, in part because those with the greatest influence there – the colliery companies – were instrumental in fostering and maintaining aspects of all three. They provided the work, they built the villages, they negotiated (from strength) the social relations at the pits, they encouraged a particular form of unionization, and they discouraged (implicitly if not explicitly) Labour party activism in any form. (And those who didn't like it could leave; many did, as Waller's data show.) In this, the companies were aided and abetted both by the dislocating and isolating processes that impinged on the people who came to their villages and by the key agents in both pits and communities (the buttymen and the Spencer group) who contrived a particular mixture of deference, self-interest and non-political association in the locally-constructed significant reality of the working people.

This interdependence was not simply the outcome of company imposition: had direct compulsion by the employers been the crucial mechanism, political quiescence would probably not have resulted, as illustrated by the resistance of Kent miners to buttyism (Goffer, 1977) and that of Doncaster area miners to village strategems (Gibbon, 1988). The miners and their families were themselves implicated in the creation of their coalfield culture, through the operation of hegemonic processes by which relations of domination and subdomination came to imbue the entire lived experience – the social practices, relationships, expectations, and dominant values. Thus the individualist ethos which characterized the social relations at the workplace in the Dukeries was as much a survival mechanism developed by the miners for the competitive milieu underground as it was imposed by the employers.

Both coercion and consent were typical of the Dukeries villages, therefore, and the mechanisms instituted by employers and their employees were integral to daily life and the maintenance of the former's hegemony. According to Waller (1983, p. 105):

> In the mining villages . . . can be found both deference and powerless resistance. There are residents of the private company villages who maintain a hatred for the system of tied housing and restriction, embodied in the figures of the colliery manager and the company policeman, the deputies and the butties. Such men would recognize the traditional ability of the agricultural labourer to tip his cap to the employer while raising two fingers behind his back.

The salient causal processes in the creation of this deferential coalfield culture are the subject of considerable debate. Some, e.g. Krieger (1983) and Sunley (1986), stress the crucial role of work organization, and the butty system in particular, whereas others – Waller (1983) and Rees (1985, 1986) – emphasize the power of the colliery companies over their villages, and their monopoly of local labour markets. Whatever the cause, however, there is no doubt that a separate culture was established in the Dukeries – very different from that in adjacent South Yorkshire, for example, as both Krieger (1983) and Waller (1983) emphasize – and that this has remained, in remodelled form, to the present day. As such, the continued separate attitudes of Nottinghamshire miners towards the working practices implemented by the NCB (see Krieger, 1983) point to the fact that the Dukeries culture has lasted long after the events and institutions that created it, and provide a basis for appreciating why Nottinghamshire was different in 1984–5.

Some of the features typical of the Dukeries can be found elsewhere, and enhance the argument presented here. In their study of Yorkshire during the 1984–5 strike, for example, Winterton and Winterton (1989: see also Waddington et al., 1990) found that the strike breakers were more likely to live outside the mining communities, thereby producing a geography whereby the strike was strongest (and longest) in the pits whose labour came mainly from local, closed communities: in Nottinghamshire, of course, the opposite occurred, with the closed communities being solid against the strike. (Waddinington et al., 1990, show that in the Nottinghamshire community which they surveyed the immigrant and the 'local' miners were spatially segregated within the housing stock and that most of the miners who joined the strike were among the recent immigrants whose home lives were somewhat separate from those of the rest of the community.) The separate culture was most clearly developed in the Dukeries; it was there that the Conservative party and the NCB rested their hopes of defeating the NUM and that the union itself invested so much energy in picketing to try and close the crucial pits. That Nottinghamshire went on working reflects not simply the self-interest of its miners but more importantly the culture that their predecessors (many of them their ancestors) helped to create and transmit to the present.

THE STRIKE AND AN UNDERSTANDING OF PLACE

The work on which much of this chapter was based (Griffiths and Johnston, 1991) was oriented towards answering a geographical question concerning the relative lack of support for the 1984–5 NUM strike in Nottinghamshire. As many observed at the time, the question could have similarly been asked nearly fifty years earlier with regard to the relative lack of support for the 1926 General Strike in the same county: as Sunley (1990) describes the two geographies, they have 'striking parallels'. One could argue that the similarity is coincidental; alternatively, one could claim that similar conditions have evoked a similar response to two events separated by half a century. The latter is Sunley's position. He argues that 'the failure of both disputes revealed and reproduced the regional nature of management-labour relations in the industry' (p. 35), because 'miners' interpretations of the two disputes, and of the underlying arguments, are understood as embedded in the nature of collective social relations at work ... the constitution of workplace relations has varied between coalfields and ... variations in management and labour strategies have been central to this process' (p. 36). This conclusion is somewhat at odds with Waller's (1983) contention (written before the 1984–5 dispute) that it was company control of the villages and of the politics there which made the Dukeries a quiescent region. Our case is that, while the nature of the social relations at the workplace is clearly an important differentiating characteristic of the Dukeries field, they are probably a necessary but insufficient factor to account for the response of miners there to the 1926 and 1984 calls to strike.

To some extent, the relative importance of the three components of a place identified here as contributors to an understanding of the strike in the Dukeries is secondary to our main purpose. The goal here is to illustrate the general contention set out in this book that in order to use regions in geography (as against practising regional geography) it is necessary to appreciate what the salient features of a region (or place) are – some of which may be more important to particular research tasks than others. The Dukeries field was (and still is in many respects) different from many others on all three of the components of a place, as illustrated not only by Sunley's arguments (following Krieger and others) regarding the different social relations at the workplace, but also Waller's (1983, p. 235) that whereas the Dukeries villages were praised for many of their design aspects, 'the social and political institutions of the miners in the new South Yorkshire villages left much to be desired compared with traditional and long-established coalfields'.

A separate coalfield culture developed in the Dukeries in the 1920s, and we have suggested (as do Krieger, Sunley, Waller and others) that the milieu within which that culture was set has been the transmission agent for ensuring that a separate culture remained in the Dukeries in the 1980s. The precise transmission mechanism has not been explored, although the oral histories on which Krieger and Waller rely are vital in tracing not only the nature of the current culture but also its roots. Within that culture the precise reason for the Nottinghamshire miners deciding not to strike remains a matter of contention for further study – were they simply self-interested and unprepared to show solidarity with the miners of other fields?; were they so concerned for solidarity within the union that they would not strike unless its rules (Rule 43 in particular) were upheld?; or what? Further study of the strike and the place will suggest the answers. For the current purpose, demonstrating that they were different is sufficient to illustrate two main points: that understanding a place involves uncovering the multivariate and inter-related nature of its culture, for which the three components of the schema in chapter 3 provide a valuable framework; and that without understanding the nature of a place in all its complexity, it is difficult to appreciate what happens there during particular events – simple, monocausal explanations (often located in the sphere of production) are usually insufficient.

5

The United States South:
Exploring a Paradox

... no other part of the nation became more conscious of its identity
or more passionately asserted its homogeneity. Belief in uniformity
tended to create uniformity. There were many Souths, but after about
1830 leading white Southerners could see only one. Theirs was a
triumph of history over geography, of imagination over reality. While
these southern Americans believed their region unified by its homogeneity, what actually drew it together and made it conscious to itself
was its deep and (according to white Southern belief) ineradicable,
division – into white and black.

D. J. Boorstin, *The Americans: The National Experience*

Many studies of the geography of the United States identify the southern
States – basically those of the former Confederacy south of the
Mason–Dixon line and east of the Mississippi – as a separate region or
place, with its own particular characteristics. Many of those studies use
the States themselves as their organizing units, if for no other reason than
the convenience that data are readily available for mapping at that scale.
Thus a cultural region is often circumscribed by a set of administrative
boundaries, a practice which fails to conform with other attempts to define
the country's cultural regions. Zelinsky's (1973) cultural region 'The South'
(figure 5.1), for example, includes parts of both east Texas and Oklahoma,
and several States north of the Mason–Dixon line (Virginia, West Virginia,
Delaware, Maryland and Kentucky) plus parts of southern Ohio, Indiana,
Illinois and Missouri, though it is divided into a northern and a southern
'second-order region'. The South's distinctiveness, he argues (p. 122), stems
from differences between its settlers and those on the coast further north,
in 'motives and social values'. In addition

> The immigration of African slaves may have been a factor, as might
> also a degree of interaction with the aborigines that was missing
> further north. And certainly the unusual (for Northwest Europeans)

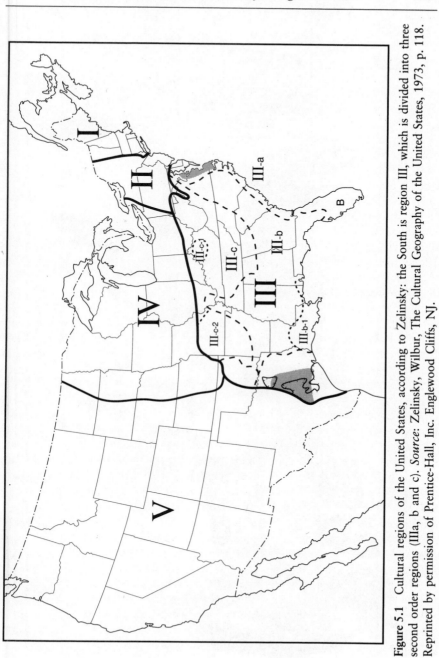

Figure 5.1 Cultural regions of the United States, according to Zelinsky: the South is region III, which is divided into three second order regions (IIIa, b and c). *Source:* Zelinsky, Wilbur, The Cultural Geography of the United States, 1973, p. 118. Reprinted by permission of Prentice-Hall, Inc. Englewood Cliffs, NJ.

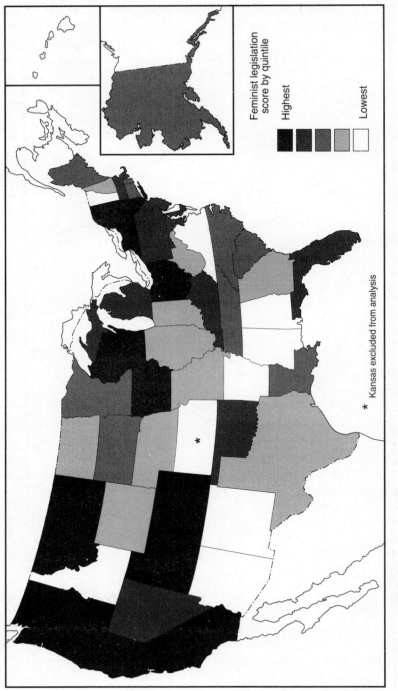

Figure 5.2 An index of women's legislation, by State. *Source:* Holcomb et al., 1990, p. 183.

Feminist legislation
score by quintile

Highest

Lowest

* Kansas excluded from analysis

pattern of economy, settlement, and social organization, in part a matter of a starkly unfamiliar physical habitat, may have prompted a swerving away from other culture areas.

Zelinsky's description of the South as 'so distinct from the non-South in almost every observable or quantifiable feature and so fiercely jealous of its peculiarities' (p. 122), at least until the present century, suggests a place with a clearly identifiable culture of its own, even though it is large and, on many criteria, heterogeneous. Similarly, when we look at the South in contemporary perspective, we can identify a wide variety of indicators on which it stands out. Those indicators to some extent point in different directions and pose something of a paradox for explanation. To resolve that paradox, it is argued here, requires the same type of analysis of the components of a place as illustrated in the previous chapter.

THE PARADOX DEFINED

A selection of mapped examples illustrates the nature of the paradox that the South sets. These provide neither an exhaustive listing nor even a wide range of examples, but clearly identify the differences that mark out the South in the contemporary United States.

Women's rights

Social and political attitudes in the South seem very different from those elsewhere, especially the country's northeast – the traditional 'Manufacturing Belt'. This is illustrated by attitudes to women. Holcomb, Kodras and Brunn (1990) selected 26 variables representing various aspects of women's legal rights in 49 of the 50 States (Kansas was excluded because of incomplete data: the source was Cherow-O'Leary, 1987). The South doesn't stand out in the resulting map (figure 5.2), although none of the States of the former Confederacy falls in the top 40 per cent on their ranking, except Florida whose population character and structure has changed very substantially in recent decades as a result of imigration, especially of the elderly. In part this is because the 26 variables aggregate several different dimensions of discrimination against women; a factor analysis identified ten significant factors, which 'vividly demonstrates a lack of consistency among the states in support of women's legal rights' (p. 192). The first three separate out issues relating to abortion, to economic discrimination, and to male-female relationships respectively. Most

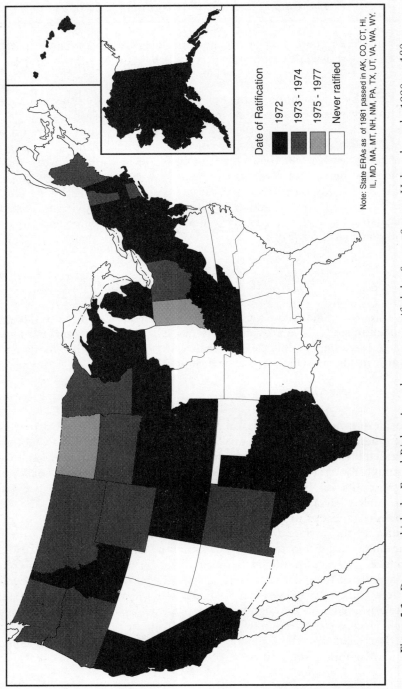

Figure 5.3 Dates at which the Equal Rights Amendment was ratified, by States. *Source:* Holcomb et al., 1990, p. 180.

Date of Ratification

1972

1973 - 1974

1975 - 1977

Never ratified

Note: State ERAs as of 1981 passed in AK, CO, CT, HI, IL, MD, MA, MT, NH, NM, PA, TX, UT, VA, WA, WY.

of the southern states score particularly badly on economic discrimination, but only a minority do so on the third and none do on the first.

The particular features of southern culture are better illustrated by individual attitudinal variables, therefore, even though this runs the risk of over-generalizing from limited data. Figure 5.3 shows support for the Equal Rights Amendment (ERA) to the United States Constitution, proposed in 1972 but never ratified because although it passed through both houses of Congress it did not receive the positive vote of three-quarters of the State Legislatures within seven years, as required by the Constitution. Most northeastern State Legislatures ratified the Amendment in 1972, with three smaller New England States following in the next two years. Further west, only Illinois and Missouri in the centre of the country plus a block of three in the far west (Arizona, Nevada and Utah) failed to give the Amendment support by the due date. In the 'old south', on the other hand, only Tennessee provided ratification (in 1972), along with the 'border States' of Texas, Kentucky, West Virginia, Maryland and Delaware. (By 1981, sixteen States had passed Equal Rights Amendments to their own State Constitutions, only one of them in the South – Arkansas: interestingly, Illinois passed its own, while failing to ratify the Federal amendment.)

This denial of equal political rights to all American women, largely because of the intransigence of southern legislators, was a response to a contemporary political movement that represented deep-seated attitudes towards gender differences. The right for women to vote for the President of the United States was introduced in Wyoming in 1869, when, according to Abler, Adams and Gould (1971, p. 446) 'frontier men and women chafed under archaic and undemocratic laws carried earlier from the East'. By the end of the nineteenth century all of the western States save New Mexico had granted women's suffrage, which then spread rapidly eastward through the northern States. In 1920, the Nineteenth Amendment to the United States Constitution was ratified, having reached the necessary three-quarters support among the State Legislatures: as figure 5.4 shows, however, all of the recalcitrant Legislatures were in the country's southeast, with only Tennessee in the area of the Confederacy voting for the Amendment. (Abler, Adams and Gould show that the same southeastern States were also among those that were late in the reform of their divorce laws.)

Much of the opposition to the ERA came from adherents to fundamentalist religious movements which take literally Biblical statements such as St Paul's to the Ephesians – 'Wives, be subject to your husband as to the Lord' and 'As the church is subject to Christ, so let wives also be subject in everything to their husbands'. As Wohlenberg (1980, p. 677) expresses it:

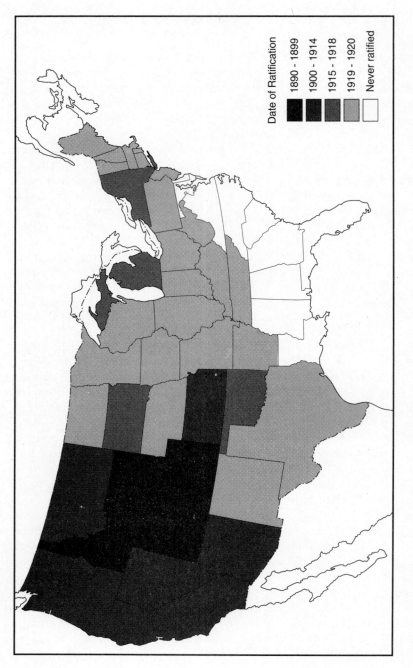

Figure 5.4 Dates at which the 19th Amendment to the US Constitution (giving women the vote) was ratified, by States.
Source: Holcomb et al., 1990, p. 179.

> Such people [i.e. religious fundamentalists] may believe that the elevation of a wife to equal status with the husband is tantamount to subversion of the divine will for the hierarchy and hence integrity of the family. If persons holding such views are sufficiently powerful in a state, they may be able to prevent ratification of the ERA by that state

Adherents to such faiths are small in number in the United States, and insufficiently substantial to achieve non-ratification because of the direct influence. So Wohlenberg developed several other hypotheses relating the fate of the ERA to aspects of State political culture. He found that not only did the States that failed to ratify the amendment have larger populations of both religious fundamentalists and political conservatives, but also that States which had opposed earlier civil rights amendments (the 19th on women's suffrage and the 26th on youth suffrage) also tended to oppose the ERA. Of the fifteen States which had not ratified the amendment by 1979, he predicted that five (Alabama, Louisiana, Mississippi, South Carolina and Utah) almost certainly would not, five (Arkansas, Georgia, Missouri, North Carolina and Oklahoma) might, whereas Arizona, Florida, Illinois, Nevada and Virginia possibly would. Southern States dominate the first two of those lists.

These more conservative positions towards women's rights in the southern States are far from an isolated example of regional differences in social attitudes. Abrahamson and Carter (1986), for example, examined data on tolerance, using four scales concerning attitudes to civil liberties, euthanasia, epileptic workers, and prohibition. On all four they found that tolerance increased nationally in the four decades after the Second World War. There were strong regional differences (with the south being the least tolerant region) after individual social and economic characteristics had been taken into account, however, and those regional differences did not decline over the period.

Social policy and Federally-funded welfare programmes

A characteristic feature of the response to the major economic depression of the 1930s in most of the 'developed' countries of the world was the rapid growth of what was termed the 'welfare state' – which is now under severe attack as a political response to the recession of the 1970s and 1980s. Most countries had some welfare system in place, more so in some (such as Germany) than others; the United States had a relatively poorly-developed system. It rapidly instituted one under the New Deal administrations of Franklin Roosevelt, however, despite the problems of Federal

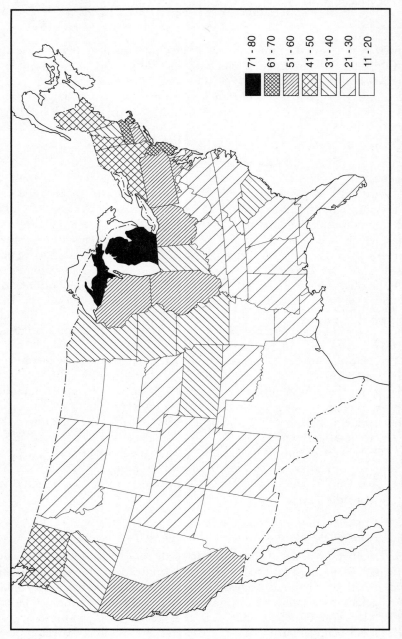

Figure 5.5 The percentage of people in poverty who were receiving AFDC benefits in 1980. *Source:* Johnston, 1990d, p. 46.

initiative in what was deemed by the Constitution to be an area of State responsibility, plus the challenges to the legality of much that was initially proposed and enacted.

The New Deal welfare state initiatives, which were extended by some of the successor administrations, notably Lyndon Johnson's, involved complex Federal–State inter-relationships. The United States' Constitution includes the clause (in the Tenth Amendment) that 'The powers not delegated to the United States by the Constitution, nor prohibited by it to the States, are reserved to the States respectively, or to the people'. Thus, since nothing in the Constitution allows the Federal government to create a welfare system, whereby payments (or payments in kind) are made to the residents of the various States, a welfare state system could only be established either through Constitutional Amendment (which would be difficult both to write and then to enact) or through successful negotiation with the State governments. The latter has been the chosen course, with the Federal government establishing welfare programmes, and guidelines for their operation, whereby part (if not all) of the costs of programme implementation are met from Federal money, and allocated to the State governments to be used for the defined purposes. Since most of the money being offered was raised through Federal taxation, especially income tax, these mechanisms were being used to try and ensure that State governments did operate the welfare programmes seen as desirable by the Federal government; if they did not, then their residents were paying taxes to Washington, but receiving relatively little in return. (For relatively poor States, whose residents would benefit most from programmes designed to aid those suffering from poverty, refusal to participate would mean losing out in a potentially redistributive process.) Nevertheless, some States either failed to enact the programmes or, more commonly, were less active than others; the recalcitrant ones have largely been in the South.

This conclusion is illustrated by one of the largest welfare state programmes instituted for the relief of poverty, specifically that of children. Aid to Families with Dependent Children (AFDC) is Federally funded but adminstered by the State governments, within rules provided by the funding agency. This programme has been the subject of several pieces of geographical research, notably by Wohlenberg (1976a, 1976b, 1976c) and Kodras (1986a). Its implementation and relative impact show substantial variation among the States.

Since AFDC is specifically directed at the relief of poverty, one would expect a correlation between the level of poverty in a State and the number of recipients there. That correlation is very weak, however. Figure 5.5 shows the percentage of people in poverty (i.e. below the Federally-defined

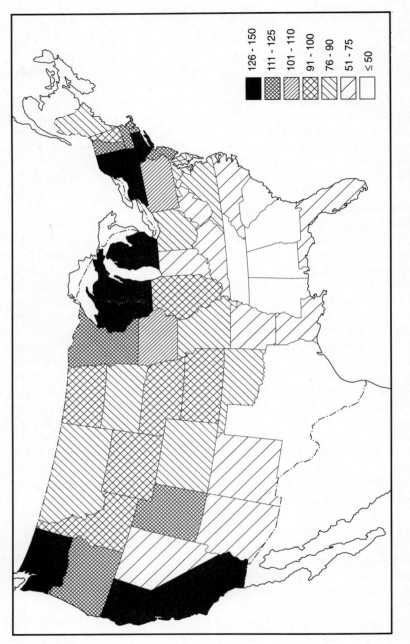

Figure 5.6 The average monthly AFDC payment, by State, as a percentage of the US average in 1980. *Source:* Johnston, 1990d, p. 46.

Legend:

- 126 - 150
- 111 - 125
- 101 - 110
- 91 - 100
- 76 - 90
- 51 - 75
- ≤ 50

povery level) in each State who were receiving AFDC benefits in 1980. It varied from 80 per cent in Michigan and 73 per cent in the District of Columbia to only 17 per cent in Idaho, North and South Dakota and Wyoming. Many of the High Plains States had low percentages, as did all of the southern States. South of the Mason–Dixon line and east of the Mississippi the largest percentage was recorded in South Carolina (31) and the average for the nine (North and South Carolina, Georgia, Florida, Tennessee, Alabama, Louisiana, Arkansas and Mississippi) was 26; in New England, on the other hand, the average was 49 per cent, and it was 56 per cent in both the Mid-Atlantic Statistical Division (New Jersey, New York and Pennsylvania) and the five East North Central States.

The differences in the percentage of their poor receiving AFDC payments reflect both varying eligibility criteria and the rigidity of their implementation among the States (Wohlenberg, 1976a). In addition, States also vary in the amounts paid to successful applicants. In general terms, the States which benefit fewest poor people also pay them least, as Figure 5.6 indicates. For the United States as a whole, the average monthly AFDC payment in 1980 was $313; no southern State paid above 75 per cent of the national average, however. These differences partly reflect variations in basic needs and in the cost-of-living, but the fivefold variations suggest the operation of other factors too. Overall, we are led to the conclusion that State governments differ very substantially in their relative generosity (using Federally-raised money) towards their poor residents.

Why should this be? In unitary states, governments must evaluate the trade-off between higher taxes and higher welfare benefits. High welfare benefits may attract electoral support from the recipients, but the high taxes to pay for them may lead to electoral unpopularity with the wider population; balancing the two is a difficult political act. (Przeworski and Sprague (1986) have some interesting data and suppositions about this.) But the balancing act does not have to be done in the United States with regard to AFDC (and other programmes, such as Medicaid), because the government which distributes the benefits (at the State level) is not also responsible for raising most of the money to pay for them (which comes from the Federal government). So why are some State governments, notably those in the South, apparently unprepared to spend 'other people's money' on some of their residents?

Part of the answer is provided by variations in attitudes towards the advantages of a welfare state system and specifically towards the major beneficiaries of that system in their context, blacks, especially black, female-headed families. As figure 5.7 taken from Jones (1990) shows, very high percentages of black female-headed families in the South are in poverty.

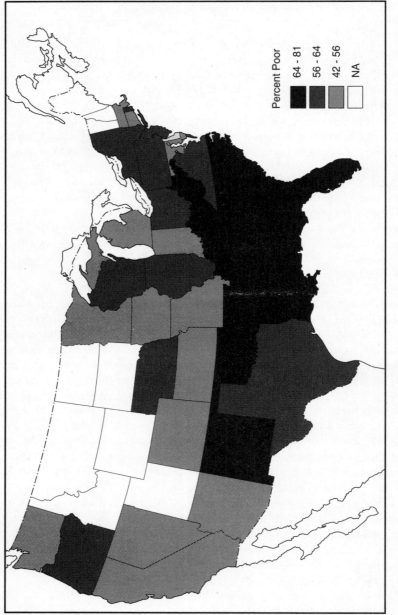

Figure 5.7 Percentage of black female-headed families in poverty, by State, in 1979. *Source*: Jones, 1990, p. 201.

Many southerners are apparently against provision of large-scale welfare support for these people, however; they apparently believe it will both encourage them to have more children, especially children not in a male-headed, nuclear family, and thus increase the State's welfare load, and also because they think it will reduce the incentive for them to work, and thereby solve their problems themselves. The latter is a widespread contemporary attitude among those known as members of the 'New Right', which condemns the 'culture of dependency' that they believe the welfare state engenders and instead favours a market economy in which initiative is rewarded. According to their argument, above a certain level greater welfare benefits can act as a work disincentive, encouraging people to remain below the poverty line and be supported by the state rather than by their own efforts, which would have to be the case if benefits were lower. (In a similar analysis, Kodras (1986a) has produced a geography of the 'work-disincentive effect' of the level of AFDC allocations – figure 5.8 – in which the lower the parameter the smaller the effect. In most of the southern States, therefore, the level of AFDC payments is much less likely to contribute to the generation of a 'culture of dependency' on the state than is the case in many further north – especially in the Upper Great Lakes region – and west.) But people can only provide for their own welfare in a capitalist society if opportunities are available for them in the labour market – and for most, because of transport and accessibility problems, child-care issues and constraints on long-distance migration, it must be the very local labour market. Therefore, according to Kodras (1986b, p. 82) 'the decision between work and welfare is not voluntary, nor is it aspatial . . . it varies according to the context in which one lives'.

Jones (1990) has evaluated the relative importance of labour market conditions and AFDC payment levels as contributors to the levels of poverty among black, female-headed households. Both prove significant, and he can therefore counter arguments that the work-disincentive effect alone is sufficient to account for the poverty levels. Where jobs are available, there is evidence that higher AFDC payments do apparently encourage more people to remain dependent on the state than where they are lower, but overall variations in labour market buoyancy mean that 'analyses which place the blame for poverty among these families upon the welfare "largesse" are deficient' (p. 210). From this conclusion, he estimates the 'equilibrium benefit level' for AFDC recipients in each State, given its labour market conditions, and from that derives the adjustments which would have to be made in payment levels to reach those equilibria. Figure 5.9 shows the outcome. The southern States, plus Texas, New Mexico and Arizona, would have to make the largest positive adjustments (i.e. the

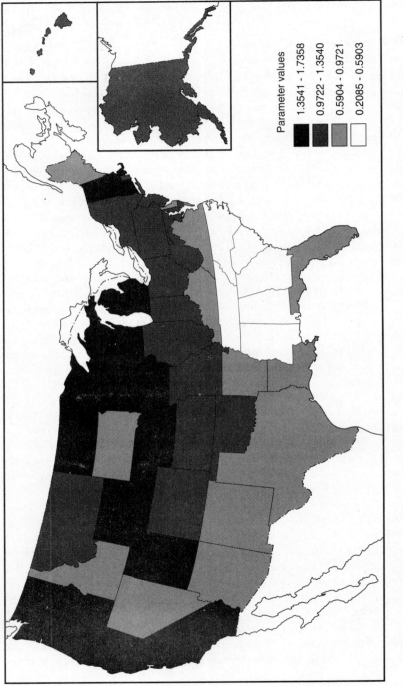

Figure 5.8 Interstate variations in the 'work disincentive effect' of AFDC payments, by States, in 1979. The lower the parameter, the smaller the effect. *Source:* Kodras, 1986a, p. 238.

Parameter values

1.3541 - 1.7358
0.9722 - 1.3540
0.5904 - 0.9721
0.2085 - 0.5903

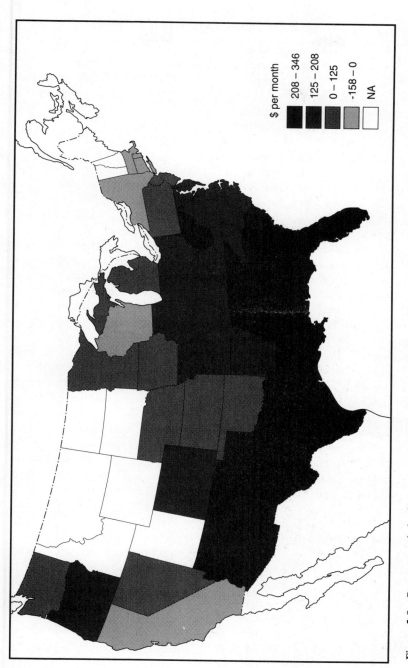

Figure 5.9 Recommended adjustments to the average monthly AFDC payment rate in order to produce equilibria between payments and 'labour market buoyancy'. *Source*: Jones, 1990, p. 214.

largest increases in payments), whereas a number of northern State governments would have to reduce their levels. (The reductions would be as large as $158 per month in Wisconsin and $113 in Connecticut, compared to increases of over $300 in each of New Mexico, Arizona, Mississippi, Louisiana, Alabama and Tennessee.)

The conclusion to be drawn from these analyses is that whereas in some States, mainly in the northeastern United States, governments are generous both in the number of welfare recipients and in the amount of support allocated, those in others, mainly in the South, are much less generous. Three reasons are often suggested for this, one strictly electoral, one relating to the fiscal situation in each State, and the third reflecting wider attitudes, in particular attitudes of southern whites towards blacks. All three are inter-related, however, since State fiscal problems are in general greatest in the South, where discrimination against blacks has traditionally been greatest, and where the electoral situation for long favoured one party.

The *fiscal* argument is that welfare state benefits for the poor cost relatively less in the more affluent States, because they are drawing on a larger tax base; the higher the average income in a State, the smaller the effort required to finance a programme at a given level of payments (because presumably there will be both fewer recipients plus more rich people to tax than in States with low average incomes). Thus, the richer States of the north and west should be more generous than their poorer contemporaries of the South, a conclusion that has been sustained empirically, e.g. Magull (1978), Fenton and Chamberlayne (1969). This holds even though much of the money for welfare programmes such as AFDC comes from the Federal exchequer; the larger the average payment, above a Federally-prescribed minimum, the larger the proportion of it which has to be met from State revenues, so that generous State governments are taxing their own residents in order to support their generosity (see Tresch, 1975).

The empirical correlation between spending and wealth fails to provide a convincing explanation for inter-State variations in welfare allocations, however; why should some State governments tax their residents more than others in order to provide such a good welfare state, it is asked, unless there are pressing political, and especially *electoral*, reasons, to do so? (Apart from electoral reasons, there could be moral ones, reflecting inter-State variations in beliefs concerning the 'rightness' of a generous welfare state programme.) Spending should only be high on welfare, it is argued, where this is perceived as necessary in order to woo voter support (Sharkansky, 1971; Wright, 1975). States certainly vary, and have varied even more in the past, in the degree to which such voter-wooing is necessary. This is illustrated by figures 5.10 and 5.11 which show the percentage of the seats in each house of the various State Legislatures won by the Democratic Party in 1972–6. The southern States stand out very strongly as having experienced a Democratic hegemony then, as they did for the entire century beforehand. With over 80 per cent of the seats in each house, many of them won by very large majorities indeed and a not insubstantial number having been uncontested by the Republican Party (see Key's (1949) classic volume on southern politics), did the Democratic Party need to pay large welfare benefits in order to win votes?

But one-party dominance of State legislatures was not confined to the South, as Ranney's (1971) classification (figure 5.12) indicates. Although there were few States where the Republicans were as deeply entrenched as the Democrats were in their southern strongholds, there were several where the need for large welfare state payments to win votes for a marginal government was low. Thus, despite a clear relationship between electoral marginality and welfare payment levels – payments were highest in the more marginal States, even when fiscal effort was controlled for – this explanation is also seen as insufficient.

The final variable introduced in many studies is *discrimination against blacks*. This has always been strongest in the southern States, with their history of slavery and the implicit belief, well-established in the local culture, in black inferiority – a belief capitalized on for more than a century after the Civil War by the Democrats (see below). Thus, for example, Cowart (1969, p. 223) suggested that welfare programmes are 'perceived as a "gravy train" for low income Negroes' by white southern politicians and as 'a promoter of illegitimacy' amongst them. (Jones and Kodras, 1986, p. 52, suggest a more economic interpretation, involving the white population attempting 'to preserve a low-wage labor-force for agriculture and labor-intensive industries by, among other things, ensuring that welfare programs present no viable alternative to labor in the fields or factories'.) If this is so, then southern, one-party States with large black populations should be even lower welfare spenders than others where the electoral need to spend is weak, although statistically it is hard to separate out this effect because all of the extremely safe Democratic States are relatively poor, have large black populations and are in the South (Johnston, 1983b).

The generally-accepted explanation for welfare payment levels in the South is that they are, and have been, low because of: the relative poverty of the southern States, which would call for a high fiscal effort if payments equivalent to those made further north were to be offered to the larger number of poor there; the electoral safety of the Democratic party with regard to the southern State legislatures and governorships, for over a

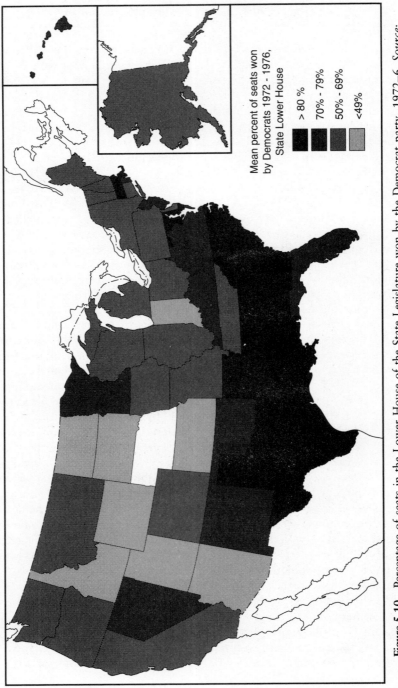

Figure 5.10 Percentage of seats in the Lower House of the State Legislature won by the Democrat party, 1972–6. *Source:* Johnston, 1980, p. 131.

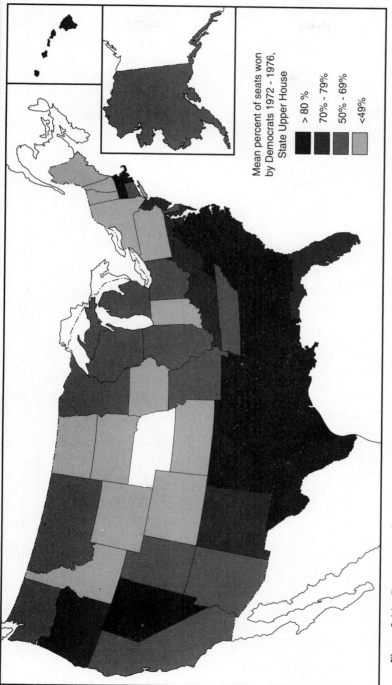

Mean percent of seats won
by Democrats 1972 - 1976,
State Upper House

■ > 80 %

■ 70% - 79%

■ 50% - 69%

□ <49%

Figure 5.11 Percentage of seats in the Upper House of the State Legislature won by the Democrat party, 1972–6. *Source: Johnston, 1980, p. 131.*

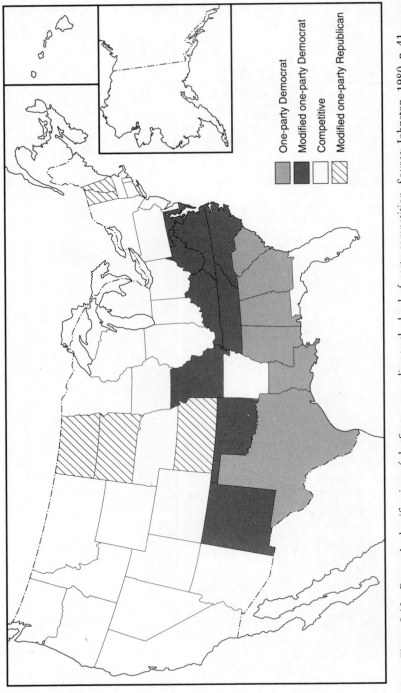

One-party Democrat
Modified one-party Democrat
Competitive
Modified one-party Republican

Figure 5.12 Ranney's classification of the States according to the level of party competition. *Source*: Johnston, 1980, p. 41.

century – sustained by discriminatory practices which prevented many blacks becoming registered voters despite their legal achievement of civil rights; and the widespread belief among southern whites in the racial inferiority of blacks – who are the main recipients of welfare benefits – coupled with the perceived work-disincentive effects of substantial payments and the encouragement to have even larger, and thus more dependent, families than they are believed to provide. But why have these three conditions arisen?

Federal non-grant expenditure in the States

Grants to State governments to cover parts of the costs of welfare and other programmes (such as those for the construction of the Inter-State Highway system) comprise only one of the elements of Federal spending which has an uneven impact on the various parts of the United States. The other main component comprises direct Federal payments to individuals or groups, either in grants, in wages, or in expenditure on goods and services. The decisions on how much to spend, on what, and where, are made in Congress itself, through the mosaic of committees and subcommittees of the Senate and the House of Representatives which both legislate for and make appropriations to the particular programmes operated by the more than 30 separate departments of the Federal state apparatus.

A large number of studies has looked at the geography of those spending patterns, and attempted to account for the spatial variation in how much is spent, where (for example, Johnston, 1980; Archer, 1983). Their focus is usually a series of maps showing spending on individual programmes or of particular types. Figures 5.13 and 5.14 provide two examples of these, referring to spending by the Department of Defense in fiscal year 1979. Figure 5.13 shows spending on defence contracts, for the purchase of equipment and other supplies – large and small. (The data only show the States where the contracts were placed. The company with the contract may spend the money, or part of it, at its plants in other States, or it may subcontract part of the work out-of-State.) A few States benefit most from this expenditure, notably those around Washington DC itself (where potential contractors may gain advantages from locating in proximity to the Pentagon), plus Massachusetts, Texas, California, Washington, Maine and Missouri. Several of these are the homes of major defence contractors (such as Boeing in Washington), and should be among the major beneficiaries of the defence appropriation process; some of the links are less obvious, such as that between the alfalfa producers of inland Texas and the production of military uniforms.

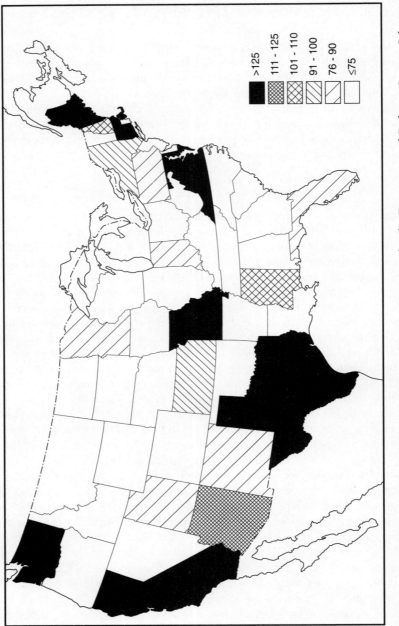
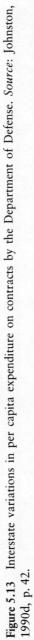

	>125
	111 - 125
	101 - 110
	91 - 100
	76 - 90
	≤75

Figure 5.13 Interstate variations in per capita expenditure on contracts by the Department of Defense. *Source:* Johnston, 1990d, p. 42.

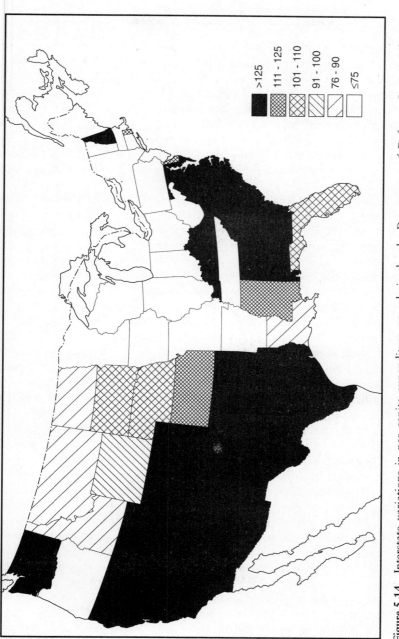

Figure 5.14 Interstate variations in per capita expenditure on salaries by the Department of Defense. *Source:* Johnston, 1990d, p. 42.

The second map (figure 5.14) shows the geography of the Department of Defense's spending on salaries (for civilians and service personnel together), and indicates that the great majority of the southern States (with the exceptions of Louisiana and Arkansas) were substantial beneficiaries, whereas northeastern States got much less than the national average per capita expenditure in this category. In part, this was because the southern States offer a better environment for certain types of defence base, but this is not a full explanation. To most analysts, the way in which Congressional committees operate provides the key to understanding maps such as those displayed here.

The geography of Federal spending is the result of two distinct decision-making processes. In the first, a bill is passed which allows for certain actions to be taken, such as the establishment of a space agency, the construction of a national highway system, the provision of agricultural price supports, and so on. Such enabling legislation may be introduced in one or both of the houses of Congress by individual elected members, or may be sent there by the Executive. It must be approved, in the same form, by both houses and ratified by the President (whose power of veto can be over-ridden by two-thirds of the members of both houses). The second process involves the allocation of funds to implement part or all of the legislated programme. This is done through the annual budget procedure. The budget originates in the Executive branch and is sent to both houses for approval; it can be amended by both – and usually is, very substantially – but the final version must be approved by both the President and the two houses acting jointly.

Appreciating what bills get enacted, in what form, and then what monies are appropriated to fund their implementation requires an understanding of how Congress conducts its business, and how its members are influenced, by the President, by other members, and by outside interests, including their own constituents. Much of the power in both the House and the Senate resides not on the floor of the relevant house (though the ultimate veto is there) but rather in the various standing committees of each. Whenever an enabling bill is submitted, it is passed to the relevant committee or committees for detailed scrutiny and recommendations; in turn it may be sent to one or more subcommittees. The committees are empowered to suggest amendments, and the bill which is returned to the house (if it ever is) may be substantially different from its original form; there may be a long period of debate between representatives of the two houses of the Legislature and the Executive before consensus can be reached.

The budget is treated similarly, although many more members of the Legislature are likely to be involved. Each house sends the Executive's proposed budget to its Committee on Appropriations, which divides the various parts among its subcommittees. These return the parts – amended if they see fit (and they often do, very substantially) – to the full committee, which then recommends a revised budget to the house. The revised format produced by the Senate is very unlikely to agree with that produced by the House of Representatives, so a joint Senate/House committee is then established to negotiate an agreed document, which the President then has to decide to accept, renegotiate, or veto (usually in part rather than in its entirety). Throughout, the legislators concerned will be subject to a great deal of explicit lobbying, and will be aware of the political debts they are expected to settle through the budget, as well as the importance that their decisions may have for their own political futures.

In both processes, and especially that relating to the budget, immense power lies with the Senators and the Representatives on the relevant committees and subcommittees. Assignments to important committees are thus actively sought by members of Congress, through their party leaders who allocate them. In seeking committee positions, most will at least in part opt for those which match their personal political interests – someone interested in foreign affairs, for example, would probably not actively canvass for a seat on the House standing committee concerned with the Post Office and the Civil Service. But personal interests may come second behind political realities for most, especially for Representatives, whose term of office is two years only. They will want to be on committees and subcommittees where they can advance the interests of both their sponsors – those who have contributed to the costs of their, usually expensive, election campaigns and, it is hoped, will contribute to those of the next as well – and their constituents; to some extent, these will be the same. Thus a Representative from a Midwestern State will not want to serve on the Merchant Marine and Fisheries Committee, but would probably covet a place on either the Agriculture Committee or the Appropriations Committee (especially its Agriculture Subcommittee). For the party leaderships, of course, it is important to get representation across the board, so a Democrat Representative from a large State such as California may find that the Agriculture Committee contains sufficient California Democrats already, and he/she may then be allocated to the committee concerned with the work of the Department of the Interior instead.

Each committee's membership is allocated between the two parties proportionally to their membership of the full house so that, for example, if the Democrats have 60 per cent of the Senate seats they will get approximately 60 per cent of each committee's seats. In every case, the chair of the committee or subcommittee will go to a member of the majority party;

since the chair has very substantial power in directing how the business is conducted, occupancy of commitee and subcommittee chairs is among the most significant roles within Congress. In general terms, such roles are attained through seniority. Although it is less the case now than in the past, the longer a person has been on a particular committee the greater the likelihood that he or she will eventually succeed either to its chair or to the senior minority party position. Thus power comes with political longevity, and once appointed to a coveted committee, a Senator or Representative will be loathe to accept, let alone seek, reallocation to another with the more junior status that will ensue, unless the move is clearly likely to be politically beneficial in the medium- if not the short-term.

What we would expect to find therefore is:

1 Representatives and Senators serving on committees and subcommittees whose spheres of influence coincide with those of their constituents, so that they can promote local interests within Congress; and
2 the senior positions being occupied by those members who have been in Congress longest.

Both expectations are empirically valid. The pattern of recruitment to committee assignments very clearly indicates over-representation from geographical constituencies (Rundquist and Ferejohn, 1976; Johnston, 1980). For example, the States of Indiana, Ohio, New York, Pennsylvania, New Jersey, Maryland, Delaware, Connecticut and Rhode Island were not represented on the House Committee on Agriculture in 1985 (Johnston, 1988c), and of those only Indiana was represented on the Senate's Subcommittee on Agriculture, Nutrition and Forestry. Within the House Committee, whereas Minnesota, Iowa, Illinois and Missouri each had two Representatives on the Soyabeans and Feed Grain Subcommittee and California and Texas had none, the latter had three and two members respectively of the Cotton, Rice and Sugar Subcommittee.

One obvious consequence of this pattern of representation should be the flow of funds towards the States whose members are there to promote local interests. This is known as the politics of the pork barrel. It has achieved a great deal of support from anecdotal evidence (see Johnston, 1980, for example), which clearly suggests that Senators and Representatives have been able to channel very substantial volumes of Federal money towards their home States, thereby promoting their political reputations, assisting them in the search for campaign funds, and enhancing their re-election prospects. (Incumbents have a massive advantage in Federal election races.) But this anecdotal evidence is not always supported by more rigorous statistical analysis. Where it is (as in Ferejohn, 1974; see also

Johnston, 1980), the southern States usually come out as major beneficiaries – because their Senators and Representatives tend to be among the longest-lived politically; the Midwest States, on the other hand, tend to benefit much less, which is a source of much local concern (Murphy, 1971). Where it is not supported, the reason is often, as suggested by Rundquist (1980, 1983), because the spending patterns are already set by the geography of demands (one would not expect large spending on subsidies for cotton farmers in New Hampshire, for example) and the goal of the pork barrellers is rather to get plenty of money for the programme than to direct it to certain areas rather than others.

Overall, the southern States are major beneficiaries of Federal spending, especially so relative to their contributions to the Federal exchequer, in considerable part because of the success of their Senators and Representatives in the pork barrel. In order to achieve this, they must attain seniority, with the implication that the South does well out of the Federal budget because its members of Congress are more likely, on average, to be reelected and therefore climb the seniority ladder. This has come about because southern politics were so dominated by the Democratic party in the century after the Civil War that many of its Senators and Representatives faced sterner re-election contests in the Primary elections within their own party (i.e. for the right to stand for the Democrats again) than they did against the Republicans in the election itself. Elsewhere in the country, seats were more marginal, defeat somewhat more likely, and thus power in the Congress less easily retained. This situation has changed somewhat since the 1960s as a consequence of:

1 the growing strength of the Republicans as a conservative force among whites in the South; and
2 the greater advantages reaped by incumbents in all parts of the country.

Thus the South as a region had power in Congress much greater than its relative representation implied; this was crucial in the 1930s with the expansion of the welfare state and the growth of support for agriculture, and in the 1950s and 1960s with the growth of the defence and space budgets.

The South as Sunbelt

The final element of the geography of the South which contributes to this chapter's paradox concerns its growth as a major manufacturing region of the United States since about 1960. Growth there complemented decline

elsewhere, notably in the traditional manufacturing core of the country's
northeast: this led to the development of the shorthand term Sun-
belt:Frostbelt (or Sunbelt:Snowbelt, or Sunbelt:Rustbelt) to represent the
shift of manufacturing jobs away from the climatically less attractive parts
of the United States and towards those earlier identified by Ullman (1954)
as having attractive climates.

This regional restructuring has involved relative growth in the South
(and the west, but the focus here is on the South alone) complementing
decline in the northeast. Markusen's (1987) data on changes in non-
agricultural employment, for example, demonstrate striking variations
among the standard census regions (table 5.1). These clearly differentiate
the Sunbelt (the bottom five regions) from the Snowbelt (the top four) in
terms of relative growth in jobs. The South Atlantic region (Delaware,
Maryland, Virginia, West Virginia, North and South Carolina, Georgia
and Florida, plus the District of Columbia) performed much better than
the national average, especially in the first two decades when growth rates
were half as large again as those for the United States as a whole.

Peet's (1983) explanation for this regional variation is based in differences in the 'class struggle'. As capitalist industrialization developed so, he
argued, did forms of collective working class resistance to it. Such development was uneven:

Table 5.1 Regional variations in non-agricultural employment change

Region	Percentage change		
	1950–60	*1960–70*	*1970–80*
New England	10.6	23.0	18.9
Middle Atlantic	9.5	18.4	5.4
East North Central	12.3	25.3	15.4
West North Central	16.2	27.9	27.9
South Atlantic	29.6	46.5	36.8
East South Central	22.8	38.6	34.5
West South Central	28.1	40.1	54.3
Mountain	46.7	42.2	66.6
Pacific	49.2	41.2	41.8
United States	20.2	31.0	27.4

Source: Markusen, 1987

Factors determining the strength of organized worker resistance are complex, but large industrial plants with many similar boring tasks, such as automobile factories, seem to favor the building of strong labor organizations. Similarly, workers living in homogeneous communities centered around one particular kind of work, like mining, also tend to have high levels of collective resistance to capital. . . . By comparison, heterogeneity of work experience and worker characteristics weaken resistance, while labor segmentation and stratification have similar effects. (p. 120)

When faced with strong collective resistance – almost certainly mobilized through widely-supported trades unions – capitalist organizations may well seek to locate their operations in places where collective struggle is weaker. As Massey and Meegan (1982) have argued, relocation away from intense class struggle is just one option facing employers; they also contend that consideration of the various options is most likely in periods of recession when profitability is low and some form of restructuring crucial, and that relocation may then be part of a composite strategy involving restructuring of the labour process.

Peet's analysis of labour unionization in the United States noted that rates of union membership have traditionally been much lower in the southern States than elsewhere (figure 5.15). On that criterion alone they were more attractive areas for investment, especially in labour-intensive manufacturing and other industries, than States with much higher unionization levels. That relative advantage was enhanced after the passing of the 1947 Taft–Hartley Act, which allowed States to pass 'Right-to-Work' legislation prohibiting unions from insisting on 'closed shops' at plants, even those at which a majority of the workers had voted in favour of union representation in collective bargaining (on which see Clark, 1988).

Differences in wage levels parallel the regional differences in unionization. The two are intimately related, according to Peet (p. 124):

While wage rates depend on productivity, and the degree of competition in an industry, they are also influenced by the organized force exerted by labor on capital: unionism has a significant direct effect on wages and fringe benefits. . . . Hence the geography of earnings in manufacturing parallels unionization

creating a further advantage for the South. (Tabb (1984) shows that in 1978 one in three of all manufacturing jobs in the South was in an industry with a wage rate below the national average for all manufacturing, indicating that low-wage jobs in particular had been attracted there.) Furthermore, energy was over 30 per cent cheaper in the South than in

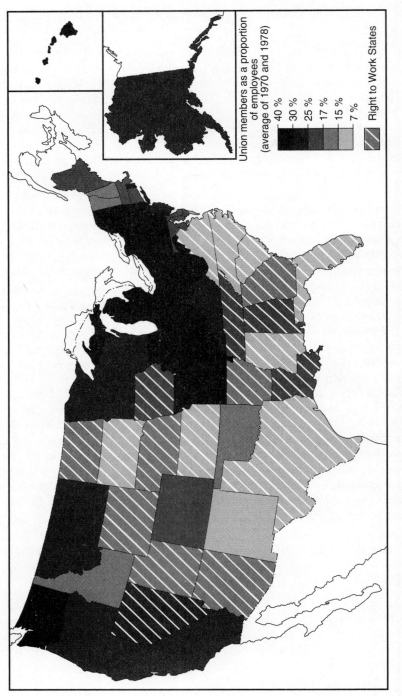

Figure 5.15 Average union membership, by State, 1970–8. *Source*: Peet, 1983, p. 123.

Union members as a proportion
of employees
(average of 1970 and 1978)

40 %
30 %
25 %
17 %
15 %
7 %

Right to Work States

the northeast in 1980, according to Agnew (1987b, p. 174), who draws on Bensel's (1984) work, which combines the energy and unionization advantages of the South, to illustrate the growing gap in growth rates over the post-war decades between, on the one hand, the energy-rich/right-to-work States and, on the other, the energy-disadvantaged (high cost, mostly imported) and heavily-unionized. He concludes, from this, that 'The combination of an anti-union environment and energy-cost advantages offers a most plausible explanation for the increasing appeal of the periphery in the 1970s' (p. 174).

Agnew, Peet and others also argued that southern State and local governments are more favourably inclined towards capitalist interests, and provide a facilitating 'business climate'. The southern States had the lowest effective tax rates (for local and State corporate and property taxes) in the 1970s, for example, and many local governments there have fewer controls on development (Houston's lack of a land-use plan is frequently cited in this respect). Further, the growth of Federal expenditure, in support for agriculture and in the expansion of the aerospace and defence industries (see above) have all favoured the South.

The outcome of all this, Peet contends, is a clear 'geography of class struggle' (figure 5.16) in the United States in the 1970s, in which the southern States (with the exception of Louisiana and, to a lesser extent, Alabama) have the lowest values (i.e. the least conflict), along with the Dakotas. (Peet's class struggle index combined data on union membership, work stoppages, average wage rates, and the 'business climate' ratings of States, which in turn combine information on tax levels and legislation.) The Frostbelt to Sunbelt shift of capital can thus be portrayed as the movement of money away from areas of intense class struggle to States where it was much lower, and potential profitability was consequently much greater. Such movement was especially great in the 1960s and 1970s because this was a time of rapid change in industrial technology, calling for new investments, and capitalists preferred to make 'drastic adjustments, such as massively replacing living labor by machines and/or disciplining their labor forces' (p. 129) in areas of low-intensity class struggle. He concludes that

> the change in manufacturing employment during the 1970s and 1980s *is* a move from Frostbelt to Sunbelt so long as 'frost' and 'sun' refer to the *social* conditions for profit making. . . . More accurately, we have witnessed a reaction by increasingly competitive producers to the uneven spatial development of class struggle, resulting in the migration of all types of employment, but especially manufacturing,

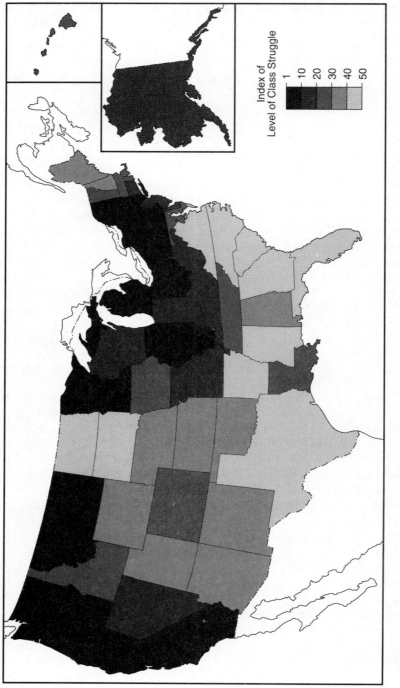

Figure 5.16 Interstate variations in the intensity of the 'class struggle' in the 1970s; the higher the value, the lower the intensity. *Source:* Peet, 1983, p. 132.

Index of
Level of Class Struggle

1
10
20
30
40
50

from areas of high class struggle to areas where the struggle is less developed. (p. 131)

And this is, of course, not the final shift, for growing class struggle in the currently favoured areas, combined with a 'fighting back' by the presently disadvantaged, will see the creation of a new pattern of uneven development (Smith, 1984): Boston, for example, has regained competitive strength (Ganz, 1985; though see Fincher, 1982, on the social consequences of its policies).

ACCOUNTING FOR THE PARADOX

As with the example of the Dukeries coalfield in the previous chapter, appreciation of aspects of the geography of the United States of America, and in particular the distinctiveness of the southern States in a variety of ways, calls for an understanding of cultural variations between places. And similarly also, it appears that appreciation of the South's peculiar characteristics with regard to its receipt of different types of Federal funds and its role in the recent restructuring of the American economy requires particular study of social relations in the sphere of consumption (with special focus on gender and race relations), of the organization of conflict within the state apparatus (the role of trades unions and the dominance of the Democratic party in electoral processes), and of social relations at the workplace (wage rates, for example). All of these have been taken into account to some extent by the authors quoted above, but very few have looked at the culture of the South as a whole – how it was created, how it is different, and how the particular components of a place identified here are related to that whole which is 'southern culture'. And yet the example of the changing geography of the south is a paradigm case for using the approach fostered in this book.

Cultural regions in the USA: Elazar's contribution

One of the most influential contributions to the understanding of American cultural geography – at least outside the discipline of geography itself – is Daniel Elazar's (1984) book *American Federalism: A View from the States*. (Although the first edition of this book was published in 1966, it is not referred to in Zelinsky's (1973) book on *The Cultural Geography of the United States* nor, even more surprisingly, in any of the relevant chapters in the 840-page compilation on *Geography in America* edited by Gaile and

Willmott (1989). Elazar's other books introducing his ideas – *The American Partnership* (1962) and *Cities of the Prairie* (1970) – are similarly ignored in the geographical literature. Interestingly, Elazar quotes Zelinsky in the third – 1984 – edition of his book, and his collection of readings on the subject – Elazar and Zikmund (1975) – includes extracts from both Zelinsky's (1961) paper on the country's religious geography and Ward's (1971) book on immigrants in nineteenth century American cities.) Elazar is a political scientist, and his ideas have been used mainly by others from his discipline interested in variations among the American states, e.g. Sharkansky (1969) for whom, as Nardulli (1990, p. 288) expresses it:

> Daniel J Elazar's . . . research represents the most comprehensive attempt to delineate the content, distribution, and implications of political subcultures in the United States.

Elazar himself is among the ten most cited scholars in American politics (Klingeman, 1986).

Elazar's concern in *American Federalism* was to understand why each of the fifty States interacts with the Federal government, both influencing it and adapting its programmes to perceived local needs. He suggested that how individual States acted was the result of three especially important 'overarching factors':

1 sectionalism – involving the ties of 'groups of contiguous states with bonds of shared interests' (p. 109);
2 the frontier – the continuing conflict between Americans and their environment, which periodically required reorganization of social and settlement patterns; and
3 political culture – 'the particular pattern of orientation to political action in which each political system is embedded'.

The last was seen as

> particularly important as the historical source of differences in habits, perspectives, and attitudes that influence political life. (p. 110)

American political culture contains three especially influential components, according to Elazar (p. 112):

1 the 'set of perceptions of what politics is and what can be expected from government';
2 the kinds of people who become involved in the different aspects of political activity; and
3 'the actual way in which the art of government is practised by citizens,

politicians, and public officials, in the light of their perceptions.'

In turn, the cultural components of individual and group behavior in the various political systems make themselves felt at three levels: in the kind of civic behavior dictated by conscience and internalized ethical standards; in the character of law-abidingness displayed by citizens and officials; and, to a degree, in the positive actions of government. (p. 112)

He argued that the national political culture is rooted in two contrasting conceptions long established in the country's psyche: a conception of the political order as a marketplace, and a conception of a commonwealth. The former focuses on the individual, and the latter on cooperation 'in an effort to create and maintain the best government in order to implement certain shared moral principles'. Their relative importance varies among the States, however, leading Elazar to recognize 'three major political subcultures that jointly inhabit the country, existing side by side or even overlapping' (p. 114). Each has its hearth along one section of the country's eastern seaboard, from whence it has spread inland, mixing with the others in many places to create a series of hybrid inland cultures that are combinations of the basic three: 'Each of the three reflects its own particular synthesis of the marketplace and the commonwealth' (p. 115).

In the *individualistic political culture* the conception of the democratic political order as a marketplace predominates. Private concerns and decision-making are central to society's operations, and community intervention with those concerns and decisions, via the state apparatus, is to be kept to a minimum. In a phrase reminiscent of 1980s 'New Right' thinking, 'government action [in this culture] is to be restricted to those areas, primarily in the economic realm, that encourage private initiative and widespread access to the market place'. (As Elazar points out in a footnote to that statement, views on desirable intervention have changed with time. In the nineteenth century, the state was considered by those adhering to the individualistic culture to have only very limited police powers, whereas today the regulation of monopolies, the oversight of product quality, the maintenance of minimum incomes and a variety of fiscal controls are all accepted as necessary by those of a similar persuasion. 'Culture is not static. It must be viewed dynamically and defined so as to include cultural change in its very nature' (p. 145).)

Politics in this individualistic culture is 'just another form of business', in which people participate if it is seen to be in their personal interests; it competes for talented individuals with other activities, and offers rewards accordingly. In a large, complex society, the delivery of political services cannot be organized on a one-to-one basis, and so political parties are formed to act as the 'political business corporations'. True to the general ethos of business corporations, those parties are pragmatic rather than ideological – which can lead to a certain amount of corruption.

Although all Americans are to a considerable extent influenced by the individualistic culture, there are substantial variations from it in particular respects in the other two. In the *moralistic political culture*, politics 'is considered one of the great activities of humanity in its search for the good society – a struggle for power, it is true, but also an effort to exercise power for the betterment of the commonwealth' (p. 117). Government exists not so much to promote the interests of individuals in the market place as to further the public or general good, acting for the welfare of all. The definition of the 'public welfare' can vary substantially (Elazar quotes the support for Prohibition at certain times to exemplify this). But whatever the extant definition, politicians are expected to see government service as public service (as a moral obligation to act in certain ways), even at the cost of individual loyalties and friendships; citizens are similarly encouraged to see political participation as a moral obligation (in voting, for example). Parties are probably necessary to the organization of politics, but ties to them are less than in the individualistic culture: not only may politicians and others shift parties if necessary in the pursuit of the general good but also 'nonpartisanship is not instituted to eliminate politics but to improve it by widening access to public office for those unwilling or unable to gain office through the regular party structure' (p. 118) and 'where the moralistic culture is dominant today, there is considerably more amateur participation in politics . . . [and] less corruption'.

The *traditionalistic political culture* 'is rooted in an ambivalent attitude toward the marketplace coupled with a paternalistic and elite conception of the commonwealth' (p. 118). Its roots are in a largely pre-commercial, hierarchical social organization, in which it is considered 'natural' for those at the top of the social structure to play the dominant role in political life, where a major task is to protect the interests of the existing social order. Family ties thus prevail in the allocation of political power, and those outside the approved elite are not expected to participate in political life – not even to vote. In this conception of politics, therefore, those exercising power are expected to advance self-interests, as do those in the individualistic culture, but not necessarily for direct personal pecuniary gain in the market place. For them, political parties are somewhat dangerous because they may encourage the participation of 'outsiders'; they are tolerated only to the extent that they facilitate the mobilization of the elite for whom 'Good government . . . involves the maintenance and encouragement of traditional patterns and, if necessary, their adjustment to changing conditions with the least possible upset . . . political leaders play conservative and custodial rather than initiatory roles unless they are pressed strongly from the outside' (p. 119). Similarly, bureaucracy is mistrusted because it interferes with the established social networks.

Elazar summarized the political characteristics of these three cultures in a table (pp. 120–1) reproduced here as table 5.2. Although this focuses on politics, and thus on only one of the three main dimensions of a place identified in chapter 3, nevertheless several of the characteristics have important implications for the other spheres. In the traditionalistic culture, for example, the focus on maintaining the existing order and the importance of the elite suggests that social relations at the workforce are unlikely to allow strong trade union activity and are probably paternalistic in form, whereas in the community gender relations are likely to be patriarchal. In the individualistic culture, on the other hand, the strong concern with the market is likely to stimulate very different patterns of social relations in both spheres. In more general terms, Elazar (1984) characterizes the three cultures thus:

> The moralistic political culture . . . is the primary source of the continuing quest for the good society. At the same time, there is a tendency towards inflexibility and narrow-mindedness noticeable among some of its representatives. The individualistic political culture is the most tolerant of out-and-out political corruption, yet it has also provided the framework for the integration of diverse groups into the mainstream of American life. When representatives of the moralistic political culture, in their striving for a better social order, try to limit individual freedom, they usually come up against representatives of the individualistic political culture, to whom individual freedom is the cornerstone of their pluralistic order, though not for any noble reasons. Reversed, of course, the moralistic political culture acts as a restraint against the tendencies of the individualistic political culture to tolerate anything as long as it is in the marketplace. The traditionalistic political culture contributes to the search for continuity in a society whose major characteristic is change, yet in the name of continuity, its representatives have denied blacks (or Indians, or Hispanic-Americans) their civil rights. When in proper working order, the traditionalistic culture has produced a unique group of first-rate national leaders, but without a first-rate elite to draw upon, traditionalistic culture political systems degenerate into oligarchies of the lowest level . . . . (pp. 141–2)

Table 5.2 Characteristics of the three political cultures

Concepts	Individualistic	Moralistic	Traditionalistic
	Government		
How viewed	As a *marketplace* [means to respond efficiently to demands]	As a *commonwealth* [means to achieve the good community through positive action]	As a means of maintaining the *existing order*
Appropriate spheres of activity	Largely economic [encourages private initiative and access to the marketplace] Economic development favoured	Any area that will enhance the community although nongovernmental action preferred Social as well as economic regulation considered legitimate	Those that maintain traditional patterns
New programmes	Will not initiate unless demanded by public opinion	Will initiate without public pressure if believed to be in public interest	Will initiate if programme serves the interest of the governing elite
	Bureaucracy		
How viewed	Ambivalently [undesirable because it limits favors and patronage, but good because it enhances efficiency]	Positively [brings desirable political neutrality]	Negatively [depersonalizes government]
Kind of merit system favoured	Loosely implemented	Strong	None [should be controlled by political elite]
	Politics		
	Patterns of Belief		
How viewed	Dirty [left to those who soil themselves engaging in it]	Healthy [every citizen's responsibility]	A privilege [only those with legitimate claim to office should participate]

Table 5.2   Continued

Concepts	Individualistic	Moralistic	Traditionalistic
Patterns of Participation			
Who should participate	Professionals	Everyone	The appropriate elite
Role of parties	Act as business organizations [dole out favours and responsibility]	Vehicles to attain goals believed to be in the public interest [third parties popular]	Vehicle of recruitment of people to offices not desired by established power holders
Party cohesiveness	Strong	Subordinate to principles and issues	Highly personal [based on family and social ties]
Patterns of Competition			
How viewed	Between parties; not over issues	Over issues	Between elite-dominated factions within a dominant party
Orientation	Toward winning office for tangible rewards	Toward winning office for greater opportunity to implement policies and programmes	Dependent on political values of the elite

Source: Elazar, 1984, pp. 120–1

The cultures are ideal types, of course, and in a society as mobile as America's (both regarding social and spatial mobility within the country and with respect to the volume, and diversity, of immigration to its 'melting pot') it is unlikely that individuals and places can be firmly put in any one of the three. Elazar himself warns of this, suggesting that individuals' immediate political responses may not reveal their political culture (p. 142), and in what he claims to be one of the few studies to test Elazar's ideas rigorously at the individual level, Nardulli (1990) concluded that the scheme 'lacks an empirical foundation at the individual level' (p. 302): people who gave the expected response for a particular culture on one item were unlikely to give the expected response for that culture on another item. Nevertheless much more consistency has been found at the aggregate scale.

The normal method of analysing aggregated data involves investigating States as cultural units, because Elazar's work clearly identified each of the three cultures with a geographical hearth on the country's eastern seaboard. As he puts it:

> the three political subcultures arose out of very real sociocultural differences found among the peoples who came to America over the years, differences that date back to the very beginnings of settlement in this country and even back to the Old World. Because the various ethnic and religious groups that came to these shores tended to congregate in their own settlements and because, as they or their descendants moved westward, they continued to settle together, the political patterns they bore with them are today distributed geographically. Indeed, it is the geographic distribution of political cultures as modified by local conditions that has laid the foundations for American sectionalism. (p. 122)

The moralistic culture had its roots in the New England States, where its proponents 'established several versions of their commonwealth' (p. 127). Further south, in coastal New York and Pennsylvania, New Jersey, Delaware and Maryland, were concentrated immigrants for whom 'the search for individual opportunity in the New World' was the common bond that led them to establish the base for the individualistic culture. And further south still, those who sought individual opportunity within a system which denied it to others established the plantation-based economy of the southeastern States on which the traditionalistic culture is founded.

Settlers streamed westward from these hearths, extending the spheres of the various cultures and, where they merged in certain localities, created hybrid forms which combined two of the originals. The general pattern was of a direct westward movement, but not entirely so: Elazar argues that earlier patterns have been reinforced in the twentieth century moves to California, so that whereas 'Midwesterners from moralistic culture states continued to seek the Los Angeles area . . . individualistic culture types, particularly from the east, flocked to the San Francisco Bay area' (p. 132). The result was a complex cultural map (Elazar's pp. 128–9), which he summarized in State format (figure 5.17). In this, the east-west banding of the country is clear: the moralistic culture is most likely to be found in the northern tier of States, for example, with Wyoming and Nebraska the main exceptions; the individualistic culture is predominantly in the central band extending west from the Middle Atlantic seaboard – with its presence in

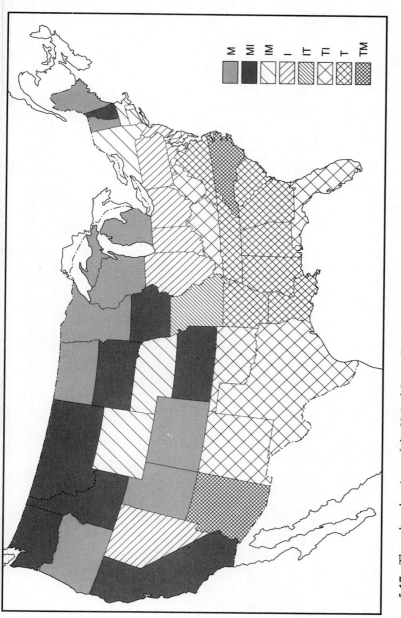

Figure 5.17 The cultural regions of the United States, by States, according to Elazar. Key: M – moralistic; I – individualistic; T – traditionalistic. *Source*: Johnston, 1990d, p. 54.

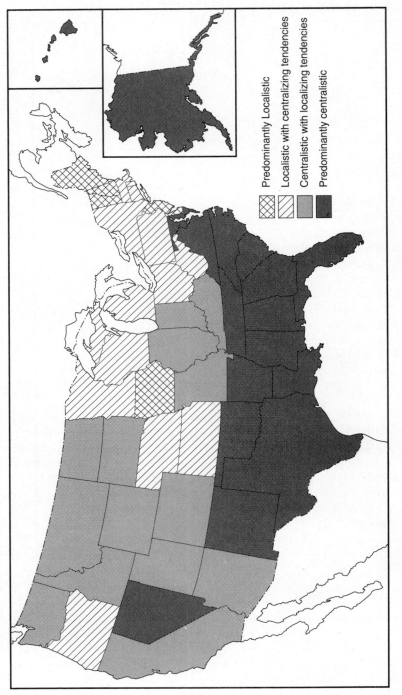

Figure 5.18 State traditions of centralism-localism. *Source:* Elazar, 1984, p. 222.

Predominantly Localistic

Localistic with centralizing tendencies

Centralistic with localizing tendencies

Predominantly centralistic

Florida the result of relative recent immigration; and the traditionalistic culture dominates the South, especially the southeast.

A more detailed investigation of the mixture of political cultures consequent on the westward spread is given in Elazar's (1970) account of the cities of Illinois. The State is dominated by the individualistic culture, but the moralistic has been strong in some areas, and its southern third has 'elements of a traditionalistic cast . . . the rights of traditional local elites [are] strongly protected' (p. 283). Because of the individualistic preeminence, State politics are dominated by the patronage system typical of that culture; in the northwestern counties where moralistic settlers congregated, however, the minority culture is strong in local government, which has 'a strong public service orientation, which places heavy obligations upon those who participate in government to maintain community goals. . . . Politics in these moralistic enclaves is viewed as a practical vehicle for coming to grips with the issues and concerns of civil society' and 'not just for ad hoc responses to immediately pressing problems' (p. 284).

Having established the existence of a clear geography of political culture, Elazar tested for its impact on various aspects of political behaviour (albeit relatively informally: Sharkansky, 1969, points to the subjectivity of Elazar's methods, including the way in which he defined an area's culture). For example, he looked at innovatory social programmes in the States, including civil rights legislation prior to the 1960s, and concluded that the least innovative were the traditionalistic whereas the most 'advanced' were largely moralistic: 'it was a combination of a high degree of ethnic diversity that led to this kind of legislation. The affected ethnics, in effect, challenge the majority to live up to the demands of their political culture and virtually embarrass them into doing so' (p. 169). He also showed that the three cultural realms differ substantially in the relative importance of centralism and localism in the internal operations of the States (figure 5.18). The moralistic States in general have strong local traditions, as to a slightly lesser extent do the individualistic States; centralization of State governance is common in the southern States, however, where it is consistent with the traditionalistic culture.

Elazar's pioneering work has been taken forward by a number of authors, with Sharkansky (1969) providing an important initial formal analysis. He argued that the three cultures can be arranged linearly along at least three dimensions. The moralist culture regards *political participation* as a duty, and the individualist sees it as a way of advancing self-interest, whereas the traditional culture reserves it for the elite (at least in an ideal situation). With respect to *bureaucracy*, the moralist respects a professional, well-rewarded administrative corps, but the individualist sees it as a fetter to

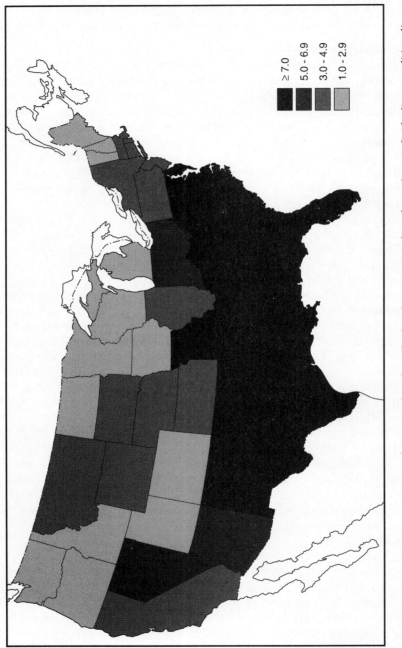

Figure 5.19 A classification of American states based on Sharkansky's (1969) index of moralism–individualism–traditionalism.

personal freedom, and for the traditionalist, bureaucracy is a constraint to the elite's activities. Thirdly, moralists welcome *government intervention in the community* where it is for the good of the commonwealth, individualists would minimize it 'to permit a balance of satisfactions from activities in the private and the public sector' (p. 69), and moralists oppose all except that which maintains the existing power structure. Within this last dimension, the moralists' culture would clearly welcome all State initiatives designed to promote the public good, the individualists would welcome only those that could be interpreted as political favour from which they could benefit, and traditionalists would only accept those designed to sustain the status quo.

From these general derivations linked to Elazar's arguments, Sharkansky identified three formal hypotheses. He produced a linear scale of moralism-individualism-traditionalism (ranging from 1.00 for the most moralistic state – Minnesota – to 9.00 for the most traditional – Arkansas and Mississippi: figure 5.19) and correlated this with 23 variables selected to represent aspects of political participation levels, the size and perquisites of the government bureaucracy, and the scope, magnitude and costs of government programmes. (Per capita average income and percentage urban in each State were held constant to remove any independent effects for socio-economic conditions, and regional locations were also controlled, to cover the separate effects of sectionalism.) The results showed strong partial relationships between culture and measures of participation, moderate relationships (partial correlations between −0.11 and −0.57) with those relating to bureaucracy, and strong relationships with certain variables representing government programmes (notably those representing taxation levels, and expenditures on education and welfare). These led Sharkansky to conclude that

> The evidence presented . . . lends some weight to the designations of political culture made by . . . Elazar. . . . the . . . scale of political culture shows important relationships with several traits of state politics and public service . . . independent of both the social-economic characteristics of personal income and urbanism, and other features of each state's regional history and traditions. The findings indicate that Elazar is a perceptive – if sometimes abstruse – observer of state cultures.

These relationships are especially important with regard to political participation, he argues, because culture has its most direct impact on popular behaviour. Nevertheless, despite these findings Sharkansky believes Elazar's designations to be 'of questionable reliability' in some respects, leading to a representation of his results as 'more suggestive than definitive' and a call for more research.

In later work following that call, Stonecash and Hayes (1981) argued that the shared learning which takes place within a culture (i.e. a place, in the context being argued here) means that 'How one expects government to behave, and the kind of world one would like to see government foster surely constitute an integral part of this cultural baggage' (p. 686). To measure cultural dispositions, by States, they followed Hutcheson and Taylor (1973) by using membership of certain religious groups to create a composite 'index of fundamentalism/liberalism'. They found that State responses to the Medicaid and AFDC programmes varied according to both their wealth and the power of the Governor to achieve legislative change. In addition, the more liberal the State, the greater the response, with the greatest impact of liberalism being found in the wealthiest States with the most powerful governors. Johnson (1976) extended this work by attempting to replicate Elazar's classification of the States (figure 5.17) through a discriminant analysis using religious affiliation data; he concluded that these do provide valid measures of the cultural differences. He then looked at the relationship between political culture and eight aspects of political activity in the States: extent of economic and welfare programmes; local emphasis in government; government centralization; innovation; encouragement of political participation; political participation rates; the importance of political parties; and the amount of inter-party competition. Only with government centralization and the importance of political parties did he find no relationship to the cultural variable (when socio-economic characteristics were held constant), leading to a conclusion regarding the importance of local political culture in understanding the geography of political activity.

Cultural regions and regional variations

Elazar's work, and that flowing from it, is crucial to the present argument because it broadens the concept of cultural regions very substantially from that normally employed by geographers to incorporate many aspects of the society in a place as well as the artefacts in its built (often rural) environment. As Sharkansky (1969) pointed out, it is relatively narrowly founded in aspects of a place's political culture. Nevertheless, because it is based on an appreciation of a place's history and socio-economic structure, it forms a firm base for resolving the paradox regarding aspects of the recent changing geography of the United States, and especially of the role of the South.

The particular features of the South identified above were: rapid indus-trialization in the 1960s and 1970s; the relative poverty of civil rights; substantial flows of Federal funds for certain programmes; and low levels of take-up of Federal funds for other programmes, notably those providing welfare payments for the poor. Partial 'explanations' for each have been offered in a wide range of studies; what we get from Elazar's work is a synoptic view of the role of cultural variations as underpinning those 'explanations'; the latter are the proximate rather than the full accounts of why the maps displayed earlier in this chapter showed the South to be distinctive on so many separate dimensions.

Elazar portrayed the South as dominated by a traditionalistic culture in which rule by a landed elite was for long the norm. (The history of the development of that culture is portrayed in many books: Boorstin's (1965) trilogy on *The Americans* contains several essays relating to aspects of the region and its particularities.) For that elite, widespread participation in political life was antithetical to their view of the 'good society', hence their attitudes towards equal rights for women, for example. Similarly, they were opposed to state welfare provision, preferring the paternalistic – and therefore repressive and oppressive – provision typical of the dominant unit of economic organization in the region – the plantation; from this we can derive the anti-trades unions attitudes that developed there, and the attractions of the region for investors looking for cheap labour in the late twentieth century.

The repressive and oppressive paternalism of the South is most apparent in elite attitudes towards the black population, brought forcibly to the region to work as slaves on their plantations. From this developed a general feeling of white superiority and the belief that blacks were a feckless race who would accept a 'culture of dependency' upon the state and its welfare payments rather than promote their own well-being. Hence the low take-up of Federal funds for welfare programmes. That paternalistic, white superiority view was challenged by the events leading up to the Civil War, however, and by the abolition of slavery which followed the South's defeat. The traditionalistic elite's reaction to that defeat was to re-erect their paternalistic culture in a slightly different form, replacing slavery by share-cropping, for example, and thus retaining their power over production and profits. The Democratic party became the mobilizing force for all whites, with its commitment to white superiority over-riding other issues. The resulting century of Democratic hegemony over southern politics (achieved, for example, by the many strategems devised to prevent blacks from registering as voters and from obtaining other civil rights such as equal opportunity in education) ensured the low take-up of Federal funds for welfare. It also, most importantly, gave the southern Senators and Representatives great power in the Federal Congress because of their control (obtained through seniority – itself a consequence of the Democratic hegemony in the South) of most of the important Congressional committees with regard to spending on defence and space contracts and the provision of subsidies to agriculture, the oil industry, and other aspects of the South's economy.

Only by appreciating the full nature of southern culture is it possible to account for its position in the changing geography of the United States. The traditionalistic form penetrated all aspects of the various dimensions of a place set out in this book, creating a cultural milieu which remains potent to the present day, despite the increased melting-pot nature of the region following greater immigration in recent decades. Similar cases can undoubtedly be made for the study of other areas of the United States, where other cultures dominate.

PLACES AND REGIONAL MODES OF PRODUCTION

In her book entitled *Regions: The Economics and Politics of Territory*, Markusen (1987) has portrayed the United States South not just as a separate place, along the dimensions used here, but also as a 'dominant and distinct mode of production' (p. 58), based on slavery. The slaves were not free to sell their labour power, as in a capitalist mode of production, but were a commodity bought and sold (along with their families, through which the slave culture was reproduced) by the slave-owners in the same way that they owned, bought and sold land. (A result of this was that the owners extracted absolute rather than relative surplus value from their slaves, which retarded both any increases in productivity and developments in agricultural diversification.) Furthermore, the slave-owners differed from capitalists in the strength of their drive to accumulate capital; they were only concerned to sustain their assets and earning capacity, rather than to expand them, and so 'squandered' much of their profit on conspicuous consumption rather than invested it in further rounds of accumulation. Thus the South developed a separate business ethic from the capitalist regions further north and west, with growth a relatively low priority and the lack of major programmes of investment and diversification (outside agriculture as well as within) – thus:

> Lack of an indigenous capital market separate from the plantation system curtailed credit to smallholders. As a result of these supply and demand inadequacies, small farmers in the South remained largely

marginal and subsistence producers up through the Civil War period. (p. 61)

The entire southern economy was 'backward', therefore, because of the ethic set by the elite, and not just the plantation component.

In contrast to the slave mode of production in the South, the northern States were clearly capitalist. This, among other things, accounted for the north's success in the Civil War, according to Markusen. The diversified northern economy meant that it had a manufacturing base on which to draw, and also that it had a better communications infrastructure. Its social relations aided its Civil War campaign too.

> Whereas workers and farmers could be drafted in the North, planters dared not permit their primary labor force, slaves, to fight, for it would be too dangerous to arm them. (p. 75)

Further, the north had a strong state tradition which enhanced its ability to wage war successfully, whereas the South was a 'decentralized, anarchic slavocracy' in which squabbling was rife. The South lost, but in the restructuring that followed the slave economy was replaced by sharecropping, which was almost as repressive and oppressive, and few other cultural changes were attained.

Markusen concludes this part of her discussion by arguing that:

> It is impossible to interpret contemporary regional antagonisms without taking into account these products of the Civil War era. . . . The underdevelopment of southern agriculture and industry, the one-party political system, the South's unique version of racism, and the culture of defeatism are powerful forces distinguishing the South from the rest of the country and prompting regionalism well into the second half of the twentieth century. (p. 77)

It was only then that change began, with the emergence of what Markusen terms the 'New South', when:

> The South's appeal for profit-squeezed northern sectors consisted precisely in the underdevelopment of both its labor force and its local state, traceable in turn to slavery and the subsequent agricultural reconstruction compromise. (p. 184)

A north–south (or Sunbelt–Snowbelt) conflict developed, in which struggle over economic policies was enhanced because of the 'long-standing cultural antagonism between these two groups of states . . . [and] the political structures and indigenous parties that facilitated it' (p. 189).

Markusen's interpretation is very similar to that developed here, therefore. She focuses more on the role of a slave mode of production that was slowly incorporated into a burgeoning capitalist one, however, and less on the cultural variations linked to that initial difference in the mode of production (which of course also means that she pays no attention to differences between the moralistic and individualistic cultures within the north).

Markusen's emphasis on mode of production is taken much further by Brustein (1988) in his attempt to answer the question 'why do the cultivators of western France continue to support the French Right while the cultivators of Mediterranean France continue to support the French Left?' (pp. 27–8). For him, that basic difference in perceptions of which party best represents the individual self-interests of French farmers can be accounted for by the mode of production concept. Each mode, he argues, following Marx, can be characterized on two components – the productive forces ('the social and technical means by which production is carried out') and social relations ('the institutions and practices associated with the production, exchange and distribution of goods'). From these it is possible (and again, Marx is cited as the authority) to predict 'the superstructure, or ideological nature, of society'. Marx did not suggest empirical indicators for the two components, however. Brustein chose to represent them by *economic activity* and *property rights*, and from these he claims it is possible to derive an area's settlement pattern and class composition, and also its residents' voting behaviour, the last because 'the mode of production affects political preferences by determining the universe of specific interests – interests on which individuals base their action' (p. 31).

France has three dominant modes of production, according to Brustein: in the west, characterized by subsistence, medium-scale tenancies and dispersed settlement; in the Mediterranean, with market-scale owner cultivation or wage labour, a concentrated settlement pattern and an absence of elites; and in the northeast, where there is large-scale commercial tenancy and/or ownership with wage labour. He then tested his propositions using a battery of variables, and concluded both that his index of the mode of production accounted for regional variations in voting for left-wing parties in 1849, 1914 and 1981 and also that it provided a better account than the 'traditional' theories of Siegfried (1913). He then expanded his argument to cover voting patterns in Italy (on which see also Dogan (1969) who advances arguments linked to religious practices, which Brustein claims are inferior to his own; see also Derivery and Dogan (1986) Judt (1986) and, on the geography of support for the Socialist and Communist parties, Giblin (1984)), Nazi Germany, India and the United States.

Regarding the United States case, Brustein focuses on the Populist movement of the 1880s and 1890s, which 'had three regional centers. Each was
overwhelmingly rural and each was associated with a product whose price
had fallen catastrophically; the mountain states were based mainly upon
silver; the South was based chiefly upon cotton; and the four trans-
Mississippi states of Kansas, Nebraska, and the two Dakotas were based
principally upon wheat' (p. 175). He accounts for the Populist candidates'
success in the last of these three by the economic situation in the areas at the
time, and suggests that their lack of success elsewhere reflected economic
differences, so that in

> the midwestern states of Iowa, Illinois, and Wisconsin . . . farmers
> specialized in dairying and growing corn as feed for hogs, both more
> stable than growing wheat since neither was as dependent upon
> exports, the world market, and the weather as growing wheat.
> Because of their mode of production these farmers were not particu-
> larly affected by the agricultural crisis of the 1890s. Thus the agricul-
> tural program of the Populist party did not reflect the material
> interests of midwestern farmers. (p. 177)

From this and his other case study material, he concludes that the mode
of production theory can not only account for past regional variations in
voting behaviour but also that its greatest potential 'may lie . . . in its ability
to explain present and to predict future patterns of political behavior,
from electoral outcomes to regional variation within revolutionary social
upheaval' (p. 182).

Brustein's definition of the concept of mode of production differs from
Markusen's, and from that of most other researchers whose work is
stimulated by Marx's writings. He is concerned with variations within the
capitalist mode only. Furthermore, his is a more deterministic model even
than that employed by many Marxian writers, which is the base of much
that has been presented in this book. The case argued here is that within
the capitalist mode of production, cultural differences between places can
lead to outcomes that are not readily predicted from knowledge of their
dominant economic activities; thus Brustein may claim that Utah residents,
because of their great dependence on defence-related employment and
the predominance of Mormons there, might 'continue to support the
conservative wing of the Republican party as long as that wing forcefully
advocates a strong military and lower federal taxes' (p. 182), but the
geography of voting in the United States reflects much more than just
economic self-interest. Whilst much of Brustein's work is of substantial
interest to the general case being developed in this book, therefore, his

argument regarding regional modes of production is not a viable development of Markusen's regarding the origins of the separate nature of the American South. Cultural variations among places reflect much more than economic functions and the political self-interest that may follow therefrom. By its lacunae, Brustein's argument sustains the case developed here for a holistic approach to the study of place and its culture, which does not privilege any one component of that whole.

6

Bounded Places

Man . . . is as much a territorial animal as is a mockingbird singing in the clear California night. We act as we do for reasons of our evolutionary past, not our cultural present. . . . If we defend the title to our land or the sovereignty of our country, we do it for reasons no different, no less innate, no less ineradicable, than do lower animals. . . . all of us will give everything we are for a place of our own. Territory, in the evolving world of animals, is a force perhaps older than sex.

R. Ardrey, *The Territorial Imperative*

Throughout the preceding four chapters places have been discussed as elements of a complex cultural mosaic, but with no reference to their boundaries. In some circumstances this is an entirely valid approach, since the boundaries between places are at best imprecise; one place slowly merges into another. But in other cases, clear boundaries are both defined and defended, so that people not only know that they are residents of a place, they also know where that place starts and finishes, and thus who is not of it. This may be unimportant, but in many aspects of life identification with a place, and the consequent feelings against other places (or, more precisely, against their residents plus others who identify with them but now live elsewhere), is salient. In such situations, appreciating the definition of a place's boundaries and their use in the promotion of people's identification is important to the task being set in this work. Thus the present chapter explores how such appreciation can be advanced, using the concept of territoriality as its organizing focus.

TERRITORIALITY

Territoriality as a concept has been used in discussions of the nature of behaviour in a variety of social and natural sciences. As Sack (1983) pointed out in his important theoretical essay on human territoriality, some writers – notably those drawing on certain ethological work, e.g. Ardrey (1969) – present it as a biological drive or aggressive instinct, a genetically transmitted behavioural trait which humans share with other animal species. Sack rejects that view, as illustrated above by the quotation from Ardrey's work, however, preferring to present territoriality, as defined in his later book (Sack, 1986, p. 2), as 'a human strategy to affect, influence and control'.

Smith's (1986a, p. 482) definition of territoriality underpins the present discussion:

> The attempt by an individual or group to influence or establish control over a clearly demarcated territory which is made distinctive and considered at least partially exclusive by its inhabitants or those who define its bounds.

He closely follows Sack in emphasizing the importance of power as a human relationship, in the exercise of which territoriality is an important strategy: Sack's definition (1986, p. 19) is that territoriality is

> the attempt by an individual or group to affect, influence or control people, phenomena and relationships, by delimiting and asserting control over a geographic area.

Smith goes further, however, observing that people use territoriality strategies to promote 'identity, defence and stimulation' and also stressing that those three needs are socially produced not biologically given. As a consequence, use of the territoriality strategy is 'conditioned primarily by cultural norms and values which vary in structure and function from society to society, from one time period to another, and in accordance with the scale of social activity'. At the societal level, he argues that

> territoriality becomes a means of regulating social interaction and a focus and symbol of group membership and identity, ranging from the scale of urban gangs and their turf, through patterns of territorial regionalism, to the compartmentalization of the world into a system of states.

Sack's theory of human territoriality

Sack's theory of human territoriality is non-deterministic, as emphasized in his statement (1983, p. 57) that

> under certain conditions territoriality is a more effective means of establishing differential access to people, or resources, than is nonterritoriality

and he suggests ten reasons why this is so. Those ten (he calls them 'tendencies') refer to two major characteristics of territory: it can be bounded, and thus readily communicated; and it can be used to displace personal relationships, between controlled and controller, by relationships between people and 'the law of the place' – territory is thereby reified in order to promote personal ambitions impersonally.

Of the ten tendencies, Sack (1986, pp. 31–2) refers to the first three as 'logically (though not empirically) prior. They are the bases by which the other seven potentialities of territoriality are interrelated, and any or all of the ten can be possible reasons for its use'. They are termed classification, communication and enforcement, and these, because they are part of the definition of territoriality, must be present: 'territoriality must provide classification, communication, and enforcement, but it can be "caused " by one or several of all ten' (p. 32). The meanings of the three terms are straightforward. *Classification* refers to the categorization of people and/or things by location in space: it is easier to apply than many other categorizations which relate to individual characteristics and criteria. *Communication* refers to the ease of transmitting the classification: 'it requires only one kind of marker or sign – the boundary' (p. 32). And *enforcement* relates to the efficiency of using location as the criterion for indicating whether or not people are subject to certain exercise of power. (As he puts it, territoriality is especially efficient 'if the distribution in space and time of the resources or things to be controlled fall well between ubiquity and unpredictability': when within the bounded space, you are subject to the rules that apply there.)

The other seven tendencies relate to: the reification of power, by making an abstract concept tangible; the displacement of attention from interpersonal relationships to the apparent role of the territory as the power-enforcer – 'it is the law of the land'; the impersonality that these relationships engender; the apparent neutrality that territoriality suggests; the provision of containers, or moulds, to which all people and things can be allocated, when required; the possibility of places being empty; and the space-filling consequences of territoriality – new territories may be engendered for new events, as with the creation of the European Communities embracing a larger territory than that associated with any individual state. Any one or more of the seven may be the reason(s) why a territoriality strategy is selected in particular situations, but whenever they are the outcome necessarily involves classification, communication and enforcement. In the operation of a library, for example, the librarian's rules are usually presented impersonally – this is what you will do while in this building, which involves classification (presence in the building), communication (clear identification of the boundaries), and enforcement (these are the rules that you will obey).

Sack then sets out a variety of combinations of the ten tendencies which illustrate the various uses of a territorial strategy. Splitting up a factory into a series of separate workshops whose members are in competition, for example, facilitates a policy of 'divide and conquer' — as with the 'butty' gangs at separate locations on the coalface in Dukeries' collieries (described in chapter 4).

Sack (1983) ends his seminal introductory essay by pointing to the criteria that must be met if his general theory is to be vindicated. A large number of cases must be studied, he argues, in order to achieve four goals: to assess whether the adduced reasons for territorial rather than nonterritorial behaviour are valid; to determine the precise conditions under which the operation of a territoriality strategy becomes an advantage; to identify whether there are conditions under which territoriality is a necessary strategy; and to set out the advantages that a territorial strategy can bring to an organization. His later book (1986) focuses in part on these issues. An initial essay looks at the increasing use of territoriality over time, and this is followed by detailed analyses of: the organization of the Roman Catholic Church; the territorial organization of local government in the United States; and the spatial structuring of workplaces. (In the 1983 essay, he used the example of the organization of the United States' Army.)

Although the 1986 book is not set out explicitly to assess his arguments against the criteria set out at the end of the 1983 essay, there is no doubt that Sack's conclusions are almost entirely positive with regard to his theory's potential. Thus he claims territoriality to be

> the basic geographic expression of influence and power . . . [it is] an essential link between society, space and time. Territoriality is the backcloth of geographical context — it is the device through which people construct and maintain spatial organizations. . . . [It] is not an instinct or drive, but rather a complex strategy to affect, influence, and control access to people, things and relationships. (p. 216)

He doesn't identify exactly the conditions in which territoriality will be used as a strategy, but does implicitly conclude that it is a necessary one.

> Whatever the goals of a society may be . . . and whatever the geographical scale . . . a society, simply as a complex organization, will need territoriality to coordinate efforts, specify responsibilities, and prevent people from getting in each other's way. And since terri-

toriality of one sort or another will likely be employed, we must be aware . . . [that it] is not only a means of creating and maintaining order, but is a device to create and maintain much of the geographic context through which we experience the world and give it meaning. (p. 219)

That final sentence provides the basis for extending Sack's treatment here.

Territoriality is used as a strategy at a variety of spatial scales. At the smallest, for example, individuals may define and 'bound' their territory within an otherwise shared space, such as a dormitory or a reading table in a library. Within dwellings, they may have rooms which are clearly identified as their 'private property', entry to which they control and within which their rules obtain – as with 'no smoking'; the same is true of separate rooms and suites in office buildings. More broadly, property rights over bounded territories are basic to the operation of capitalist societies; individuals or corporate bodies own land and have the right to determine what may be done with it, who may enter it and under what conditions, and so forth, subject only to decisions of the state regarding the wider public good (what are known as police powers). Such properties are normally organized to keep unwanted people out, and unauthorized entry, or trespass, is an offence punishable under civil, if not criminal, law. Others are 'constructed' to keep people in – as with prisons and asylums: to some extent Sack's definition of territoriality is more suited to this use of bounded places for surveillance, as argued in more detail below. Finally, at the largest scales, states are, by their very nature, bounded places which operate both surveillance (keeping people in) and defensive (keeping people out) functions. (Elsewhere in this chapter these two are referred to as inclusionary and exclusionary versions of the theory.)

In looking at the use of territoriality strategies, most attention will be paid to the state and to its component local state apparatus, though several elements of the arguments have wider relevance. In addition, consideration will be given to the use of bounded places, and the creation of identity with them, in the creation and recreation of personal and collective identities.

THE STATE AS A TERRITORIAL CONTAINER

States are widely recognized as territorially-defined institutions. Dunleavy and O'Leary (1987), for example, define a modern state with regard to five characteristics, and include statements that (p. 2):

The state is sovereign, or the supreme power, within its territory and

> The state's sovereignty extends to all the individuals within a given
> territory.

But the relationship between a state's sovereignty and its territory is not
discussed (territory and territoriality are not listed in the book's index), a
feature shared with other texts on the nature of the state.

Alford and Friedland (1985) have two entries for 'territory' in the very
full index to their book entitled *Powers of Theory: Capitalism, the State,
and Democracy*. Both refer to territory as a basis for 'premodern' (their
term for 'precapitalist') social organizations, which were only incompletely
destroyed by the alterations in social relations wrought by the introduction
of capitalism (p. 51). The process of state-building under capitalism – a
necessary element of the emerging mode of production, according to Lipset
and Rokkan's (1967) classic work, on which they draw – frequently
stimulated territorial conflicts because of this nature of its foundation:

> Because of the territorial location of cultural, religious, and linguistic
> groupings, conflicts with the state sometimes redefined the boundaries
> of the nation through civil war, secession and mass migration. . . .
> The national revolution involved conflicts over cultural values
> between central elites and peripheral cultures. (p. 256)

But they fail to notice that the state-building processes that are at the heart
of Lipset and Rokkan's theorizing were themselves based on the importance
of territory to the exercise of power which is at the heart of the contemporary capitalist state: although they note that 'the international relations of
capitalist states occur on the basis of the securely established sovereignty
of each state over its territory and population' (p. 291) they do not explore
the importance of territoriality to the establishment and sustenance of
sovereignty.

Clark and Dear's (1984) book on *State Apparatus* was written by two
geographers, and one might expect it to contain a fuller account of the
nature of sovereignty as a set of power relationships exercised through
territoriality than is found in contributions by political scientists. But
territory is not in their index either, although at the outset it is identified
as one of their book's two major themes.

> The second theme concerns the territorial manifestations of state
> involvement in national, regional and urban processes. In this instance
> we focus on the spatial structure of capitalist society which occurs
> as a result of state actions. These two themes [the first is the theory

of the capitalist state] intersect throughout the book and, as a result, a concept emerges of geographical structure as a composite product of state action and sociospatial processes under capitalism. (p. 2)

Their index thus contains many entries for terms with 'spatial' as an introductory adjective, but their approach largely involves 'reading off' spatial structures from political processes and very little of the book addresses the importance of territory in operating those political processes.

Exceptions to the general tendencies set out in the previous paragraph are provided by the works of two social theorists. Giddens, in *The Nation-State and Violence* (1985), defines the state as 'a political organization whose rule is territorially ordered and which is able to mobilize the means of violence to sustain that rule' (p. 20), and argues that the growth of the absolutist state, with its much wider span of power than its feudal predecessor, required a clearer definition of territorial structures. With the replacement of absolutist by modern nation-states territory became even more important: a nation-state is defined (p. 120) as 'a bordered power-container . . . the pre-eminent power-container of the modern era'. In this, he works from Weber's identification of three elements that distinguish states from other organizations:

(i) the existence of a regularized administrative staff able (ii) to sustain the claim to the legitimate monopoly of violence and (iii) to uphold that monopoly within a given territory. (p. 18)

That monopoly in the use and/or licensing of violence in the exercise of sovereignty within its 'power-container whose administrative purview corresponds exactly to its territorial delimitation' (p. 172) is allied to territoriality in Giddens's presentation. A major activity within nation-states (by other, licensed, agencies as well as by the state apparatus) is *surveillance* – 'control of information and the superintendence of the activities of some groups by others' (p. 2). This process is much facilitated by a territoriality strategy. The nature of the territorial container is central to the definition of the state itself, hence the importance of boundary disputes and cross-boundary incursions to modern nation-states: as Giddens expresses it (p. 291), they provide 'challenges to its administrative and cultural integrity'.

Although territoriality is central to the concept of surveillance in his work, and it is thus an example of Sack's theory – Giddens (1985) does not refer to Sack's (1983) essay, and Sack (1986) does not refer to Giddens's (1985) book – Giddens does not directly address most of the central issues of the importance of territoriality to the nature of the state. This is the focus of an important essay by Mann (1984), however, which provides the clearest statement of the necessity of territoriality not only for the definition and operation of the nation-state but also for its autonomy in contemporary capitalist society.

The state, according to Mann, exists to perform four tasks that are necessary either to society as a whole or to interest groups within it: to ensure internal order; to sustain military defence and aggression; to maintain communication infrastructures; and to achieve economic redistribution. These are most efficiently performed by the personnel of a state apparatus, he contends (p. 197), whose superior efficiency is a consequence of its territorial definition. The state, he argues, differs from other organizations in which power (economic, political, military and ideological) is exercised.

> the state does not possess a distinctive *means* of power independent of, and analogous to, economic, military and ideological power. The means used by states are only a combination of these, which are also the means of power used in all social relationships. However, the power of the state is irreducible in quite a different *socio-spatial* and *organizational* sense. Only the state is inherently centralised over a delimited territory over which it has authoritative power. Unlike economic, ideological or military groups in civil society, the state elite's resources radiate authoritatively outwards from a centre but stop at defined territorial boundaries. The state is, indeed, a *place* – both a central place and a unified territorial reach. (p. 198)

In its regulatory activities, the state operates what Mann terms infrastructural power, which refers to its ability to penetrate everyday life within civil society and implement political decisions (p. 189). Territoriality is crucial to this: the greater the infrastructural powers of the state, he argues (i.e. the greater its need to penetrate everyday life), 'the greater the territorializing of social life' (p. 208).

Territoriality is not only a necessary strategy in the operation of modern nation-state apparatus, however; according to Mann it is also the basis of its relative autonomy within capitalist societies, and hence its ability to act independently of various interest groups within those societies. Once the territorially-centralized state is established, he argues, civil society loses control over it; the state becomes an autonomous force, and its territorial definition is the basis of its autonomy. As Mann puts it, the achievement of territorial sovereignty by the state, with which is associated the monopoly of legalized violence as identified by Giddens, gives those controlling the state apparatus an advantage over others, some of whom may have access to greater stores of economic and other power. The latter may endorse the use of that state power, because they benefit from its exercise in general, if not on every occasion, and thus are prepared to sustain its legitimacy. When they do not, then there may be a challenge to the state, as illustrated by Habermas's (1972) work on crises in capitalist societies. Whilst society in general is prepared to legitimate the state because of the benefits that it brings, then the state elite is empowered to act autonomously, to do things that are not necessarily desired by those who still support it, but which are accepted because of the other benefits that the exercise of state power provides.

Laws, territory and the state

The identity of the state may be maintained through its monopoly over violence, but that monopoly is always open to challenge. (Here, and throughout much of the chapter, the state will be reified as a shorthand way of referring to those who exercise power within the state apparatus.) That autonomy can be contested by the population subject to the state's power (both the population of the state's territory and the population beyond its territorial reach, with the latter probably represented by another state). The state determines the rules by which society will be organized and individuals must operate their daily lives. Those rules may be accpeted and observed because of the coercive powers of the state, but in complex societies the extent to which the state can coerce is limited – in the medium-if not the short-term – by the potential of its population to 'revolt' against them in a challenge to the state's legitimacy. The continued existence and acceptance of rules reflects individual and collective recognition of the need for order. Some anarchist theorists argue that if all agree to abide by rules enacted by everybody, for the benefit of everybody, then this is sufficient; a state with coercive powers is unnecessary. To others, however, a state is necessary to ensure that collective action is taken which is in the interests of all. In many circumstances, individuals may act in ways that represent their own short-term best interests but which are against their long-term interest. Only with a collective organization imposing rules will the general good be assured: the alternative, in the absence of a state or similar body, in the words of Hobbes's (1651) classic. work *Leviathan* is a life that is 'nasty, brutish and short' (see also Johnston, 1989c).

The rules that the state enacts and enforces are generally known as laws, which are designed, enunciated and operated for the purpose of social control. Laws are special cases of rules because the state is – necessarily according to Mann's definition – a territorial body. The ability to exercise sovereign power over a defined area is the hallmark of a state, so laws as its means of exercising that power are territorial too (Johnston, 1991b). The nature of those laws – what they are for – is the focus of the next section.

THE ROLES OF THE STATE AND THE USES OF TERRITORIALITY

Giddens and Mann have added to Sack's work by providing an answer to a question which he poses but does not address, relating to the necessity of territoriality in certain circumstances. Territoriality is a necessary element of the definition and operation of the capitalist nation-state, and a basis for the autonomous power that is exercised by the elite in charge of the state apparatus.

But why is the nation-state necessary, thereby making a territorially-based institution and a set of territorially-enforced laws necessary to capitalist societies? Many authors have concluded that the continued survival of a capitalist mode of production requires an autonomous institution such as the state. Drawing on the work of O'Connor (1973), Clark and Dear (1984) have identified three basic state roles. First, it is required to secure social consensus, whereby all groups within the society agree (implicitly if not explicitly) to accept the way in which it is operated (what they term 'the prevailing contract': p. 43). This is its primary task, since unless the state 'provides order, stability and security' it is impossible for 'production and exchange [to] take place with any degree of continuity'. Consensus is achieved, they contend, by three sub-apparatus within the state: the political sub-apparatus provides an organizational framework, via liberal democratic forms of government at national and local levels, for wide participation in, and therefore explicit acceptance of, the state's exercise of power; the legal sub-apparatus mediates in disputes and allows all to achieve their state-defined rights; and the repressive sub-apparatus (the police and the military) limits opposition and undertakes surveillance. All three combine to create an essential social consensus, without which 'the fabric of social relations and capitalist exchange would collapse' (p. 43).

The second role is to secure the conditions of production, by investment that will increase production in both public and private sectors of the economy and by regulating patterns of consumption so as to ensure the reproduction of the labour force. The state in a capitalist society is involved in providing 'the infrastructure for economic growth and coordinated market exchange', according to Clark and Dear (p. 43), and by doing that it 'provides the conditions for creating profit, and hence ensures the allegiance of the capitalist elite' which 'reinforces its [i.e. the state's] own power and legitimacy'. This involves sub-apparatus which produce public goods, which contract with private sector organizations for the provision of other goods and services, and which regulate money through the treasury. Together these create an infrastructure within which profits can be made and capitalism can flourish, an infrastructure which individual capitalist organizations could not provide, either separately or together.

The final state task involves securing social integration, by ensuring the welfare of all, and especially the subordinate groups within society who are economically relatively powerless. Whereas the second role (securing the conditions of production) involves the state's participation in and contribution to the creation of wealth which is unequally distributed, this third ensures the redistribution of some of that wealth towards the relatively underprivileged in society, so as to sustain their support for an economic system in which they do less well than others. This legitimation is achieved, Clark and Dear argue, by five sub-apparatus: those that deliver health, welfare and education services, those that distribute information, and those which facilitate communication. Whereas a major task of the sub-apparatus involved in the legitimation of an unequal economic system is the distribution of a range of services, thereby winning support through the provision of material gains, they are also involved in what is termed 'some degree of regulation or control over the serviced population' (Clark and Dear, 1984, p. 52). This is an ideological task:

> Ideologies tell people what exists, what is possible, and what is right or wrong. They structure the limits of discourse in society, and are present in all aspects of everyday life, including family, school, neighborhood and workplace. . . . The integrative purpose of ideology is therefore to promulgate the belief that the 'system' is capable of overcoming the contradictions of capitalist relations.

This may require a separate sub-apparatus, or it may be achieved by the others, as in the role of a state education system in the promotion of an ideology, for example, and of the mass media in sustaining a culture which lauds the capitalist system.

Clark and Dear's detailed analysis of the structure and functioning of the state in capitalist societies is not accompanied by an examination of the use of territoriality as a strategy by which its roles are exercised. Their only discussion of territory is concerned with the local state segment of the state apparatus (as examined in greater detail in Johnston, 1990e). They ask 'Why should it be necessary to create a small-scale spatial analogue of the national state?' (p. 133), and answer by asserting that it is because of the requirement for the state to be involved in 'long-term crisis avoidance at the local level' (p. 133) in ways that 'effectively co-opt and thereby control the local population' (p. 134). They do not address that need in detail, however, nor do they enquire why it is a necessarily spatial means of control. Their main interest is in the relative autonomy of the local state (see also Clark, 1985), and in establishing that the local government/administration systems are simply part of the state apparatus and in no way independent of it. By decentralizing at least part of the state structure and encouraging democratic participation in its activities, the central state elite wins the consent of the population and furthers the legitimacy of the entire state apparatus.

The need for the state to perform the above three roles is widely accepted, though the terminology may be different. It is also agreed that:

1   there is no one way in which the state apparatus in a capitalist society must act in order to perform its tasks; and
2· the state apparatus is not limited to those three tasks alone.

Those who control the state apparatus both interpret the situations they encounter to determine how they should promote social consensus, advance accumulation and ensure legitimation and use their power to promote other economic, social and political goals in which they are interested. Thus the state is an arena within which power can be 'captured' by groups with agenda other than those associated with the three necessary tasks, as in the recent rise of Islamic fundamentalism as a political force in states such as Iran. Alternatively, groups which achieve control over the state apparatus may then use their power to promote beliefs which lie outside the main spheres of political activity and which may be only incidental to their obtaining power − as with debates on degrees of censorship in many countries.

There is no determinism, therefore, no need for the state apparatus to act in particular ways. Even with the exercise of economic power, which is primary since it is concerned with the long-term sustenance of the mode of production, although those in power within the state apparatus are constrained to promote and legitimate accumulation there is no single route to those ends. Indeed, the nature of the dialectic that is at the heart of the capitalist mode of production is such that new solutions are frequently being required for new problems. How those in control react will reflect their socialization in place (as illustrated at another scale in chapter 4), their perceptions of the issues they face, their accountability to the population of their own state, and the perceptions and actions of other actors in the arena, including those in control of other states. Within the constraints of ensuring continued profitable conditions, therefore, the degrees of freedom for the state apparatus are many; they are both constrained and enabled.

THE ROLE OF TERRITORIALITY IN STATE ACTIVITY

The authors reviewed here provide elements of an approach to understanding the state through the concept of territoriality. None brings the various parts together in an holistic argument which addresses the necessity of territoriality for an institution that is itself necessary to capitalism's long-term survival. Sack has argued that territoriality is a sound strategy for the pursuit of control, and control is central to the state's operations, but others have not incorporated that case into their work on the state itself.

Territoriality and the three state roles

Territoriality is a viable, and probably necessary, strategy for pursuit of each of the three state roles identified by Clark and Dear. The justification for that assertion is the purpose of this section.

Concerning the securing of social consensus, capitalism cannot flourish without order, stability and security. People will not invest capital if the probability of making profits is small, because their assets may be confiscated, for example, or their workforce may be ill-disciplined and its productivity low. In consequence, certain countries may be much more attractive to outside investors and providers of development aid than others, with possible implications for the nature of the state apparatus and in particular the operation of democracy there (Johnston, 1984d, 1989d). The state must provide a secure environment within which wealth accumulation can be successfully prosecuted.

Internal disorder must be at a minimum and external threats few, if any, in that secure environment. The state must be able to deliver security and stability through 'the rule of law', in which people either accept and operate within the existing laws or are coerced into so doing, usually with some promise that this will produce economic, social and political benefits in the future. In other words, the state apparatus must operate a successful surveillance function, which requires an efficient and effective police force. As Giddens argues, such an operation calls for a territorial strategy, with the rule of the state's law prevailing throughout its defined sovereign area. That territorial strategy will undoubtedly involve a hierarchy of areas within which control is exercised, as made clear in Sack's examples. Similarly with external threats, the state must be able to defend itself against potential adversaries; its borders must be secure, which again requires a territorial strategy. To some, the state's military strength should be apparent but preferably not demonstrated. That a state apparatus is ready, willing and able to defend its territory should be sufficient to deter any would-be invaders. If it is called upon to demonstrate its preparedness, the costs of waging war may be a deterrent to investors because of the high taxation rates that could then prevail; the decline of major political powers on the world scene is associated by some with the costs of waging expensive wars (Kennedy, 1988; Taylor, 1989).

The surveillance function extends beyond defence and law and order, however, to embrace what is generally termed the civil law. The stability that participants in capitalist markets require includes the assurances that contracts will be fulfilled and that disputes between signatories to an agreement will be arbitrated fairly by a neutral body. They may recognize that laws about certain aspects of contracts vary from place to place, and that interpretations of the same laws may also vary spatially (as illustrated by Blomley, 1990), but as long as individual courts and other arbitrators are consistent, they provide a secure context within which investors will operate. Guaranteeing that security is a crucial state role; without it, the capitalist mode of production cannot flourish.

With regard to securing the conditions of production, provision of an infrastructure is the central task. That infrastructure will have two components: a physical framework – including transport and communications networks, for example, plus basic utilities such as power, water and waste removal – and a facilitative milieu. The latter is the more important according to political theorists of the 'New Right' who dominated the capitalist world during the 1980s. Their particular concern was with the role of the state as a guarantor of the operation of 'free markets', to be achieved in a variety of ways but with control of the money supply one of the most crucial (Gamble, 1988). Inflation was identified as the scourge of capitalist economies then considered to be in crisis, and the proper role of the state apparatus was to remove it, thereby providing the conditions for substantial investment in the means of future wealth accumulation. If those conditions prevail, not only will investment be forthcoming, jobs created and prosperity assured but private investors will also provide the physical infrastructure, according to some theoreticians, thereby leaving the state's primary role as creating and sustaining a facilitative milieu for capitalist profit-taking.

Arguments for the state as a regulatory body creating and sustaining a favourable environment for capitalist operations do not also call for a mosaic of nation-states such as that currently in place. One state regulating the whole world might suffice. However, capitalism is built on competition between investors in different parts of the world, and while they all want a stable milieu in which to operate they also prefer one in which their own interests are protected against those of their competitors elsewhere. Hence, as Harvey (1985b) argues, groups in particular areas will probably cooperate in what he terms a 'regional alliance' to promote their competitive advantage.

Harvey's argument regarding the need for such regional alliances is based on his wider analysis of the necessity of uneven development in the spatial structuring of capitalism (Harvey, 1982). In order to accumulate wealth, those investing capital in production and/or distribution have to 'freeze' it in a place, where they create fixed resources (such as factories) and employ others (such as labour). Their basic 'materials' – capital and labour – are inherently mobile, but for accumulation strategies to succeed that mobility must be restrained by investment in what he termed 'fixed and immobile infrastructures' (p. 150). Those structures must then be protected, until such time as investors decide to replace them (probably by withdrawing their investment – or declining to renew it – and instead placing it elsewhere). The result is that 'capitalist development must negotiate a knife-edge between preserving the values of past commitments made at a particular place and time, or devaluing them to open up fresh room for accumulation'. There is a continual state of tension, therefore:

> All economic agents (individuals, organizations, institutions) make decisions on the circulation of their capital or the deployment of their labour power in a context marked by a deep tension between cutting and running to wherever the rate of remuneration is highest, or staying put, sticking with past commitments and recouping values already embodied. (pp. 150–1)

The 'cutting and running' strategy involves the devaluation of assets, and the consequent depreciation of investments is therefore undesirable; investors want to maximize their returns, which means reaping their potential gains for as long as possible. To achieve that, they want their investments protected through measures that will promote, if not guarantee, continued profitability. A regional class alliance is one way of approaching this. Indeed, according to Harvey

> regional class alliances, loosely bounded within a territory and usually (though not exclusively or uniquely) organised through the state, are a necessary and inevitable response to the need to defend values already embodied and a structured regional coherence already

achieved. The alliance can also actively promote conditions favourable to further accumulation within its region. (p. 151)

Both those already present in a region and those to be attracted to it can
benefit from such an alliance if it is successful, therefore.

It is possible to have alliances within alliances, regional groupings promoting local interests (perhaps through the local state apparatus) within a
national alliance, for example. And in building an alliance, the investors
may make common cause with those in whom they invest – the workers.
Local solidarity is promoted where it is perceived as necessary to local
prosperity, leading to Harvey's opinion that

> The conclusion is inescapable: if regional structures and class alliances
> did not already exist, then the processes at work under capitalism
> would necessarily create them. (p. 152)

The state is particularly appropriate as the crucible within which such
alliances can be forged, for five reasons: its territorial definition, which
provides an integrity other types of alliance would lack; its authority,
through its monopoly of coercive power; its boundedness, so that 'it
can impose relatively firm boundaries on otherwise porous and unstable
geographical edges' (p. 152); its fiscal and monetary powers; and its ability
to foster a nationalistic ideology.

> The upshot is a regional class alliance that typically builds upon the
> apparatus of state power, engages in community boosterism and
> strives for community or national solidarity as the means to promote
> and defend an amalgam of various class and factional interests within
> a territory.

In this way, capitalist competition takes on the appearance of competition
between states.

The pattern of nation-states inherited from the pre-capitalist era has in
some cases provided not only a useful set of bounded territories within
which those alliances can be formed but also a set of institutions which,
because of their relative autonomy (itself a function of their territorial
identification), are able to undertake the regulation and to sustain it
through their legitimacy. The existence of a mosaic of states thus allows
both the regulation of local populations in a whole variety of ways and
the provision of an infrastructure within which accumulation can be
advanced. The elements of that mosaic may not always be well suited to
the task, as illustrated by the growing importance of the European Community in the regulation of the economic, social and political affairs of

twelve formerly independent states; the Community is itself the successor to previous nation-state-building efforts, such as the creations of Germany and Italy in the nineteenth century. Restructuring the map of states is part of the restructuring of regional alliances.

The state is not just an institution for the promotion of capitalist interests, therefore, but rather one which in particular furthers the interests of those domiciled within its territory. It regulates the activities of individuals and corporate bodies through its sovereign control over that territory, using the strategies outlined by Sack. The same is true for its work in securing social integration. State redistribution of portions of the wealth created as a consequence of its activities under the previous function is confined to its territory's residents: normally only a state's nationals are allowed access to its subsidized (even free) education and health services, for example. In this way, the labour force that is crucial to the accumulation strategies can be committed to the regional class alliance.

One particular feature of this third state role is that it is ideological in content, promoting within the population a set of beliefs that supports the operations of capitalism in general and of local capitalist interests in particular. (The same was true, and perhaps even more so, of the socialist states – dubbed by some as the welfare-state dictatorships – of eastern Europe between *c*.1950 and *c*.1990.) Thus during the 1980s there was a major government-led campaign through all levels of the educational system in the United Kingdom, stimulating a pro-capitalist ideology which praised the benefits of entrepreneurship and individual self-responsibility and which involved Ministers denigrating the views of many in the academic world.

Nationalism as territoriality

The promotional campaigns discussed in the previous paragraph are an example of the general concept of nationalism, defined by Smith (1986b, p. 312) as:

> (a) A feeling of belonging to the nation; [and] (b) a corresponding political ideology which holds that the territorial and national unit should be allowed to coexist in an autonomously congruous relationship.

Johnston, Knight and Kofman (1988), drawing on the work of Anderson (1986), identify two types of nationalist campaign, which differ in the relationship between territory and nation set out in Smith's definition.

In the first type, the territory of a nation and the territory of a state are

not congruent, and the nationalist movement's goal is to achieve congru-
ence by a reordering of territorial boundaries. Their strategy is clearly
based on territoriality though, as will be elaborated later, it does not
necessarily imply control over individuals. The nation is defined in cultural
terms (such as common language, religious and ethnic bonds), and its
representatives lay claim to a territory in which the nation will be autonomous, if not independent. That territory is currently occupied by others,
however, and the goal is either to remove them or to encourage them to
yield at least some, if not all, of their power to the nation whose land they
occupy.

The second type of nationalism refers to situations in which there is no
incongruity between national area and state territory, but the link between
nation and state is weaker than some would wish. There is a territory over
which the state has sovereign power, but its residents do not strongly
identify themselves with it; there is no enduring national sentiment. Thus
the goal, usually of the elite controlling the state apparatus, is to generate
and sustain national sentiment among the territory's residents, in part to
legitimate the state itself and in part to promote the interests of the regional
alliance(s) that it represents. This has been so in many newly-independent
ex-colonial states, for example, where the territories defined by the colonial
powers bore little resemblance to the often weakly-defined pattern of
national territories preceding colonial invasion. By the time independence
was achieved the possibility of returning to those earlier boundaries was
remote, and so new national identities had to be built based on the colonial
territories, a process usually initiated by the pro-independence movements
that led to the creation of the new states.

The nationalism in countries like the United Kingdom during the 1980s,
referred to above, is a sub-category of that described in the previous
paragraph. The sense of nationhood among a substantial proportion of
the population was considered insufficiently strong by those in control of
the state apparatus to sustain their programme of economic, social and
political restructuring, which was designed to promote the interests of
capital in general and the local regional alliance(s) in particular. An ideological strategy was thus initiated to enhance people's sense of identification
with the national territory.

Nationalism may be used as a strategy through which some people can
achieve control of others, involving them winning consensus support for a
programme whose benefits will be unequally distributed. In this sense it is
a clear example of territoriality as defined by Sack. But nationalism is also
an example of the need for identity, recognized in Smith's definition of
territoriality. If people do need to identify with groups in order to define

themselves (and social psychologists have shown that group identity is important to people's perceptions of the world), a territoriality strategy may provide an effective focus for their self-identification. It is almost certainly not a necessary strategy, for many people successfully identify themselves with groups that have no territorial associations, such as religions (although, as Sack shows, most of these are territorially structured in their organization, with territorially-defined locales being used to mould people into communities with common interests: Sack, 1986, p. 87). In part it depends on the nature of the group and its goals. If members wish merely to provide a social focus to parts of individuals' lives, and if the group is neither antagonistic towards nor antagonized by other groups in the same territory, then territoriality could be an unnecessary strategem. But if there is antagonism, either one-way or mutual, territoriality may become necessary, as was the case in the cities of Northern Ireland after the onset of increased tensions in 1969 when people retreated into separate 'religious ghettos'. Further, if a group wishes some degree of autonomy or self-determination (Knight, 1988), then territoriality may be a necessary strategy: for groups lacking a territorial base, self-determination ambitions are likely to be thwarted by the absence of a mobilizing focus that occupancy of land can give, which is the situation for many indigenous peoples throughout the world.

TERRITORIAL CONTAINERS WITHIN STATES

Sack uses the American system of local government as an illustration of a territoriality strategy, concluding that:

> The development of hierarchies of territories has defined communities to contain, channel, and mold the geographically dynamic processes; has heightened the effect of impersonality; and, in many cases, has increased the bureaucratization and centralization of power. (1986, p. 167)

Much of his discussion focuses on the provision of 'public goods', for whose provision he believes that 'Territorial hierarchy is . . . thought to be unavoidable in complex capitalist political systems.'

Sack's discussion includes no reference to the plethora of separate local governments typical of virtually every American metropolitan area, and which provides a further, distinct, example of the operation of a territoriality strategy. A theorist who has focused on this plethora is Tiebout (1956), who has provided a case for the fragmentation of the state apparatus in that way.

The number of necessary state activities is very large in modern liberal democracies, and the number of possible other state activities is even larger. Furthermore, within many of those activities, of both types, the nature and extent of state action can also vary substantially. The need for the state is not equivalent to a need for the state to do particular things in particular ways and to particular degrees. With regard to the AFDC programme discussed in chapter 5, for example, there was no need for such a policy – it was enacted by the Federal government as a way of tackling a perceived social problem. Nor, having determined the programme's desirability, was there any need for a particular level of commitment to it and, as shown in chapter 5, State governments have differed very substantially in both how and the extent to which they have implemented the AFDC programme.

State government responses to AFDC provide an example of the sort of system of government that Tiebout advances, with people able to decide locally on their priorities. With a centralized government it is impossible to cater for all opinions across the immense range of the policy agenda. The party (or parties) elected to power act according to their perceptions of what the people wish them to do. With a wide range of issues and a wide range of views on those issues, no one government can satisfy all demands; it is also unlikely that all shades of opinion on every issue will be reflected by the small number of parties which contest an election (and which may therefore exclude from the agenda what some people would see as salient issues: Schattschnieder, 1962). As Downs (1957) showed in his classic model of the operations of democracy, electors are then 'forced' to vote for that party perceived to be closest to them on the issues that they consider salient. Whereas parties will position themselves to be close to a substantial body of voters, the almost certain outcome is a compromise: the elected party (parties) is closer to the voters on the salient issues than is any other, but many voters (perhaps even a majority?) will have been unable to choose a party which best represents their views on some, if not most, issues.

Tiebout's case for the fragmentation of government seeks to correct this defect of centralized democracy. With certain state functions, such as national defence and macroeconomic control, centralization is necessary. But for many others it is not, especially in the delivery of most public goods and services. Some people in a metropolitan area may want a large public library service, for example, and be prepared to pay for it in their taxes. Others may want a smaller and therefore cheaper service, while a third group may see no need for public libraries at all. If the metropolitan area were governed by a single local government, then a decision would have to be made on which group's desires should be met, with the consequence that a large proportion of the electorate will be dissatisfied. If a large service is provided, those opposed to it will resent paying for something they view as unnecessary, for example, whereas if a small service is all that is available, those wanting more will feel underprovided for.

This problem could be overcome, according to Tiebout's argument, if instead of one local government serving the entire metropolitan area there were many. Each would then decide what services to provide, and to what extent, and people could determine which to live in. People would also be deciding what taxes they were prepared to pay, because the cost of local services fell on local residents, so each local government would be offering potential residents a services-and-taxes package. There would thus be a market in local governments and people would be offered a choice of public services in the same way as they are offered a choice of others in the private sector markets.

Tiebout's model appears at first glance to be a rationalization of the current situation in most United States' metropolitan areas, each of which has a plethora of local governments offering a wide range of services-and-taxes packages. There were 380 separate multi-purpose local governments serving parts of the Chicago Standard Metropolitan Statistical Area (SMSA) in 1977, for example (six counties, 261 municipalities, and 113 townships). In addition there were 315 school districts providing education to different parts of the SMSA and 419 Special Districts, most of them single-purpose authorities only and providing services for territories which did not conform to those of any other local government (including the entire SMSA in some cases). Of those 1214 local governments, 1166 had property-taxing powers, and raised their income against the value of properties within their territories. Chicago was far from atypical (as the data in Johnston, 1981, 1984c show), so a major characteristic of United States local government is its fragmentation and its apparent ability to provide customer choice in the provision of public services for which they pay in property taxes.

The reality is that few have a great deal of choice, however, and most are severely constrained. This is because local government powers have been used by groups within society to promote their own ends. The residential separation of socio-economic, racial, religious, socio-demographic and other groups has been observed in all capitalist cities. People in the more affluent groups tend to prefer to live apart from any others, in order to create local milieux in which they can share community life with their peers, and within which their children can be socialized (in each others' homes, in the neighbourhood and at local schools) into a culture consistent with that which the parents wish to promote. This distancing is

achieved through the operations of the housing market, whereby the richest
bid up the prices in their preferred areas to levels above those which any
other group can afford, the next richest do the same with their areas, and
so on down the income scale. Separation by income and wealth is thus
achieved. Separation on other criteria is advanced by a range of separate
mechanisms, whereby for example members of certain cultural groups are
kept out of some areas and those of others choose to congregate together.
  In the United States, as Danielsen (1976, pp. 22–3) notes:

> Income differences and housing costs, as well as racial, ethnic, and
> other social considerations, would produce spatial differentiation . . .
> even if local government policies had a negligible effect on where
> people live.

In other societies, however

> spatial separation is far less pervasive than in the United States . . .
> [where] the exclusionary policies of local governments, particularly
> in the newer suburbs, produce far more spatial separation than
> would be the case if only economic and social factors influenced the
> distribution of people in the spreading metropolis.

That spatial separation is not simply a reflection of choice, as Tiebout's
model depicts it, but rather of the promotion of congregation and segregation by those who do not wish to share their residential areas with
people considered inferior on social and other grounds.
  Promotion of residential separation in American suburbia involves the
use by municipalities of what is known as the police power, the ability of
the state to limit individual freedoms in the interests of the greater public
good. Among the recognized elements of the police power is land-use
planning and its central task of zoning, which indicates what can and
cannot be done with all land within a municipal territory. The basis for
zoning is the promotion of public health and safety, and it is a power
which most State governments have devolved to the municipalities. These
thus have autonomy to define land-use patterns within their territories (on
which see Clark, 1985), which they do by regulating the density and type
of land use, the size and standards of buildings, and so forth.
  Whilst overtly zoning is used to promote public health and safety, in
very many municipalities it is being employed to ensure the socio-economic
character of the local residents. For example, if the white affluent residents
of an area wished to zone out the poor (who would make more demands
for locally-provided public services than they contributed for in property
taxes), large families (who would put demands on local schools inconsistent

with their fiscal contributions), and the blacks (who are considered socially-inferior and thus undesirable neighbours), they couldn't do so by defining residential zones the criteria for which were that people had to be white, have no more than y children, and earn an income of more than $x. What they could do, however, was make it impossible for such people to afford to live in the area. Such a policy has been widely promoted by what is known as *exclusionary zoning*, and Danielsen (1976, p. 51) argues that 'the power to zone becomes a mandate to exclude land uses which threaten community character, property values, or the fiscal well-being of the locality'. This has been done by designing zones with housing which the poor, and especially the black poor, could not afford, using very low densities (lots of a minimum size of one acre or more are common) and excluding cheaper building types (such as mobile homes and apartments). As Downs (1973, pp. 51–2) expressed it, the police power was thus abused because:

> No household 'must have' a one-acre lot for healthful living, since millions of healthy Americans live on far smaller lots. . . . Thus, nearly all suburban minimum lot size requirements lack any relation whatever to health or safety needs. The same thing is true of minimum set-back and building placement requirements. . . . most residential zoning regulations prohibit mobile homes. Yet there is absolutely no evidence that it is more healthful to live in a conventionally built home than in a mobile home.

Exclusionary zoning is an example of a territoriality strategy, though slightly different in type from those discussed by Sack. He concentrates on what I have termed 'inclusionary' strategies (Johnston, 1991a), whereby power over people is exercised by concentrating them in certain areas. The zoning process described here is an 'exclusionary' strategy, however, with power being used to keep people out. (In the end the two strategies are complementary, because those excluded from all other areas are as a consequence included only in those they are allowed access to. Thus the black ghetto in American cities may not, as some argue, be the result of an explicit inclusionary goal – see Hogan (1985) – but rather the consequence of an exclusionary strategy – or a large number of them in a myriad separate municipalities.) It enhances the processes of distancing through the property market, so that Plotkin (1987, p. 113) could conclude that 'By supplementing the inner workings of capitalist property with some new outer limits of social control, public zoning helped everyone stay in line with the basic patterns of social restrictions and private growth'.

Residential separation is the basis for much local political activity, with people defending their neighbourhoods against changes in either or both of land use and land users – as Cox (1989) illustrates in his developing theory of the 'politics of turf'. The zoning powers available to local governments in the United States, and upheld by the Courts so long as they are not used explicitly to discriminate by race (discrimination by wealth and income is not unconstitutional: Johnston, 1984c), permits a particular territorial strategy to be used. Elsewhere, other territoriality strategies have been developed outside the state apparatus, as with the notorious walls built across two roads by the residents of an Oxford middle-class suburb to prevent the inhabitants of a neighbouring council-housing estate from even walking through (and thereby presumably contaminating!) the 'higher status' area (Collison, 1963), a similar wall erected in a Memphis suburb (Fleming, 1989), and the 'Bodley barricade' across a road dividing two very different types of residential area in Stockport (Robson, 1982). All are examples of an exclusionary territoriality strategy, whereby a spatial structure is designed to keep people out. Space is divided up into a series of territorial containers, and power is exercised through denying entry to members of certain groups within society.

TERRITORIALITY AND THE DEFINITION OF SELF AND OTHERS

The previous section illustrates one use of territoriality in a strategy which extends Sack's theory. As he presents it, territoriality involves people being controlled through inclusion, via surveillance mechanisms. By incorporating people within a territory you make them subject to the rules that apply there and so control their behaviour.

But there is also control by exclusion, as, for example, with the creation of separate residential areas for different religious groups in Belfast. The social relationships between the two groups are controlled by restricting, and in some cases preventing, contact between them. Such a strategy may be operated without using any of the state apparatus, through 'voluntary' procedures by which people agree not to let members of certain groups into an area, but these may be difficult to police in certain circumstances. Use of the state apparatus can sustain such strategies, however, as in the use of land-use zoning practices allied to the incorporation of independent municipal entities discussed above.

Employment of the state apparatus to promote residential congregation and segregation not only assists in the operation of social control via territoriality but also promotes the longer-term processes of unequal social reproduction, in two ways. First, it facilitates the uneven provision of public goods, to the benefit of some and the detriment of others, as with the reproduction of social class differences through locally-provided education services in American surburbia (Johnston, 1984c). Secondly, because separation restricts contact, it assists the development of inter-group stereotypes based on ignorance and fear rather than contact and knowledge (Johnston, 1989f). Those stereotypes promote images of a divided society, in which to identify oneself positively with the people in one territory is complemented by negative identifications of others, who live in other territories.

One of the outcomes of territoriality is thus the segmentation of society, with important consequences for individual and social behaviour. Such segmentation is a necessary solution to the problems of coping with an extremely complex society, according to some writers. A society is an interdependent whole, and yet people are unwilling to partake in it as such, according to Tuan (1982, pp. 196–7):

> As self-knowledge increases, so does a critical knowledge of nature and society, or the world. The world, subjected to critical evaluation, loses its objectivity and cohesiveness. An individual finds it more difficult to accept society's values and to partake in its affairs as a matter of course. . . . Given the freedom and the opportunity to explore self and world, few individuals in fact do do.

Instead, Tuan argues, they retreat into segmented worlds to keep melancholy and boredom at bay.

Tuan further argues (p. 7) that 'The human mind is disposed to segment reality' and that complex societies encourage this.

> A civilized society is large and complex. . . . Group cohesion and shared myths are tenuous, especially in times when external threats do not exist. A modern society's cohesion is almost constantly under the stress of questioning by its component parts – institutions, local communities, and individuals. The material landscape itself provides suggestive clues. A primitive village gives the impression of being a single and rather simple entity if only because few man-made barriers such as curbs and walls are visible, and few places are reserved for exclusive functions. By contrast, in a large city the innumerable physical boundaries that keep people and activities in discrete areas forcefully remind us of the city's delimited and segmented character, its complex hierarchies of space.

People accommodate to such large, dense congregations by fragmenting them, it seems, and then withdrawing, in part at least, to one fragment.

(That fragment may be the context for their operation in civil society, but they may have to go outside it to participate in both the world of work and the worlds of politics.)

The segmentation of society, and its influence on individual behaviour, has been the subject of social psychological research, such as Tajfel's. These studies of individual prejudice and discrimination have explored the group dynamics that underpin such behaviour, arguing that there is a complex 'interweaving of individual and interpersonal behavior with the contextual social processes of intergroup conflict' (Tajfel and Turner, 1979, p. 33). They contend that

> Opposed group interests in obtaining scarce resources promote competition. . . . Conflicting interests develop through competition into overt social conflict . . . intergroup competition enhances intragroup morale, cohesiveness and cooperation. . . . Thus, the real conflicts of group interests not only create antagonistic intergroup relations but also heighten identification with, and positive attachment to, the in-group.

Their definition of an in-group can be equated with co-residence in an area, at any scale, from neighbourhood to state. Although they focused on ethnic and social class criteria for group membership, Tajfel and Turner recognized nation as a further criterion, but not any smaller-scale spatial unit. They further claimed that 'Similarity, proximity and situational salience are among the variables that determine out-group comparability, and pressures towards in-group distinctiveness should increase as a function of this comparability' (p. 41). Co-residence in an area can clearly meet the criteria of 'similarity, proximity and situational salience', so their theory of intergroup conflict has considerable relevance for the present work.

The basis of the theory is the distinction between a pair of ideal types – interpersonal and intergroup behaviour.

> At one extreme . . . is the interaction between two or more individuals (or groups of individuals) that is *fully* determined by their interpersonal relationships and individual characteristics, and not at all affected by various social groups or categories to which they respectively belong. The other extreme consists of interactions between two or more individuals (or groups of individuals) which are *fully* determined by their respective memberships in various social groups or categories, and not at all affected by the individual personal relationships between the people involved. (Tajfel and Turner, 1979, p. 34)

(In the latter, for example, two groups may interact as employers and trades unionists respectively, with the nature of their contacts in no way reflecting the interpersonal feelings of any pair drawn from the two groups.) For intergroup behaviour to dominate, people must perceive that to act as group members rather than as individuals is beneficial to them. This involves group identification processes, which may be voluntary (i.e. similar people agree to act as a group), the result of persuasive processes of socialization and mobilization (which is what political parties do in their attempts to build cores of electoral support), or involuntary (as with coercion by a state to act in certain ways). In the second case, the creation of a belief system whereby one group's members see themselves in conflict with others for scarce resources (such as power, prestige and wealth) can generate intergroup ethnocentrism and antagonism: this is especially so, Tajfel and Turner argue, if one group perceives itself as receiving inferior treatment.

Group membership is part of an individual's striving to achieve a positive social identity, according to Tajfel and Turner (1979), and the resulting

> Positive self-identity is based to a large extent on favourable comparisons that can be made between the in-group and some relevant out-groups; the in-group must be perceived as positively differentiated or distinct from relevant out-groups. (p. 40)

The pursuit of positive self-identity leads to the development of in-group: out-group comparisons, and thus the polarization of society into mutually-opposing groups. Individuals must internalize their group membership as part of their self-definition: 'It is not enough that the others define them as a group, although consensual definitions by others can become, in the long run, one of the powerful causal factors for a group's self-definition' (p. 41). The separate nature of the groups must be apparent also, so that in-group members can readily identify those belonging to out-groups, and the latter must be perceived as relevant comparators.

Two major conclusions of this body of work are of particular relevance here. The first is that group identification is linked to competition and conflict. As Tajfel and Turner express it:

> The aim of differentiation is to maintain or achieve superiority over an out-group on some dimensions. Any such act, therefore, is essentially competitive. This competition requires a situation of mutual comparison and differentiation on a shared value dimension. (p. 41)

Secondly, once group memberships are allocated (i.e. the individuals accept their own in-group identifications, and those of the comparator out-groups), then in many situations people will act according to the group norms, even though the nature of the conflict is not explicit: experiments have shown

> that intergroup discrimination existed in conditions of minimal in-group affiliation, anonymity of group membership, absence of con-flicts of interest, and absence of previous hostility between the groups. (p. 34)

Socialization into a group identity is thus all-important as an influence on behaviour.

National identity is one aspect of intergroup behaviour that has been investigated by social psychologists, including work on the polarization of views that results from representation of an out-group – the residents of another state – as an enemy (Holt and Silverstein, 1989). Silverstein and Flamenbaum (1989), for example, have looked at the biases in the percep-tion of information about out-groups perceived as enemies, evaluating hypotheses such as (p. 53): 'benign acts will not be seen as evidence that the enemy is conciliatory while aggressive acts will be seen as evidence that the enemy is hostile' and 'Apparently friendly actions of enemies may also be attributed to hostile motivations, such as the desire to deceive or manipulate others' (both were found to be valid). These 'value-guided attributions' are defined by Sande et al. (1989) as 'maintaining the moral self-image and the diabolical enemy-image', and they are led to the con-clusion that

> One of the most unfortunate consequences of the tendency to attribute evil motives to all or most of our enemy's actions is that we may blind ourselves to legitimate opportunities for conflict resolution. (p. 116)

Intergroup divisions are not only the bases for conflicts, therefore, but also barriers to their resolution.

The basis for such intergroup divisions at the neighbourhood rather than the national scale has been explored by Sennett (1973), whose analysis is based in psychiatry. He argues that individuals have to discover their own identity during adolescence, in order to recognize, create and sustain their own self-images. This is partly achieved by creating opposing 'other images', stereotyped representations of groups to which they do not belong, or to which they do not wish to belong. This is one element of a process of purification, of defining oneself by segmenting the world. (Sennett defines purification as involving 'an attempt to build an image that coheres, is unified, and filters out threats in social experience ... the degree to which people feel urged to keep articulating who they are, what they want, and what they feel is almost an index of their fear about their inability to survive in social experience with other men': p. 19.) By defining segments (or fragments in Tuan's terminology) and retreating into one of them, thereby avoiding contact with others from outside that segment, the individual

> has learned how to insulate himself in advance from experiences that might portend dislocation and disorder. . . . the adolescent can sustain a purified picture of his own identity; it is coherent, it is orderly, it is consistent, because he has learned how to exclude disorder and painful disruption from conscious consideration. (Sennett, 1973, pp. 27–8)

To survive in a complex society, we classify its members, associate with those in groups we identify with and shirk from contact with all others. To the extent that individuals from the latter impinge on our lives, we treat them as typical of the group to which they belong. The characteristics which we ascribe to such groups are thus social constructions; they are the myths that we generate about those who are not 'of us' and on which we base our behaviour towards 'them'.

Adolescence is a period of immaturity, which should be succeeded by maturity, when such simplifications are removed and people are able to accommodate the complexity and diversity (or disorder) in society. Sennett argues that the transition never comes, however, so that modern societies comprise not mature individuals participating in a wide variety of interactions beyond their own 'segment' but rather a series of segmented, purified communities in which people develop self-identification through identification with specific groups. Societies are thus ossified collections of purified communities, some of which are territorially defined. Instead of people letting 'a series of painful, confused and contradictory experiences enter their lives' (p. 39), communal solidarity is linked to patterns of avoidance. Order is imposed on society, at least in part, through the creation and maintenance of a particular spatial form (Sibley, 1981).

In creating their segmented selves, individuals are not operating in a social vacuum; rather they are acting in a well-defined social context. Most are socialized in local milieux, places with clearly-defined cultural characteristics with which they are encouraged to identify (usually implicitly): people create themselves by their own decisions, but not in conditions of their own choosing. Most of those conditions are inherently local in scale, but they may also be influenced at a larger scale by a state ideology which promotes not only particular interpretations of 'us' – the members of our state – but also of 'them' – the residents of others.

Purified communities are thus the outcome of a continued structuration of community influence, whereby fragmented societies are reproduced.

Segmented communities and conflict

Purified communities contain within themselves the seeds of social conflict, as Sennett recognized. He was writing in the aftermath of the riots that occurred in many American cities in the late 1960s. The analysis summarized here was the precursor to his promotion of an anarchic approach to city planning which would dismantle the segmented, purified communities typical of those urban areas. Cities currently comprise complexes of safe and comfortable segmented worlds with people retreating into districts containing others similar to themselves. (In effect, most people are raised in such segmented worlds and socialized into the desirability of reproducing them.) Sennett would put people into areas where they felt different, where the complexity of the society offered no easy sanctuary.

> Such a community would probably stimulate a young person, and yet scare him, make him want to hide, as it would everybody else, to find some nice, untroubled place. But the very diversity of the neighborhood has built into it the obligation of responsibility; there would be no way to avoid self-destruction other than to deal with the people who live around the place. The feeling that 'I live here and I count in this community's life' would consist, not of a feeling of companionship, but of a feeling that something must be done in common to make this conflict bearable, to survive together. (p. 178)

Dissolution of purified communities would, he hoped, both create tension within society and yet defuse conflict: tension would be present because mutual accommodations would have to be achieved, but conflict would be reduced because the mutual stereotyping of 'them' and 'us' based on ignorance would be ended.

> the experience of living with diverse groups has its power. The enemies lose their clear image, because every day one sees so many people who are alien but who are not all alien in the same way. (p. 156)

The viability of Sennett's strategy is not of concern here; in any case he accepted that its achievement would be difficult, involving

> convincing men who have succeeded quite well in isolating themselves in warm and comforting shelters in the suburbs, or in ethnic, racial or class isolation, that these refuges are worth abandoning for the terrors of the struggle to survive together. (p. 146)

What is worthy of note in the present context is that whereas Sennett's 'solution' might be viable with regard to segmented communities within urban areas, it would not be with regard to any problems at larger spatial scales, such as the 'them' and 'us' portrayal which is characteristic of the inter-relationships among states. And if conflict between communities is a possible consequence of the purification strategies at the neighbourhood scale, it is even more so at the national, since the state has the legalized monopoly on the use of violence.

The potential for geopolitical conflict between states as the containers for regional alliances was recognized by Harvey (1985b, p. 162) who contends that 'the perpetuation of capitalism in the twentieth century has been purchased at the cost of the death, havoc and destruction wreaked in two world wars'. Further, because of the growing sophistication and power of weapons, we now face 'the renewed threat of global war, this time waged with weapons of such immense and insane destructive power that not even the fittest stand to survive'. The threat of such war comes about because of the contemporary crisis of capitalism which 'disrupts regional class alliances and sours relationships between them' (p. 158). Geopolitical realignments and conflicts seem inevitable to him as governments manoeuvre to promote their residents' interests, but the now characteristic disorder carries the fear that the world order will 'dissolve into a chaos of competing and warring forces' (p. 162). Some may respond that the trend in the late 1980s, as a consequence of overstretched economies in the USA and the USSR, has been a reduction in the potential for conflict, especially as other, less stretched states (such as Germany and Japan) have renounced the sort of arsenal-building strategy that characterized the previous hegemonic powers. Only time will tell . . .

Where territoriality is used as an exclusionary rather than as an inclusionary strategy for social control, therefore, the result is likely to be heightened social tension, hence the arguments for its abandonment. One almost certainly leads to the other, however, for the creation of states using an inclusionary territorial strategy by its very nature involves the definition of 'others'. Thus the strategies identified by Sack as efficient and effective means for social control are also likely producers of social tension and conflict. They are, at a variety of spatial scales, the bases for geopolitics. If one accepts the arguments that (a) the state is necessary to capitalism, (b) the state is necessarily a territorial entity and (c) conflict between the residents of separate territories is a possible consequence of the 'them and us' stereotyping that is typical of such segmented societies, then one is pressed towards the conclusion that (d) conflict between territories is a likely outcome. Thus, the conclusion must be that territoriality is both necessary to the state and a probable cause of its demise: as in so much else that is characteristic of capitalism, it contains within itself the seeds of its own destruction.

CONCLUSION

Sack's work on territoriality, developed at least in part because of his dissatisfaction with other theories of the role of space within society and especially the 'spatial separatism' that characterized human geography in the 1960s and 1970s (Sack, 1980), offers a powerful theoretical base for geographical contributions to the social sciences. In part, the 'them and us' consequences of territorial strategies are not dependent on the existence of bounded spaces; they could just as readily arise between groups defined on criteria which lack a spatial referent (such as betwen disciplines and between groups within disciplines: chapter 1), and they could certainly arise between places, as defined and illustrated in chapter 4, between which the boundaries are imprecise. But the power of Sack's analysis, and that of others who have worked on similar topics, is the importance of territoriality as a strategy – especially to the state. From that, we can readily deduce that bounded places are important components of the spatial structuring of societies and significant contributors to many of the conflicts which are latent there.

7

Making and Remaking Places: The United Kingdom under Thatcherism

> private affluence and economic growth in the South East in the eighties were underpinned by a massive and disproportionate public expenditure. . . . the growing North–South divide was not simply a product of the hidden hand of the market, but was deliberately redefined and enhanced as part of the political strategy of Thatcherism.
>
> Ray Hudson, letter to *The Independent on Sunday*

The 1980s was a decade of major change in the United Kingdom, wrought by a radical, right-wing government. During the 1960s, when Labour was in power, elements within the Conservative party developed a diagnosis of the country's ills; in line with that analysis, policies to achieve significant changes in economic and social structures were introduced following the Conservative return to power in 1970. In 1972, however, Edward Heath's government made a policy about-turn in the face of economic difficulties. Further problems, notably those engendered by major strikes, led to the government's defeat in 1974 and the return of a minority Labour government, which obtained a small working majority at a further election eight months later.

During the five years of the Labour governments of 1974–9 not only was the Conservative party captured by a group determined to implement again the radical policies foreshadowed by the Heath government but that group was also, and more importantly, intent on seeing them through. The party leadership was won by Margaret Thatcher, who proved to be a determined exponent of the radical policies after the Conservatives regained power in 1979. Reflecting her dominance of the political scene and her determination to push forward the radical reforms mapped out (and continually extended) by the party, the programme became widely known as

'Thatcherism'. In its economic components it had much in common with parallel developments in many other countries – such as 'Reaganism' in the United States and 'Rogernomics' in New Zealand – which suggests that such reforms may have been a necessary response to the current crisis of world capitalism. Thatcherism was a much wider ideology, however, based in a determination to destroy the broad political consensus of the previous three decades and to create a new national unity through which socialism would never rise again. In a popular phrase of the time, the goal was to put the 'Great' back into 'Great Britain' (which implicitly says much about attitudes to Northern Ireland and the United Kingdom).

This ideological crusade (a hegemonic programme to some: Jessop et al., 1988) involved major shifts in the nature of British society. As such, it involved the creation of a new identity within its bounded space. Furthermore, and of particular interest for the arguments developed in this book, it involved major changes in the map of the United Kingdom, altering both the UK as a place and the places that make up the UK. This final chapter presents an impressionistic overview of the nature of Thatcherism and the new map of Britain that it has created. (As in most other writings, the noun Britain and the adjective British are used rather than the proper name – the United Kingdom – for which there is no adjective.)

THATCHERISM'S INHERITANCE

The country which the Conservative government 'inherited' in 1979 was divided in a variety of ways – by class, gender, race and location, for example, according to Hudson and Williams (1989). It was to become even more divided, on all four categories, during the 1980s, as other authors have depicted e.g. Allen and Massey (1988), Anderson and Cochrane (1989), Ball, Gray and McDowell (1989), Champion and Townsend (1990), Cochrane and Anderson (1989), Hamnett, McDowell and Sarre (1989), Lewis and Townsend (1989), McDowell, Sarre and Hamnett (1989), Massey and Allen (1988) and Smith (1989). For geographers, the division by location is of particular interest – especially the degree to which it is additional to the others (i.e. people may be disadvantaged not only by their class, gender and race but *also* by where they live). That locational division is frequently over-simplified as a North–South divide; as many careful analysts have pointed out, such as Champion and Townsend (1990), however, there are salient other divisions, notably between large cities (especially inner cities, as in Greater London) and smaller towns (as in much of North Yorkshire).

There can be little doubt that the North–South divide widened during the 1980s (see Martin, 1989), despite arguments of Conservative politicians to the contrary. What is of interest is why. Hudson and Williams (1989, p. 165) claim that it has occurred because of deliberate intent on the part of the Conservative governments.

> The growing North–South divide is commonly represented, not least by Mrs Thatcher's government, as a simple product of the operation of the hidden hand of market forces. We wish to argue, strongly, that this is not the case. On the contrary, the North–South divide has deliberately been redefined and enhanced as part of the political strategy of Thatcherism. It was and is intimately connected to its electoral prospects.

Their brief section presented to sustain this argument is unconvincing, however. For example, they quote the major cutbacks in spending on nationalized industries which differentially affected the North, the favouring of high-technology industries linked to defence, which were concentrated in the South, the encouragement to financial service industries, massively concentrated in London, and the reduction of expenditure on regional aid (which favoured the North in previous decades) concurrent with infrastructure spending in the South (e.g. on the M25 and Stansted airport). All this contributed to the outcome that 'The North–South divide ... widened with a vengeance' (p. 192). But the case that there was a deliberate intent to widen that divide is far from proven.

Hudson and Williams also claim (p. 190), slightly less assertively, that 'spatial inequality has been redefined as a result of a series of policy and political choices that are an integral part of the Thatcherite project'. This is probably closer to reality. The Conservative government's policies in the 1980s undoubtedly largely favoured the South over the North and, given their belief in the superiority of market forces, little was done directly to alter the balance through state intervention. But that is far from the same as the governments deliberately destroying the North: they set out to destroy a culture that was particularly concentrated in the North, which is somewhat different.

The foundation of that cultural divide was the difference between North and South in both their industrial structures and their social relations at the workplace. The North became the heartland of British industry from the eighteenth century on. As the twentieth century advanced, however, so its dominance was somewhat diluted: newer industries, based on modern technologies and less dependent on the natural resources of the North, were concentrated in the South, especially London and its surrounding metropolitan region. Over time, demand for Northern industrial products slackened, both with the shifts to new technologies, materials and products and with the loss of markets to cheaper producers elsewhere in the world. The North's economy was slowly eroded, and it suffered most in periods of recession – especially in the 1930s. From then on, however, successive (especially Labour) governments sought to protect the Northern economy and its residents' job prospects through regional aid programmes. Their relative success is much debated. Undoubtedly several hundreds of thousands of jobs were either created or sustained, but some – such as Sharpe (1982) – argue that, given the strength of Labour support in the North, it is surprising that when in power that party did not do more to protect the Northern regions against the ill-winds of the world economy.

By the 1970s, therefore, the North was dominated by industries which were declining both nationally and globally, and an increasing number of analysts – basing their arguments in the theories of economic cycles developed by Kondratiev and Schumpeter e.g. Hall (1988) – argued that this decline could not be halted. Policy initiatives should instead focus on creating the conditions within which new industries could flourish – recognizing that this would probably mean major shifts in the concentrations of industrial employment. The North was in general not an attractive environment for such growth because its industrial inheritance was not sympathetic to the new developments. Furthermore, the North was unlikely to contain within itself the resources on which regeneration could be based. Although much wealth had been created there during the decades of industrial prosperity, much of it had then been channelled to the South, seen as the focus of the country's social and political life: the main public schools and the fashionable universities were all there, for example, and to a considerable extent the returns from investment in the North were spent in the South by those who were educated and socialized and made their homes there, while still retaining their investments further North. And as well as a relative absence of resources to invest in the North – a situation undoubtedly exacerbated by the growth of a national banking system (at least for England and Wales) focused on London – there was a relative dearth of stimuli to new developments. The great majority of government and private research laboratories, within which many of the inventions and innovations on which new industries could be founded or developed, are in the South, and much of the basic research funded in universities and polytechnics is also concentrated in the country's Southern regions.

The North–South industrial divide involved differences in the nature of what is produced and the resources for investment in new industries and processes. Even more so, however, it involved differences in the social relations at the workplace, and in the politics there. Despite many intra-regional as well as inter-regional variations (of the types discussed in chapter 4), the basic difference was between a North dominated by large factories and plants in which trades unions were very strong and a South which was characterized by industries with much smaller plants, on average, and where unions were in general weaker and certainly less militant (even in the towns dominated by large factories, such as the GWR works at Swindon).

Paralleling these North–South differences in politics at the workplace were associated variations in party politics. From the 1920s until the 1970s, British politics were dominated nationally, as increasingly were those at local level too, by two parties – Conservative and Labour. Each drew its predominant support from one socio-economic class only – the Conservative party from the 'middle class' and Labour from the 'working class'. Given the North–South divide in terms of the country's class structure, with the 'middle class' relatively prominent in the South and the 'working class' in the North, not surprisingly Labour has traditionally been strongest in the Northern regions and its Conservative opponent in the South. Nevertheless, even when differences in class structure are taken into account, macro-regional differences remain: in broad terms, the North is more pro-Labour than expected, and the South more pro-Conservative; this is demonstrated conclusively in Johnston, Pattie and Allsopp (1988).

Reasons for this enduring North–South divide in voting patterns have been the focus of debate among political scientists, sociologists, and electoral geographers. The basic cause appears to be the role of the local milieu (defined at a variety of scales) as a socializing context within which people learn political attitudes and adopt partisan identifications, and within which parties mobilize support (or not, as with Labour in the Dukeries in the 1920s and 1930s; see chapter 4). Thus the relative preponderance of Labour supporters in the North provides milieux within which new voters, whatever their 'objective' occupational class position, are more likely to be socialized into pro-Labour attitudes than is the case in the South. Analyses suggest that this is especially so in the coal-mining areas, which are particularly strong in their support for Labour. On the other hand, Labour tends to win fewer votes than expected among the 'working class' in small towns and country areas. The result has long been a country that is spatially polarized electorally – both North–South and urban–rural: Curtice and Steed (1988) suggest that the latter became more important during the 1980s – although there were still considerable numbers of Labour seats in the South and of Conservative seats in the North until the

1980s. That polarization has been accentuated since the mid-1950s, and especially since the 1970s, with Labour losing support substantially throughout the South and the Conservative party faring similarly in many parts of the North, especially Scotland.

During the present century, local government elections have increasingly been treated by both the parties and the voters as referenda on the popularity and performance of the incumbent national government rather than as a statement of preferences regarding local issues and party performances in delivering local services. The consequence has been a 'nationalization' of local voting patterns, so that the map of voting at local elections, and the map of partisan control of local governments, is very similar to that for voting at general elections. Labour has traditionally controlled local governments in the North, especially in the large industrial cities and conurbations, whereas the Conservative party has dominated in the South. This pattern has been important, especially for Labour, because it provides a mobilizing context; voters who can observe a party acting on their behalf locally are more likely to vote for it in a national election than are those who have no direct experience of it wielding power, and parties with local control are better able to manipulate the media there in their favour when it comes to general as well as local elections.

Finally, with regard to the sphere of consumption the most important North–South variation relates to the provision of public services, and is thus closely linked to the geography of power in local governments. A range of analyses has shown that, relative to both local needs and the resources available to meet them, Labour-controlled local governments tend to spend more on public services which favour the 'working class' – such as council housing, a range of social services, public transport, and education – than do those which are controlled by the Conservative party (Sharpe and Newton, 1984). Since Labour-controlled local governments tend to be concentrated in the North, then in broad terms there is more spending on public services there, producing a North–South divide in public dependence on the state.

This very broad-brush sketch has suggested that the map of the country inherited by the Conservative party when it was elected to power in 1979 involved North–South differences on all of the components of the definition of a place developed earlier in this book. At a finer scale of analysis there were many intra-regional variations too (Champion and Townsend, 1990) – particularly those between the inner cities on the one hand and the suburbs, smaller towns and countryside on the other (so much so that Sarlvik and Crewe (1983) placed London in the North in their binary division of Great Britain for an analysis of voting patterns in the 1970s).

During the 1980s, Conservative policies exacerbated those differences in many respects as the party strove to achieve the desired fundamental changes in economy, polity and society (though Mrs Thatcher on one occasion denied the existence of society) considered necessary to halt the decline of the United Kingdom in terms of both economic prosperity and levels of living and political influence overseas.

THATCHERISM: DIAGNOSIS AND PROGNOSIS

Much was written about Thatcherism throughout the 1980s, as journalists, commentators and academics sought to appreciate the revolution that the Conservative party was promoting. Towards the end of the decade, a number of substantial volumes was produced analysing the policies and their impacts e.g. Crouch and Marquand (1988), Dunleavy, Gamble and Peele (1990), Gamble (1988), Jessop, Bonnett, Bromley and Ling (1988), Kavanagh and Seldon (1989), Skidelsky (1988), and Young (1990). Not surprisingly, with a topic that was both highly charged politically and remained current, opinions and assessments varied substantially. (This chapter was finalized in the month after Mrs Thatcher's resignation.) The present essay is not a further contribution to those debates. Its goal is rather to understand the fundamentals of Thatcherism as a means to appreciating how and why the place that is Britain and the places that comprise Britain have been changed by it.

The diagnosis

The Thatcherite analysis of Britain's economy and society began with the assumption, readily sustained by international comparative data, that the country has been experiencing long-term economic decline. Its purpose was to diagnose the reasons for that decline, so that policies could be enacted to achieve its reversal.

The starting-point of the analysis was the nature of the mode of production. Britain is a capitalist country within a global capitalist economy so its decline must reflect failure to operate capitalism successfully (in relative if not absolute terms), and its revival must involve a better performance. The Conservative party's radical policies accepted the materialist conception of how a society should be organized, and were formulated so as to improve the materialist base, not replace it. Indeed, as detailed below, the analysis identified part of Britain's weakness as its continued flirtation with a socialist alternative, via the Labour party.

Within this materialist interpretation of the 'good society', the relative
failure of Britain's economy was firmly identified as reflecting the inefficiency of many of its component parts, in both the public and the private
sector. Under capitalism, efficiency in the production and marketing of
goods and services is determined by the productivity of labour: the more
efficient producers are, relative to their competitors, the cheaper their
goods and services (holding quality constant) can be, and so the more
successful they should be in the market place. Thus, if Britain was unsuc-
cessful – at home and abroad – this must have been because its goods and
services were too expensive (and possibly of inferior quality too). In turn
this must have been because British labour was relatively inefficient, producing goods and services that were too expensive to compete in export
markets and, increasingly, in the home market too.

The analysis of why British producers were inefficient focused on both
sides of the capital–labour interaction. With regard to capital, it was
concluded that British investors were reluctant to spend on improving
their performance – by investing in new technologies that would improve
productivity, for example, and by researching new products (goods as well
as services) that could be marketed successfully and bring a substantial
return on capital. In brief, British management was not very enterprising.

Several reasons were adduced for this lack of enterprise. First, the
incentives to invest in potential profits were weak, because of the high
rates of taxation on all incomes above a relatively low theshold; there was
insufficient spur to be enterprising and to show initiative and there was a
general conservatism among the business classes relative to the situation
in the more successful countries. Secondly, the price of money was too
high to encourage entrepreneurs to borrow for investment, because of high
interest rates; in addition the high rate of inflation discouraged such
entrepreneurial activity because potential profits were low in real terms,
over even a few years. Thirdly, the British labour force was generously
paid relative to its productivity, as a result of the strength of the trades
unions in bargaining for wages and working conditions – a strength to
which the relatively moribund employers readily yielded, preferring to
retain their current rates of return than to push for more. Fourthly, there
were too many monopolies, comprising not only the companies involved
in the production of goods and services – in both the private and the public
sectors – but also the labour force, through the trades unions. And finally,
linking these together, the state was closely involved in too many aspects
of economy and society. Together with the unions and the large private and
public corporations it operated a corporatist system which was designed to

favour those interest groups and was not accountable to the public through free market mechanisms.

Linked to this interpretation of Britain's economic difficulties was an analysis of British society, and especially the influence of socialist thought on all political parties. After the Second World War the Conservative party had accepted many of the Labour government's innovations in both economy and society, and therefore to some extent was committed to the socialist view of the 'good society', based not only on equality of opportunity but also on equality of outcome. Social democracy was decried under Mrs Thatcher's leadership, not only as a restraint on individual initiative but also as a harbinger of totalitarianism. Following Hayek's (1944) *The Road to Serfdom*, Conservative analysts argued that 'there was no half-way house between even the mildest socialist measures and full-blown totalitarianism . . . social democracy was a Trojan Horse for communism' (Gamble, 1988, p. 57). To protect individual freedom and liberty, therefore, the forces of socialism must be defeated, both at home and abroad. Not only must a Conservative government effectively counter the communist and other totalitarian threats to capitalist freedom elsewhere in the world, but, in Gamble's usage of one of Mrs Thatcher's most-remembered phrases, 'Effective defence against enemies without meant first hunting down enemies within'.

Socialism, plus the milder forms of social democracy promoted by size-able elements of the Labour party and, from 1981 on, the Social Democratic party (in alliance with the Liberals), was thus a major perceived cause of Britain's problems. It had contributed greatly to the development of a 'culture of dependency', in which people relied on the state not only to help them in times of acute difficulty but also to provide them with the means for their personal advancement. While that culture remained strong, and people adhered at least in part to the belief in equality of outcome as well as of opportunity, a successful 'enterprise economy' could not be relaunched. To enable that meant not only defeating the Labour party at both general and local elections (because much of the dependency on the state was fostered by Labour-controlled local governments and their high spending on public services) but also reducing the power of the bureaucracy at the heart of the state apparatus, which had a vested interest in promoting the monopoly interests of a large state sector.

In brief, the 'New Right' analysis of the problems of British society in the post-war decades focused on the failure of market mechanisms because of two main impediments to their efficient operation: public and private monopolies, and an over-involved state. These problems were not only contributing to the steady economic decline of Britain but were also undermining the moral status of society. Only a return to free markets, with a minimal, but strong, state presence would ensure a reversal of the apparently unstoppable trends: in Gamble's very apt couplet, this called for *The Free Economy and the Strong State*.

Prognosis and implementation

Given the diagnosis, the Conservative governments set about their task of regenerating the British economy with an overall goal to put as much of it as possible into the disciplines of the market place. The role of the state would eventually be reduced to little more than an enabling structure and a regulating agency. Sound money is necessary for capitalist markets to operate properly, it was argued, and ensuring its existence requires the state to keep inflation as close to zero as possible: policies to reduce inflation through control of the money supply were central to the first years of the decade, and were widely dubbed as monetarist. At the same time, monopolies were to be destroyed, because they were inefficient.

The control of inflation and the encouragement of enterprise Monetarist – or supply-side – policies were presented as alternatives to those of Keynesian demand management which had characterized government activity for several decades. The perceived best way of emerging from a recession, according to the Keynesian analysis, was for the government to stimulate the economy by creating demand. Monetarists perceived this as inflationary, however, and argued that its use had failed to achieve that which it sought: Britain experienced both high inflation and high unemployment during the 1970s but the two, as illustrated by the classic 'Phillips curve' (Phillips, 1958), were supposed to be alternatives. Furthermore, whereas Keynesian policies may have succeeded in an era of fixed exchange rates they were unlikely to do so when those rates were subject to supply and demand in a relatively open market, as now operated (although the decision to enter the Exchange Rate Mechanism of the European Monetary System in 1990, and the possibility of a single European currency by the middle of the decade – despite Mrs Thatcher's personal opposition – signalled not so much a move away from a free market as a change in the number of traders in the market). Increasing the money supply through government stimulation of spending power in such circumstances was likely not only to be inflationary but also to generate balance of payments and exchange rate crises: the supply of money must be subjected to the disciplines of the market place, which meant that Keynesian policies were no longer viable. Stability of the currency must be the government's first concern, even if this meant a period of substantial economic restructuring and unemployment as a consequence.

If inflation can be controlled through monetarist policies – though, as Gamble (1988) makes clear, there was much debate over the correct way to implement such a goal – then a context can be created within which an economy should flourish. People are more likely to invest in the expectation of profits, it was argued, when they are secure in the knowledge that the value of money will not be so eroded that the potential return is not worth the gamble. In addition, it was increasingly claimed during the decade, there have to be incentives to encourage risk-taking. In a materialist world, those incentives must be financial. It was claimed that Britain offered insufficient such incentives, because of its high rates of income tax – especially on high incomes. People should be encouraged to take risks in order to accumulate wealth, which they could then either spend or re-invest in the search for further wealth, in each case creating employment and thereby stimulating the economy. Wealth creation was promoted as the key to economic regeneration.

The needed incentives involved the reduction in rates of income tax, thereby offering people greater rewards from hard, productive and profit-able work. The goal was to reduce all levels of taxation, but this was not possible in the early 1980s because of the demands on the exchequer (including the welfare payments to the increasingly large numbers depen-dent on the state). Thus to increase the incentives in the interim the burden of taxation was shifted from direct to indirect sources. The first budget, in June 1979, reduced income taxes substantially (especially for high-income-earners) and increased indirect taxes through the Value Added Tax. The result was a substantial shift in the tax burden away from the affluent and well-paid and towards the relatively poor, who previously had not paid income tax. This was justified on the argument that reducing taxation for the well-paid would stimulate wealth-creation, and therefore job-cre-ation; in the long run, the poor would benefit every bit as much as the rich.

The switch in the source of income from taxation was also defended as part of the government's belief in the importance of markets as the places where people indicate their preferences. If people have more to spend, markets will react accordingly; if spending decisions are made by govern-ments, however, then individual desires are often ignored because a govern-ment cannot hope to represent the views of 50 million consumers. Tiebout's (1956) argument – see chapter 6 – that the equivalent of a market could be created by having a large number of local governments competing to provide 'tax/benefit packages' to consumer-voters, who would thus 'vote with their feet' in choosing where to live, could have been linked with this. The national government would then be confined to providing those services which are largely indivisible within the country – such as national defence and macroeconomic policy – whereas those over which people could choose, both as to whether they should be provided as well as in what volume, could be the preserve of competing local governments. This model was not adopted under Thatcherism, however, except with the privatization of certain public utilities; Mrs Thatcher's governments preferred to replace local governments by firms in the market place rather than by putting local governments into the market place.

Putting greater reliance on market mechanisms involved the government opening the British economy to the world economic system more so than had previously been the case. Controls on the flows of capital into and out of the country were removed, on the grounds that if they were not the inefficiency of British producers would be protected and regeneration would be constrained. If British industry remained inefficient, then local capital would flow out and external capital would not be attracted. In a world market, it was the efficient countries that would prosper in the long term, with minimal government assistance; it was up to British management and British workers to recognize this, and participate in the economic restructuring accordingly. In Harvey's (1985b) terms – see p. 201 above – both sides of British industry were being invited to forge a new regional alliance from which, unlike the previous corporatist arrangements, the state would stand aloof.

Controls on local government High levels of government spending were a major cause of inflation, according to the 'New Right' arguments. These could only be financed by a combination of high levels of taxation, which penalized initiative and discouraged venture capital investments, and high levels of public borrowing, which forced up interest rates and made borrowing expensive, and so also discouraged enterprise. Thus along with control of the money supply the government advocated reductions in state spending, to be achieved by greater efficiency within the public sector, the return of most nationalized industries and utilities to the private sector, and reduction of public dependence on the welfare state. Only in defence and the promotion of law and order was growth at a greater rate than GDP to be allowed, so as to promote the strong state which underpinned the free market.

In the attack on public spending much focus fell on local governments, many of which – especially those controlled by the Labour party – were presented as spendthrift, inefficient and poorly accountable to the electorate. The system of funding local government via a combination of local rates, paid by property-owners according to the imputed rental value of their holdings, and central government grants, linked to the perceived spending needs and resources of the local governments, was presented as out of control and requiring strict constraints. These were introduced over a period (beginning with the 1970s' Labour governments), during which the central government increasingly determined not only what a local government ought to spend, and therefore how much central grant income it would receive, but also how much it could spend, with penalties (legally enforceable after passage of the 1988 Local Government Act) for those which overspent.

Control of the volume of local spending proved to be insufficient to meet the party's requirements, however, as a number of local councils, most of them Labour-controlled, opposed Conservative policies. To further the cause, therefore, a number of other steps was taken. Several involved the removal of certain local government functions, in part if not in total. For example, to promote the regeneration of rundown industrial areas – such as the Liverpool and London dockland areas where the experiments were first tried – control of land-use planning was removed from local governments and handed to appointed Development Corporations, which had wide powers to promote the economy of their defined areas in partnership with the private sector: an increasing number of these Corporations were established in the late 1980s, providing a larger scale implementation of area-based policies (initiated in 1980 with Enterprise Zones) from which local governments were largely excluded. Other local government functions were taken away from what was seen as the joint monopoly power of the elected councils and the strong trades unions with which they were perceived to be cooperating closely: public road passenger transport was deregulated, for example; polytechnics were removed from local control entirely; schools were offered the right to opt out of local government control through a majority vote of the parents of children currently registered there and the governing bodies of all other schools were given responsibility for fixed budgets determined by formula; the provision of other services, such as waste disposal, was to be put out to tender, with the local government reduced to the role of a regulatory agent, it was hoped; council homes were to be offered for sale to tenants at favourable terms, with their replacement prevented by spending limits; and so on. And finally, seven major local governments were abolished – the Greater London County Council and the six Metropolitan County Councils in England.

These policies were accompanied in the late 1980s by a major change in the nature of local government financing. The rates system for raising money locally was abolished and replaced by a community charge – commonly known as the 'poll tax'. This was promoted as a means of making local governments more accountable to their electorates, and thus of constraining their spending proclivities, especially those of the perceived high-spending Labour-controlled councils. The rates were paid by property-owners only, including non-domestic property-owners who had no voting rights *per se*. Renters may have paid rates indirectly, but were not necess-arily aware of their contributions; many adults were apparently excluded from contributing to the costs of local government services (except through their indirect contributions via the income tax system and central grants). For these reasons, it was argued, many local governments were elected by voters the majority of whom did not pay the bills. As a result, the elected councils were not accountable for their spending; they could set high rates, raise a lot of money from a relatively small number of domestic and non-domestic property-owners, and yet be returned at election after election by voters who were not directly charged for the services they consumed. The 'poll tax', on the other hand, was to be a levy on all adult residents within a council's territory, while at the same time the levy on non-domestic property-owners was to be limited. The vast majority of voters would then be aware of the costs of local government, because they would each receive an annual bill; to reduce that bill, they would penalize high spending councils and return representatives committed to efficient, low-cost local government.

The elimination of monopolies As described above, local governments were perceived to be inefficient, at least in part because of their monopoly status: they were the sole providers of many services in an area, and thus not subject to the disciplines of the market place. But they were not the only monopolies to be attacked during the decade.

In the first years after the Second World War several major production and service industries were taken into public ownership – some explicitly, others only implicitly. Some of those nationalized operations, such as the National Coal Board and British Railways, were accepted by both Labour and Conservative parties alike, and apart from the denationalization and then renationalization of the steel industry there was little political disagree-ment over several decades about the need for them to remain in public ownership. The same was true of major service industries, notably the National Health Service. This consensus view of the need for the state to control the 'commanding heights' of the economy, the major public utilities, and the provision of health and welfare in its many forms was challenged by the 'New Right' during the 1970s, however, and in the 1980s programmes of privatization were prepared for many of them whilst a few (such as the health service) were scheduled to remain in government control but to become much more subject to the rigours of market-place disciplines. (Even so, people were encouraged to opt out of the state systems of health care and education, for example; in education, especially higher education, the government increasingly placed the onus on the individuals who were to profit from their qualifications to invest in the potential benefits themselves.)

The perceived inefficiency of the nationalized industries was seen as resulting in part from their monopoly status, a situation which they shared with the large multinational corporations that were increasingly dominating the world economy. Both had to be returned to market disciplines through government regulation of the growth of monopoly powers: a major role of the strong state was to regulate deviations from the free economy.

One way in which the monopolies had been involved in the decline of British economic power was in their 'corporate collusion' with the trades unions which, because of the 'closed shop' agreements operating at many plants, were themselves monopoly suppliers of labour. Under the corporate system, employers were too ready to acquiesce with union demands rather than stand up to them, preferring a relatively quiet, guaranteed but inefficient production system to one in which the costs of labour were held down to those which its productivity would sustain. Employers' willingness to agree to large wage demands and other requests for improvements in working conditions were major contributors not only to the poor competitive condition of British industry in the world economy but also to the inflationary spiral. Employers had to be encouraged to resist union demands, and this called for constraints on union powers. Legislation was passed which curbed union activities – such as secondary picketing, striking without ballots and the levying of political funds without the agreement of their members – and also to make their elected officials more accountable. Furthermore, the government itself was prepared to tackle the unions – as demonstrated in its policing of a number of major strikes (such as that at Grunwick, the dispute between the Iron and Steel Federation and British Steel, and, most notably, the year-long conflict between the National Union of Mineworkers and the National Coal Board discussed in chapter 4) and by the protection it offered for employers who broke with the unions representing their workers, as in the newspaper industry.

THE OUTCOME ON THE MAP

The result of these policies has been to accentuate all divisions within British society, including those by location. Exacerbation of the North–South divide has been a major consequence of Thatcherism. It was a consequence that could have been foreseen (and possibly was) but which was in any case irrelevant to the larger goal of regenerating and restructuring the country as a whole.

To many, the clearest exemplar of the consequences of these policies that were spatially uneven in their impact was the major growth in the number of registered unemployed (to well over three million; the number was substantially underestimated by changes in the definitions of unemployed over the decade) and their concentration in the Northern regions (plus inner London). The removal of protection from internationally uncompetitive industries through, for example, the abolition of exchange controls led to the demise of many manufacturing plants and the creation of what Anderson, Duncan and Hudson (1983) graphically term 'Redundant spaces in cities and regions'. The old-established staple industries of the Northern regions – iron and steel, shipbuilding, heavy engineering, textiles, vehicle manufacture – were the main sufferers, as their obsolescent plant and relatively unproductive workers were unable to produce goods that could compete either at home or abroad. New investment was not forthcoming there, because of the uncertainties of the revised competitive situation and the perceived militancy of the trades unions. The North increasingly became an industrial desert.

It was in the North, too, that the conflict with the trades unions was most intense: to some, the policy appeared to be not only to break the power of the 'union barons' but also to destroy the role of the unions in British society. Certainly the areas in which unions were strong and militant were not those which benefited from the growth in the economy that began in the mid-1980s. As Massey and Meegan (1979) showed in their pioneering studies of company strategies during periods of restructuring, in many industries the introduction of new technology and the consequent deskilling of large segments of the labour force involved relocation of plants to, and the opening of new ones in, areas where trades unions were only weakly organized, and where it was possible for employers to insist on working arrangements which severely limited union power – if it was allowed at all. In the 1970s, this trend accelerated the process known as counterurbanization, whereby economic and population growth was concentrated in the smaller towns of regions henceforth only weakly industrialized. This continued during the 1980s; several of the parts of the country which suffered least from the recession (i.e. that had the lowest unemployment levels in 1984) benefited most from the subsequent recovery (i.e. experienced the largest drops in unemployment). The equilibrium theories of regional economists failed; the North suffered first and most, and recovered least and last (Pattie and Johnston, 1990).

Not all new investment occurred in the South, however, for as the recession bit ever harder in the North so the workers there were increasingly prepared to accept the disciplines of the new economic system. This was characterized by the decision of the Japanese car firm Nissan to open a large plant on Wearside; it was able to select its workforce carefully from among the large number of applicants, and could dictate to the trades unions terms which were far from characteristic of earlier periods. Where there were doubts about the willingness of the workforce to conform to the new employers' demands – as with a proposed Ford plant in Dundee – then the investment was not forthcoming.

The South's increasing dominance of the country's manufacturing industry was accompanied by other developments which favoured that part of the country, especially London and its commuter hinterland. The new financial freedoms, plus the increasing globalization of the world economy, encouraged by information technology, stimulated the growth of service industries. As a global financial city, with deregulation assisting its development, London became a major growth centre, far outpacing other cities in the expansion of employment in a range of industries which promoted the flow of money.

Much of the employment growth in parts of the service sector, as increasingly in the manufacturing sector too, was less secure than had characterized arrangements in the past. A relatively small proportion of the workforce – usually the professionally trained, skilled, and highly-paid – had permanent jobs in the core of the labour force. An increasing proportion were on the periphery, however, dependent on short-term contracts for particular jobs; many were employed part-time only, especially in the consumer service industries such as the growing numbers of supermarkets and out-of-town shopping centres. This was in itself a stimulant to greater discipline within the labour market: people dependent on contracts for incomes from which to meet their (increasingly large) mortgage payments would be more inclined to work hard and less inclined to join unions and go on strike.

The initial consequences of the government's economic policies were very substantial job losses in the North, therefore; that region did not then participate equally in the recovery which came in the later part of the decade. Along with this came a substantial feeling that the government was doing more than just promoting a new set of economic policies; it was widely perceived to be promoting a social as well as an economic revolution, which was having most impact on the North because one of its major elements was the reduction of power for the trades unions, for long among the salient social and political as well as economic organizations there. Most Labour-controlled local governments were also in the North, and the attack on them had its greatest impact in the Northern regions too.

The relative prosperity of the South and poverty of the North were reflected very clearly in the changing pattern of house and land prices during the 1980s. The South – especially Greater London and its metropolitan region – experienced much more rapid inflation of prices through much of the 1980s. This was initially fuelled by the relative flow of money into purchasing power there as a result of the 1979 budget (see p. 229: Johnston, 1979) and was then exaggerated by the differentials in both economic performance and earning potentials for successful workers – especially in the financial services industries of the City – during the mid-1980s. In the latter part of the decade, the differentials were reduced somewhat as, not for the first time, inflation in values continued in other regions after a slowdown in London (Hamnett, 1983, 1989), but in absolute terms the gap remained wide, posing a major problem for those wishing to move south in the search for work. Those with investments in the South obtained a windfall increase in their equity holdings compared to those in the North, and this was reflected in their greater preparedness to vote for the party which had delivered them that gain – i.e. Conservative – whatever their occupational and other backgrounds (Johnston, 1987).

The government was also perceived to be attacking the local governments in the North and the inner cities, many of whose services sustained substantial sectors of the population severely impacted by the recession, and yet at the same time was putting a greater burden on those people through the 'poll tax'. For much of the first half of the decade several Labour-controlled local councils stood against the Conservative policies for local government, refusing – until eventually forced – to reduce spending, to sell council homes at a premium, to cut services, to increase charges (for public transport in South Yorkshire, for example), and so on. And several also tried to establish alternative economic policies with which to regain and to promote jobs in the local area (Storey, 1990), whilst at the same time refusing to participate in the government's own programmes (Sheffield declined to apply for an Enterprise Zone, for example). For this, they were dubbed 'loony left' local governments by Conservative leaders and parts of the media, and were widely castigated for their perceived inefficiency and a claimed profligacy on a variety of 'fringe' activities.

Most of those local governments eventually accepted the central dictats, either because of fear of the consequence of councillors' actions being deemed illegal by the courts or because of near-bankruptcy. (Liverpool was probably the last to hold out.) In some cases, Labour councillors had long been prepared to go along with central government's requirements, as Bassett (1990) illustrates for Swindon. In others, the 'New Urban Left' – largely middle class in origin and libertarian in attitude, as opposed to the paternalism of most 'traditional' parties – stood against the Conservatives and continued to promote socialist solutions to economic difficulties. Eventually they shifted ground too, as illustrated by Sheffield where the City Council became much more involved in public-private partnerships to promote regeneration after a change of leadership in 1987 (Seyd, 1990).

This final 'defeat' of the Labour strongholds in local governments enabled the Conservative party to continue with its strategies aimed at eroding Labour's electoral base. Labour's mobilizing strength has been especially strong:

1 in the manufacturing industries (including coal-mining) characterized by large factory workforces which were hierarchically structured, heavily unionized, and in many cases very militant;
2 among certain groups of workers in the public sector, both the nationalized industries and some of the major service industries – such as the health service and local government itself;
3 among council house tenants, whose solidarity is strengthened by their co-residence of large estates; and
4 in areas where the local government was dominated by the Labour party, whose commitment to the quantity and quality of local service delivery could be presented as a clear alternative to the Conservative programme.

The restructuring of manufacturing industry, the curbs on trades union power, the privatization of some nationalized industries and the introduction of strict financial accountability in others, the sales of council homes, and the constraints on local government spending have all assisted the Conservative attempt 'to rid the United Kingdom of socialism'; by undermining Labour's electoral mobilization base, in so many ways, that opposition party's ability to respond was dealt a series of severe blows.

Electoral trends during the 1980s suggested an increasingly spatially polarized country, as more and more people voted according to their views of the state of the economy and of their personal relative positions within it. People in the South, who benefited most from the new affluence, were increasingly prepared to vote Conservative, whatever their class background and previous partisan preferences, whereas those in the North increasingly turned to Labour. But as the latter party's mobilization base was eroded, so it was pushed further back into a Northern ghetto from which escape was unlikely unless there was either or both of a major downturn in the economy affecting much of the southern half of the country and a massive reduction in confidence in the Conservative government. The Labour party responded to this by shifting its policies increasingly to the right from 1983 on, presenting itself as a party able to run a capitalist system as well as the Conservatives, and at the same time more committed to protection of those less fortunate than others. Whereas the general tenor of Conservative rhetoric was that many of the problems faced by individuals could only be solved by them changing their attitudes, Labour promoted the view that society has a greater responsibility for individual shortcomings than the Conservatives were prepared to admit. Labour's hope was that this new posture – with much of the old rhetoric of 'class warfare', nationalization, and unilateral nuclear disarmament jettisoned, for example – would enable it to win votes again in substantial numbers in the South, among those disillusioned by the consequences of Conservative policies in an increasingly divided society (see Crewe, 1986, on the electoral strategies open to the Labour party).

What we see, therefore, is a country in which the government's policies have removed, or begun to remove, many of the regional variations – notably those between North and South – in the nature of economic activity, the format of social relations at the workplace, the amount of collective provision of services through the public sector, and the organization of both workplace and party politics. The main opposition party appears to have accepted many of these changes very substantially, and to be prepared to operate within the new society created under Thatcherism.

The Conservatives have sought to homogenize the map of Britain. In many ways, therefore, it seems that Hudson and Williams are correct to claim that the Conservative policies were a deliberate attempt to polarize the country spatially, prior to homogenizing it later, as illustrated by Mrs Thatcher's 1987 claim, after her third general election victory was secured, that there remained much work to do in 'those inner cities' – the parts of the country still not dominated by the Tories. In my view the geographical elements to the strategy were largely incidental to the electoral goal, however, though they probably advanced it. It was British society that was to be altered, as a whole, and it was unlikely that spatial variations were much taken into account as the blueprint was mapped out: as Gamble

(1989, p. 14) expressed it, 'The nation of subsidy and dependence is no longer to be propped up: it is to be reconstructed. The South is to swallow the North'.

NATIONS WITHIN NATION

One element of the blueprint that was geographical in its construction concerned the Conservative governments' attitudes to nationalist movements within the United Kingdom. As theorists of the state have stressed, as well as sustaining and legitimating the mode of production, governments in control of the state apparatus must also ensure social consensus within their territory, without which the other two tasks will be almost impossible. Providing social cohesion is thus a major ideological task for the state.

The country which the Conservatives were elected to rule in 1979 was facing substantial challenges to that cohesion in each of the three minority countries within the United Kingdom – Northern Ireland, Scotland and Wales. The new government's attitude to all three was that they should be defeated, and that the United Kingdom should be presented as a single unit.

The Northern Irish challenge was by far the most difficult faced, because it involved guerilla warfare by a group – the IRA – determined to achieve the irredentist goal of separation from the United Kingdom and unification of the whole of Ireland under one government. This long-running campaign was given considerable covert support by substantial elements within Northern Ireland, as well as outside; a related political party – Sinn Fein – received sufficient electoral support to ensure victory for its candidate in at least one constituency at a general election (though the elected member refused to take the oath of allegiance and occupy his seat), and a further pro-Republican political party (the SDLP) also won, and accepted, representation at Westminster. But Northern Ireland was strongly polarized, and the 'loyalist' (Unionist) majority was unwilling either to compromise with those who wished to break from the United Kingdom or to share power with them.

The Conservative government's main response was to uphold the rights of the majority to determine the fate of Northern Ireland and to present the IRA and its supporters as criminals subject to the relevant law (and therefore lacking political status). Nevertheless, it found it necessary to continue the policy of promoting law and order there through the use of the army as well as the police, presented by its opponents in Ireland as using an army of occupation. The government was willing to negotiate with the government of the Republic of Ireland to an extent not previously typical of Conservative administrations, however, and culminating in the Anglo-Irish Agreement. This gave the impression to both the Ulster 'loyalists' and some of its own 'mainland' supporters that the Conservative party's commitment to sustaining that part of the United Kingdom was not one hundred per cent. Northern Ireland was perceived as a separate territorial problem and rarely included explicitly in the nationalist rhetoric which characterized Mrs Thatcher and some of her ministers.

This ambivalence towards Northern Ireland was not repeated in the cases of Scotland and Wales, where nationalist movements had flourished in the 1970s but had ultimately failed to achieve their goals. As economic problems mounted in that decade, so opposition to the central government in London was mobilized (by the Scottish National Party and by Plaid Cymru) in those two segments of Britain's economic periphery which had retained many aspects of their identity and territorial integrity despite several centuries of Anglicization. The two parties' electoral successes in 1974 had stimulated demands for a devolution of power, if not independence, and led some to forecast the 'breakup of Britain': the bases for those claims were somewhat different, drawing on the traditional culture of the rural areas of Wales, for example, but stimulated more by the discovery and exploitation of oil ('Scottish, not British, oil') off the Scottish coast.

These demands were especially difficult for the Labour party to deal with, since it drew substantial electoral strength in those two countries and was very unlikely to win power in England alone. Thus the party was split in each of Scotland and Wales, between those who supported greater autonomy for their national homes and those who feared a Labour decline in the United Kingdom if some form of devolution, and thus possibly reduced representation at Westminster also, were agreed. (The two nationalist parties were unable to win seats at general elections in the Labour heartlands of the two countries – Strathclyde and South Wales.) But the Labour party was operating only a minority government by 1978, and it agreed to offer Scotland and Wales limited devolution if their electorates supported it in a referendum. The terms on which the referendum would be taken to indicate a positive demand for such devolution – a vote in favour equivalent to 40 per cent of the registered electorate – virtually ensured that both countries would reject the offer, and this was the case, emphatically in Wales but less so in Scotland where a majority of those who voted were in favour. And then, a few months later, the nationalists lost several seats at the general election which returned the Conservatives to power.

For much of the 1980s the demands of Scottish and Welsh nationalists had only a weak impact on the British political agenda. Nevertheless, the two countries posed a particular problem for the Conservatives because of the party's growing electoral weakness there. Thus, whereas in England the economic policies that promoted restructuring involved substantial reductions in regional aid, in Scotland and Wales considerable help was provided through the separate offices headed by Cabinet Ministers with responsibilities for the two countries.

The Scottish and Welsh Development Agencies (and the Northern Ireland Development Agency too) had financial and other resources available to them which were not present in English regions, so that whereas in England the map of recession and recovery was little influenced by overt government policy this was not the case elsewhere. (And in Wales, the Secretary of State in the late 1980s was Peter Walker, a 'wet' rebel against many of the government's policies but who retained his cabinet position for reasons of internal party politics and was allowed to operate an interventionist policy for in excess of that in place 'over the border'.) Interestingly, however, this did not assist the Conservative party electorally in the two countries; its fortunes in Scotland were particularly damaged by its use of the country as a 'guinea pig' for certain policy initiatives, notably the 'poll tax'.

NATION AND WORLD

The creation of a national identity, as argued in chapter 6, involves stimulating both an in-group identification and an opposition to out-groups. As noted above, generating such an identity was central to the Conservative ideological task in the 1980s, because of its need to sustain a 'strong state' alongside a 'free economy'.

The Conservative party's foreign policy throughout the 1980s reflected its theorists' belief that as well as ensuring an efficient capitalist system within the country it was necessary for Britain to collaborate in ensuring capitalist survival and advancement elsewhere. Thus in the early years, before the extension of *glasnost* and *perestroika*, Mrs Thatcher took a firm stance alongside President Reagan, who characterized the USSR as the 'evil empire', against the communist-ruled countries, for which she earned the nickname 'the Iron Lady'. The expansion of communism was to be resisted strongly, hence for example the recommendation (ignored by British athletes) that the country should not participate in the 1980 Olympic Games in Moscow, in protest against the Russian presence in Afghanistan.

At the same time, encouragement was given to dissident movements, notably the Solidarity trade union in Poland. With Gorbachev's accession in the USSR and the shift towards a market economy there, the Cold War rhetoric disappeared, and the rapid changes in Eastern Europe in 1989 and 1990 saw Mrs Thatcher claim credit for the return of freedoms to those countries, and thus the reduction in the socialist threat to Britain's capitalist economy. Meanwhile, the resolve of the British state to defend the 'free world' was demonstrated in the Falklands/Malvinas in 1982 and the Arabian Gulf in 1990.

Alongside this defence of freedom, the Conservative foreign policy has also been characterized by a focus on what Smith (1990, p. 265) lists as 'terms of sovereignty, independence, and national interests'. This is best seen in the governments' attitudes to the European Community, especially in the later years of their rule when the European Commission and a majority of the member-states favoured rapid progress towards both economic and political union. The UK government was often isolated within the EC because of what Smith (p. 253) terms its 'very specific commitment to a certain type of "Europe", one that is state-based and decidedly inter-governmental rather than supra-national'. Thus whereas Mrs Thatcher and her governments have favoured deregulation and the opening-up of markets in Europe, they have opposed 'market homogenization' (Wallace, 1990, p. 164) and such developments as a single European currency and a central bank. At the same time, the Conservatives opposed many of the EC's social policies during the late 1980s; power in the Commission and Parliament was largely in the hands of social democrats, who promoted policies such as a 'social charter' which were contrary to the Conservative desire to 'roll back the frontiers of the state'. During the 1989 European Parliament elections, for example, the Conservative party campaigned, *inter alia*, on a slogan of 'Don't let Labour in by the back door' – implicitly threatening its supporters in the UK that an anti-Conservative protest vote could see 'socialist' policies which had been overthrown at Westminster reintroduced through Brussels and Strasbourg. (As it turned out, although the Conservative party did lose seats to Labour in that election the main beneficiary from the protest vote was the Green party, which obtained 15 per cent of the votes cast – in a turnout of only 30 per cent – but none of the seats.)

As part of its free market and strong state strategy, therefore, the Conservative party did a great deal to promote British sovereignty and independence within the framework of the European Community. As set out in the preceding chapter, the state has three main roles in a modern capitalist society: to secure social consensus; to promote accumulation; and to legitimate the mode of production. With regard to the promotion of accumulation, the removal of barriers to trade and the movement of capital and labour within the EC are consistent with the Conservative programme – though some of the EC's regulatory procedures (regarding environmental policies, for example) are not, because they threaten accumulation strategies. But the EC's legitimation policies are largely anathema, because they are perceived to contain within them the potential for a regrowth of a large, inefficient, monopolistic bureaucratic state and the associated 'culture of dependency'.

In the light of this resistance to aspects of policies towards unification being promoted by other member state governments and by the EC's own Commission, the ideological function of the state has been used by the Conservatives to promote the EC as a desirable loose, free amalgamation of countries to achieve economic benefits but a threat to British sovereignty if it moves further towards economic and political union. This was clearly expressed in the summer of 1990 in an interview given to a weekly journal by a senior cabinet minister, Nicholas Ridley, which was derogatory to the Germans and the French – and for which he was obliged to resign. The Prime Minister's own rhetoric continued the attack, however, with barbed comments about the President of the European Commnission in speeches to both the Conservative party conference and the House of Commons as well as in her comments to the media after a European heads of state meeting in Rome. It stimulated substantial divisions within the party, exemplified by the resignation of the Deputy Prime Minister (Sir Geoffrey Howe) in protest at her 'tone'. The Prime Minister's apparent xenophobia was taken up by elements of the media in an anti-EC campaign – notably in the tabloid *The Sun* – but it was the cause of her downfall in November 1990 (perhaps ironically, the result of the ballot for the Conservative party leadership – which she won but not sufficiently well enough to guarantee victory at a second ballot – was announced while she was in Paris).

As pointed out in chapter 6, an almost inevitable component of the promotion of a state ideology, formulated to create consensus and cohesion, is the generation of 'in-group' and 'out-group' stereotypes, in which the latter are portrayed negatively. Internal cohesion is therefore often bought at the price of external tension. This is what the Conservative governments led by Margaret Thatcher sought to do during the 1980s. Initially, the focus was on the 'red threat' to the 'free world' – although the UK's preparedness to stand up to such threats was only mild in the case of large countries such as the USSR and China (especially over the Tiananmen Square massacre in 1988) and demonstrated instead in the opposition to the Argentinian invasion of the Falklands/Malvinas in 1982, the Iraqi invasion of Kuwait in 1990, and, throughout the period, the determined policy not to bargain with terrorists in the Middle East, even over hostages. Later during the decade, as the USSR moved rapidly towards substantial disarmament (as did the USA too, because both countries were suffering severe economic difficulties as a consequence of increased spending on the arms race) the communist threat to freedom became more muted and the British state ideology less strident in its negative portrayal of 'Russian imperialists'. Nevertheless, the Conservative governments were not prepared to reduce their commitment to sustaining a nuclear deterrent, and would not include the British arsenal in the negotiations with the Russians over reductions. The 'them' and 'us' dichotomy was muted somewhat, but not erased. The UK continues to spend a much larger percentage of GNP on defence than most of its European partners, and, as Smith (1990, p. 250) expresses it: 'it is assumed that Britain is a nuclear power, that it is in a fixed alliance structure (NATO), and that the Soviet Union is the enemy'.

LANDSCAPES OF THATCHERISM

The political phenomenon widely known as Thatcherism has thus played a major part in changing the nature of places in the United Kingdom during the 1980s, and whatever the dominant (if any) political ideology of the 1990s many of those changes are likely to be long-lived in the British landscape. Within the country, the commitment to a free market and a minimal, regulatory role only for the state (at all scales) has been used to promote policies that over-ride the particularities of places and their residents' desire to sustain those features.

With the exception of Scotland, Wales and Northern Ireland, whose cultural separateness has long been recognized in special status arrangements within the British state that are too deeply ingrained to be easily removed, policies that favour individual places have been substantially reduced in importance (and local governments have increasingly been prevented from putting them in place). A free market means the removal of barriers, and for the Conservatives policies that favour certain areas of a country are comparable to trade barriers at the international scale. The consequence of this approach was initially to widen the differences between places, between the North and the South and between the inner cities and the metropolitan hinterlands, as manufacturing plants were closed in the former locations of each pair and unemployment variations increased. But this was intended to be temporary; as the residents of the 'depressed' regions realized that the fault for their plight was largely their own, they would adopt new working and other practices as a consequence and accept the government's message that a bureaucratic welfare state was a burden not an advantage. Prosperity would than return to their areas – now similar in so many ways (social relations at the workplace; the organization of civil society; the nature of political institutions) to the parts of the country which suffered less in the 'decade of restructuring'.

In the 1960s, many of the models of spatial organization promoted by geographers enamoured of the 'quantitative and theoretical revolutions' were built on the foundation of an 'isotropic plain'. Geographers then realized that the world was not an isotropic plain; cultural differences between places were substantial, which meant that the models were fundamentally flawed – until such time as those cultural differences could be eroded, as Peet (1989) argues that they were. Thatcherism has to a considerable extent sought to create that isotropic plain – or at least to make the UK, and possibly the EC (even Europe more widely), closer to that conception than it has been before. A major consequence (though neither an explicit nor an implict goal) of the Thatcherite project over more than a decade was the removal of local variations in the geography of the United Kingdom and, in Relph's (1976) phrase, to replace *place* by *placelessness*.

Against that 'placelessness' strategy, however, there has been another which has promoted place, in this case the place that is the United Kingdom. The ideology of the Conservative governments has very much promoted the view of the UK as a separate sovereign state, which intends to retain not only its identity (a patriotic goal) but also its autonomy (a nationalistic goal). Thus the isotropic plain has been interrupted by substantial barriers, not so much to the movement of people, ideas, money and goods as to assimilation into wider cultures, which may promote different views of the nature of civil society, politics and the state. These barriers are not contradictory to the isotropic plain strategy, because the latter is concerned with only one of the state's roles – the promotion of accumulation. Whereas the free economy elements of the Conservative strategy called for the creation of isotropic plains, the strong state components required the barriers. The result has been a country which was internally divided, in order eventually to achieve the elimination of differences between places, but which was externally to be unified, against the threats of outsiders. Both elements have thus produced tensions, within the country between the places that were most disadvantaged from the free market policies and those which benefited most, and between the country and others. Both tensions have enhanced the relative stereotypes – between North and South within the UK; between the UK and other countries – but have generated relatively little conflict as a consequence (though the social unrest that spilled over into inner city disturbances in the early 1980s indicated the potential). As argued earlier, the territoriality strategies employed by capitalist states contain within themselves the geopolitical seeds of their own destruction, and the United Kingdom clearly demonstrated this with the dominance of Thatcherism during the 1980s.

8

Conclusion

The only real conclusion to this book is that more work needs to be done evaluating the broad methodological framework set out here for the study of places and the focus that it might provide for diverse strands of work in a fragmented academic discipline. All that has been presented in the previous seven chapters is a case for studying places and an outline of how that might be done. As such, the book follows a trend set by a number of other authors in recent years – such as Cooke (1989a) and Entrikin (1991) – but goes further because it tries to establish a methodology as well as a subject matter. In that sense, it is more like Soja's (1989) book, but differs from it in providing empirical case studies out of which it is suggested that general guidelines for the study of place might be derived.

Having evaluated what has been presented, readers might pose two important questions. The first concerns the need for such an enterprise: how important is the study of place, as presented here, to the future vitality of geography? Whether the second is even asked depends on the answer to the first. If 'A question of place' is to be central to geography's research and teaching agenda, then: is the methodological framework set out in this book a viable way to implement that agenda item?

A need for place?

There have been few years in the last four decades when nothing has been written criticizing the current concerns of geographical researchers and suggesting new ways forward. In part this is not surprising, because those decades have seen many important changes in the worlds that physical and human geographers study – separately and together – and which have called forth responses from those geographers who believe that must be 'relevant' (or 'up-to-date') in the focus of their work. In the following paragraphs I review two particular statements regarding what geographers should be doing at present, and contrast these with the framework laid out in the rest of this book. The two have not been selected at random: rather they represent two clearly-stated positions that might be widely supported, but which are not consistent with what has been presented here.

Researchers and teachers throughout academic life in many countries are currently having their concerns and orientations challenged. Whereas the major response throughout the capitalist world to the depression of the 1920s and 1930s involved greater state involvement in most aspects of economy and society, as illustrated by the welfare states established in New Zealand and the United Kingdom, for example, and by Roosevelt's 'New Deal' in the United States, the depression of the late 1970s and early 1980s stimulated the opposite response. The viability of central planning in a capitalist system has been substantially questioned, and the withdrawal of state intervention promoted, to be replaced by much greater reliance on a 'free market' – including free markets for research and teaching in higher education. We live, to quote Bennett (1989, p. 285), in a 'post-welfarist world' which 'is seeking to roll back the boundary of government. As a new paradigm it is attracting both socialist and conservative governments as a means of better responding to customer demand' (Bennett, 1990a, p. 25).

For Bennett, the challenge of the 'culture of the times' is to be involved in the reappraisal of the welfare state and its alternatives. Geographers should be developing models using spatial information so as to enhance their contributions to the determination and evaluation of policy, especially with regard to the delivery of services, both public and private. With Openshaw (1989), Rhind (1989) and others, he sees geographers as professionals who 'add value' to data, applying what he terms (pp. 275–6) 'the 80:20 rule: that 80 per cent of the answer can be obtained in 20 per cent of the time. For many applications this is enough; high levels of technical sophistication are not required'. Openshaw (1989, p. 88) is even more determined in promoting this view of 'the geographer as applied technician':

> Many geographers have already learnt the relevant skills and the available tool kits are well understood and reasonably adequate. The loss of a largely spurious close link with theory may be sad, but it also opens up a veritable Pandora's box of new and exciting possibilities initially for inductive-based computer models in human geography and subsequently for more and better theories, if we care to look and are brave enough to try!

Here we have a pragmatic, opportunistic, and narrow definition of geography as an academic discipline. It does not need to concern itself, it seems, with why things change over time and space – why we have moved from a welfare state to postwelfarism and why eastern European countries have abandoned their centrally-planned states at the same time. We don't need to ask why the economic, social and political restructuring that occurred in Great Britain during this great shift in the 1980s was spatially uneven in its impact – as argued in chapter 7 – nor why there was a spatially differentiated mosaic of places onto which that restructuring was imposed, and which – as illustrated in chapter 4 – was unevenly resisted. We don't need theory. We take geography as given – according to the vernacular use of that word: Johnston, (1986d) – it seems, and just use our data-handling skills to assist those who will purchase our expertise to help them create new geographies. Our discipline is not about understanding, only engineering. From the perspective developed here, that is a very narrow – and, almost certainly, ultimately self-defeating – disciplinary goal. Certainly the understanding of place, as part of an understanding of an evolving world cultural mosaic, is outside the agenda.

Stoddart, like Bennett and Openshaw, also promotes a problem-oriented discipline, but the content of their geography will not be to his liking. As set out in chapter 1, he is saddened by the fragmentation of the discipline and the apparent unwillingness of its practitioners 'to tackle the real problems; to speak out across our subject boundaries on the great issues of the day (by which I do not mean the evanescent politics of Thatcher, Reagan and Gorbachov)' (Stoddart, 1987, p. 334). His criticism of works which he identifies as characteristic of the geography that he deplores is clear and unambiguous.

> I confess to a feeling of unreality about much of the literature on the philosophy, methodology and even history of the subject, much of it written by people who signally fail to practise what they preach. Meanwhile so many retreat into increasingly restrictive and esoteric specialities, where they protect themselves with secret languages and erudite techniques. (Stoddart, 1986, p. ix)

When it comes to the positive message, what might and should be done, however, Stoddart is less clear – as Bird (1989, p. 212) expresses it, after quoting Stoddart at length: 'Observe that geography is real, unified, committed but we are not told exactly what it is, though for Stoddart such a geography obviously exists. It reaches out to the future, but are there changes as it does so? And although it teaches us the 'realities of the world', whose realities?'. To those who talk of a 'formless discipline', 'lacking any rigour' and with a 'vacuum' at the discipline's heart, Stoddart writes:

> There is a simple remedy: do some *real* geography. (p. x)

What that real geography is one can only appreciate through inference. We are told that there 'is a different world, of great beauty and diversity, waiting for exploration', and are pressed to ask 'the big questions, about man, land, resources, human potential' (Stoddart, 1987, p. 334). The latter are illustrated by the example of Bangladesh and its manifold problems of feeding a rapidly-increasing population under conditions of considerable environmental adversity.

Perhaps most apposite of all for the present context, Stoddart (1987, p. 331) stresses the need to realize and study the earth's great divertiy, thus:

> All the world is not like Omaha, Nebraska, or Luton, England. If it were, geography would be a vastly less interesting subject than it is. Pretending that everywhere is like Omaha or Luton has brought geography to its present state. It is losing its distinctiveness, its historic function, its appeal.

We need regional geography to revive that distinctiveness and appeal:

> Location, position, distance, area: there are *our* basic building blocks. ... We assemble them in order to know the world in which we live. To build regional geography. To show the distinctiveness of places.

And then, once that distinctiveness is appreciated:

> The task is to identify geographical problems, issues of man and environment within regions – problems not of geomorphology or history or economics or sociology, but geographical problems: and to use our skills to work to alleviate them, perhaps to solve them. Regional geography helps to identify and specify such problems – it is, however, the beginning rather than the end.

This takes us close to the heart of Stoddart's definition, and to the reason why 'We cannot affort the luxury of putting so much energy into peripheral things' (p. 334) like 'housing finance, voting patterns, government subsidies for this and that . . . ':

> there is no such thing as a physical geography of Bangladesh divorced from its human geography, and even more so the other way round. A human geography divorced from the physical environment would be simply meaningless nonsense (p. 333).

Under that definition, the study of place as adumbrated here would undoubtedly qualify as 'simply meaningless nonsense'. Relatively little has been said in this book about the links between the human and the physical, between people and their environments (which is not to suggest, however, that such inter-relationships and how they vary between places might not be part of an understanding of places, as chapter 3 illustrates). Stoddart clearly defines any study which does not focus on this inter-relationship as not geography – which makes one wonder about his own research career spent 'in the study of coral reefs and islands . . . [as] a student of geomorphology, sedimentology, botany and zoology' (Stoddart, 1986, p. ix). He lauds Kropotkin's resolve that geography should be committed, a 'geography that will teach us the realities of the world in which we live, how we can live better on it and with each other. It is a geography which will teach our neighbours and students and our children how to understand and respect our diverse territorial inheritance' (Stoddart, 1987, p. 333).

The present book is set within that inheritance too. It also recognizes the need to appreciate the diversity of our inheritance, but it does not constrain that need to a corseted discipline which focuses on society-physical environment interrelationships alone. That diversity, as presented in chapters 3–5, reflects a complex and long history through which economic, social and political ways of organizing human occupance of the earth's surface have developed. Many of the observed differences began with variations in human response to the environment as the ultimate (and, in most of those cases, the proximate) source of survival and well-being. As those differences evolved, separately and through contact with others, so the complex mosaic that many geographers now teach about evolved too. They include relationships with nature that still vary considerably over distances large and small, but within those relationships there are many other variations, of the types illustrated here. By apparently insisting that anything which is not both human and physical is thereby not geography, Stoddart not only diminishes the important role that geographers have developed in understanding modern societies, he also promotes a geography that can only provide a partial appreciation of that world of great diversity and beauty which he so clearly enjoys.

Furthermore, as argued in chapter 6, that diversity is in itself the source of many of the problems of the world today. The problems of disaster, epidemic and famine in Bangladesh which concern Stoddart are far from entirely endogenous in their origin. Many have argued that as a whole the earth can sustain its current population without any having to suffer the privations of hunger, the scourges of epidemics and the threats of disaster. But in one, very real, sense the earth is not a whole but a series of unequally linked parts. The problems faced by Bangladesh's population today cannot be appreciated without an understanding of the history of that place – of the cultural parameters that set it apart from its neighbour, of the tensions between the two cultures that led to the creation of separate states of India and Pakistan, of the further tensions that resulted in the Bangladesh seccession to independence (each of the last two clearly illustrating the link between territoriality and geopolitics set out in chapter 6), and so on. Nor can they be appreciated without an understanding of the creation of a global capitalist economic system within which (what is now) Bangladesh was allocated a peripheral position, and of the role of territoriality which encourages competition and conflict between the residents of spatially defined countries rather than cooperation and mutual assistance – if we are to 'live better . . . with each other' as Stoddart wishes, then the role of territoriality as a catalyst for conflict must be understood. Stoddart argues that the physical of Bangladesh cannot be understood separate from an understanding of the human: that argument is entirely consistent with the one promoted here, except that I do not circumscribe the study of human geography to the direct links between people and nature only.

It is, of course, easy to poke fun at 'geographic influences on the Canadian cinema, or the distribution of fast-food outlets in Tel Aviv' (Stoddart, 1987, p. 334) as well as voting patterns – and, I guess, bellringing regions too: Johnston (1991b), Johnston, Allsopp, Baldwin and Turner (1990). Yet, in their different ways, all have value in promoting the cause to which both Stoddart and I appear to be committed. As I have argued elsewhere (Johnston, 1991b), in seeking to develop a sensitivity among students and the general public regarding the importance of place diversity, one needs to work with a range of examples that people can empathize with and from which it is possible to draw larger generalizations (as Harvey has eloquently argued with regard to Marx's detailed empirical studies: 1989c). Certainly the study of voting patterns is crucial to an appreciation of some of the constraints to tackling environmental issues in liberal democracies, as I have argued in detail elsewhere (Johnston, 1989a), and if 'green politics' are the route to the sort of problem-solving Stoddart advocates then understanding who supports them, and where, is a crucial first step (Johnston, Russell, and Pattie, 1991).

The views of Bennett and Stoddart have not been presented here simply to score points; they are cogently argued cases for what geographers should do. In my view, they are partial and they seek to constrain unnecessarily. Bennett and those who argue like him appear not to want to understand in the mode argued for here; they do not want geography to be a discipline which helps us to come to terms with the diversity of the world, a diversity to which we have substantially contributed and which in its turn substantially constrains what we can now do with the world. Stoddart's view is partial because he wants to exclude much of that diversity from geographical study because it doesn't conform with his narrow definition of the disciplinary core. Others who recognize that we are living in exciting 'new times' argue that we must appreciate the importance of locality (place in my vocabulary) in the reconstruction of society (Smith, 1989).

Place is central to geography. The diversity of place is manifold. Our mission within academia, according to Hart (1982), is to describe and account for that diversity. To achieve that mission, we must promote the study of place not ignore it; and we must not constrain our definition of the geographical content of place so as to restrict the value of our contribution to understanding. This means that the fragmentation of our discipline, necessary in order to advance specialist research interests, must be restrained. Specialists must be brought together, to realize that they have greater needs for each other's expertise than appears currently to be admitted. Only in that way will we ensure understanding of wholes – places – which are much greater than sums of parts, and then with full understanding we can move much more confidently towards the fashioning of better places: to rephrase one of Bunge's (1973) important epigrams – 'May the world be full of happy places.'

And how should we do it?

The message preached in the preceding paragraph is not mine alone. Others have been arguing along similar lines. So why the need to state the case again? The simple answer is that I am dissatisfied not so much with their presentation of the case but rather with their response to the question posed at the heading for this section.

As stressed earlier in the book, some of the advocates for a 'place-based geography' have failed to answer the question satisfactorily and even, in one case (Entrikin, 1991), have declined to tackle it at all. Of those who have tried, unfortunately most have failed to provide a convincing framework within which others can work, let alone detailed methodological guidelines.

Nowhere is this conclusion better illustrated than in the substantial volume of literature that has been produced from the ESRC's CURS initiative (see above, p. 62). In his introduction to one of the summary volumes, for example, Cooke (1989a, pp. 1–3) asks:

> why should some localities be good at mobilizing local interests and others more acquiscent towards the outside world? Why is the evenly spread presence of democratic rights unevenly acted upon? Why do some issues anger people in certain localities more than people in

others, and why do certain places tend to be associated with specific types of popular mobilization?

Eight pages later, he concludes by discussing the extent to which 'generalizations can be made about changes in the wider space economy on the basis of the locality studies' (p. 9). His goal appears to be an inductive one, using the outcomes of seven case study teams 'investigating the ways in which localities function from the same broad theoretical perspective and asking many similar questions derived from that perspective'. (The 'broad theoretical perspective' is far from clear, and no methodological framework for working within that perspective is outlined.) Cooke admits that a sample of seven is too small for safe generalizations to be made, but his long-term goal is to determine the 'extent to which localities function similarly in the face of a common, though multifaceted, experience of economic restructuring.'

Cooke's particular substantive interest, and the focus of the CURS programme, is the uneven impact of economic restructuring during the 1980s and the extent to which local alliances – to adopt Harvey's (1985) term: Cooke (see above, p. 65) does not use it nor refer to that important theoretical work – have been able to counter it by promoting new employment opportunities. This is the explicit focus of another book emanating from the same programme: Harlow, Pickvance and Urry (1990). Their conclusions are usefully contrasted with Bennett's (1990b). In his summaries of the seven case studies, Cooke refers to their particular features, such as 'A capacity for mobilizing local loyalty and political influence' in Middlesbrough (p. 41) and the 'Conservatism typical of its resort tradition' in Morecambe (p. 40), but he makes no attempt to suggest the salient elements that should be studied in any locality study concerned with the general issue of local capacity in the context of economic, social and political restructuring at a wider scale (unlike that used in chapters 4 and 5). Moreover, he appears to downplay the importance of local cultural variation: 'local distinctiveness is nevertheless confronted with powerful structural forces which can exert, at the most general level, markedly homogenizing effects' (p. 31). (Signs of reification of place here?)

Harvey (1989c) has illustrated the use of empirical studies by Marx and by himself to draw out the necessary relationships within a mode of production, and thereby to isolate those aspects of society which are contingent. Cooke, the CURS teams, and other researchers into 'localities' tend not to follow this realist view, unlike a Sussex-based team working on variations in local state housing policy (Dickens et al., 1985: see also Foord and Gregson, 1986, who have undertaken a similar task with regard to the 'necessity' of gender relations). Dickens (1990, p. 176) has recently developed this approach, with regard to the necessity of the nuclear family as a basic social unit, for example (see also p. 81 above). Most of the subject matter of the present book would be characterized by him as contingent, however, but the jury is still out on some. With regard to territoriality, for example, he refers to it (and aggression) as:

latent instincts and drives. These . . . must indeed form an important part of our understanding of individual and social behaviour. (p. 178)

Like Sack (see p. 188), however, he does not assume that these instincts and drives are biologically given rather than socially created, and concludes that even if they are 'innate drives . . . they cannot explain such diverse behaviours as "football hooliganism", domestic violence or an inner city uprising. Such concrete events must be combinations of inbred attributes and "manmade" social relations'. So if those social variations are contingent and vary between places then the realization of necessary relationships will similarly vary. If not everything is necessary, then contingency on one variable alone could be sufficient to generate spatial diversity, whatever the strong homogenizing forces that Cooke (1989a), Peet (1989) and others identify.

The goal of this book has been to identify what the major contingent features are, so as to provide a framework for the study of the interactions among necessary relations and local conditions. Chapters 3–5 in particular have focused on that goal. The case studies referred to there are few and limited to the United Kingdom and the United States, but they are used in a constructive way, unlike the work of the CURS programme referred to here, to try and advance the methodology for studying the local. Undoubtedly more studies will at least refine the framework, and perhaps even replace it, as the ideas are tried in other contexts. As they stand, however, the materials presented here offer more to the reconstruction of geography than a host of case studies presented in an empiricist way.

FORWARD?

Geography, like many other disciplines within academia, is becoming increasingly fragmented among specialists who have little contact with each other and who make little use of each other's work. Such fragmentation hinders the full advance of knowledge, because it creates parts without wholes, disciplines without cores. The case for geography developed here is that we must recognize the need to study wholes – places that are milieux (some with clearly defined boundaries, others without) within which ways of life are constructed and reconstructed and within which individuals are socialized into an appreciation of who they are and what is expected of them. Without promoting the study of those milieux in their full diversity, we will not advance understanding of the rich mosaic that is, and always will be, the world that we live in. This book is presented as a small contribution to that promotional goal, suggesting some of the salient features in the study of 'regions in geography' (while studiously avoiding the need for a 'new regional geography'). But it is only a beginning . . .

9

A Short Guide to Further Reading

The recent history of geography has been set out in a number of recent books. Most deal with part of the discipline only, however. For a partial coverage of the whole, see

Holt-Jensen, A. (1988) *Geography: Its History and Concepts* (second edition) Harper and Row, London.

On physical geography see

Gregory, K. J. (1985) *The Nature of Physical Geography* Edward Arnold, London.

And for human geography

Johnston, R. J. (1991) *Geography and Geographers: Anglo-American Human Geography since 1945* (fourth edition) Edward Arnold, London.

An encyclopaedic coverage of the main terms in the literature is given in

Johnston, R. J., Gregory, D. and Smith, D. M. (eds) (1986) *The Dictionary of Human Geography* (second edition) Blackwell Reference, Oxford.

and

Goudie, A. S., Atkinson, B. W., Gregory, K. J., Simmons, I. G., Stoddart, D. R. and Sugden, D. E. (eds) (1985) *The Encyclopaedic Dictionary of Physical Geography* Blackwell Reference, Oxford.

The most recent survey of the discipline's philosophies and methodologies is

Bird, J. (1989) *The Changing Worlds of Geography* The Clarendon Press, Oxford.

Perhaps the best way of appreciating the fragmentation of human geography is to scan the 35 separate specialist chapters in

Gaile, G. J. and Willmott, C. J. (eds) (1989) *Geography in America* Merrill Publishing Company, Columbus.

For reviews of regional geography past, present and (potentially) future, see the essays in

Johnston, R. J., Hauer, J. and Hoekveld, G. A. (eds) (1990) *Regional Geography: Current Developments and Future Prospects* Routledge, London.

Several recent volumes reviewing recent developments in the discipline and suggesting future research and teaching agenda include

Clark, M. J., Gregory, K. J. and Gurnell, A. M. (eds) (1988) *Horizons in Physical Geography* Macmillan, London.
Gregory, D. and Walford, R. (eds) (1989) *Horizons in Human Geography* Macmillan, London.
Wolch, J. and Dear, M. J. (eds) (1989) *The Power of Geography* Unwin Hyman, Boston.
Peet, J. R. and Thrift, N. J., (eds) (1989) *New Models in Geography* (two volumes) Unwin Hyman, London.
Macmillan, B. (ed) (1989) *Remodelling Geography* Basil Blackwell, Oxford.
Kobayashi, A. and Mackenzie, S. (eds) (1989) *Remaking Human Geography* Unwin Hyman, Boston.

The seminal volume introducing the approach to the study of place adopted here is

Massey, D. (1984) *Spatial Divisions of Labour* Macmillan, London.

Other important volumes on the same general theme include

Agnew, J. A. (1987) *Place and Politics: The Georgaphical Mediation of State and Society* Allen and Unwin, London.
Agnew, J. A. and Duncan, J. S. (eds) (1989) *The Power of Place: Bringing Together Geographical and Sociological Imaginations* Unwin Hyman, Boston.
Entrikin, J. N. (1991) *The Betweenness of Place: Towards a Geography of Modernity* Macmillan, London.

10

Bibliography

Abler, R. F. (1987) What shall we say? To whom shall we speak? *Annals of the Association of American Geographers* 77, 511–24.

Abler, R. F., Adams, J. S. and Gould, P. R. (1971) *Spatial Organization: The Geographer's View of the World.* Prentice-Hall, Englewood Cliffs.

Abrahamson, M. and Carter, V. J. (1986) Tolerance, urbanism and region. *American Sociological Review* 51, 287–94.

Adeney, M. and Lloyd, J. (1986) *The Miners' Strike 1984–5: Loss without Limit.* Routledge and Kegan Paul, London.

Agnew, J. A. (1987a) *Place and Politics: The Geographical Mediation of State and Society.* Allen and Unwin, Boston.

Agnew, J. A. (1987b) *The United States in the World-Economy.* Cambridge University Press, Cambridge.

Agnew, J. A. (1989) The devaluation of place in social science, in J Agnew and J S Duncan (eds) *The Power of Place.* Unwin Hyman, Boston, 9–29.

Agnew, J. A. and Duncan, J. S. (eds) (1989) *The Power of Place: Bringing Together Geographical and Sociological Imaginations.* Unwin Hyman, Boston.

Alford, R. R. (1963) *Party and Society.* Rand McNally, Chicago.

Alford, R. R. and Friedland, R. (1985) *Powers of Theory: Capitalism, the State, and Democracy* Cambridge University Press, Cambridge.

Allen, J. (1984) Introduction: Synthesis: interdependence and the uniqueness of place, in D. Massey and J. Allen (eds) *Geography Matters!.* Cambridge University Press, Cambridge, 107–11.

Allen, J. and Massey, D. (eds) (1988) *The Economy in Question.* Sage Publications, London.

Almond, G. (1988) Separate tables: schools and sects in political science. *P S: Political Science and Politics* 21, 828–41.

Anderson, J. (1986) Nationalism and geography, in J. Anderson (ed) *The Rise of the Modern State.* Harvester Press, Brighton, 115–42.

Anderson, J. and Cochrane, A. D. (eds) (1989) *A State of Crisis: The Changing Face of British Politics.* Hodder and Stoughton, London.

Anderson, J. Duncan, S. S. and Hudson, R. (eds) (1983) *Redundant Spaces in Cities and Regions.* Academic Press, London.

Appleton, J. (1975) *The Experience of Landscape.* John Wiley, Chichester.

Archer, J. C. (1983) The geography of federal fiscal politics in the United States of America: an exploration. *Environment and Planning D: Government and Policy* 1, 377–400.

Archer, J. C. and Taylor, P. J. (1981) *Section and Party.* John Wiley, Chichester.

Ardrey, R. (1969) *The Territorial Imperative.* Fontana, London.

Bacon, C. (1986) Coalmining and the housing question in Britain, 1901–39. (unpublished paper).

Baker, A. R. H. and Butlin, R. A. (1973) Conclusions: problems and perspectives, in A. R. H. Baker and R. A. Butlin (eds) *Studies of Field Systems in the British Isles.* Cambridge University Press, Cambridge, 619–56.

Ball, M., Gray, F. and McDowell, L. (1989) *The Transformation of Britain: Contemporary Social and Economic Change.* Fontana, London.

Barnsley WAPC (1984) *Women Against Pit Closures.* Barnsley Women Against Pit Closures, Barnsley.

Bassett, K. (1990) Labour in the Sunbelt. *Political Geography Quarterly,* 9, 67–84.

Beauregard, R. A. (1988) In the absence of practice: the locality research debate. *Antipode* 20, 52–9.

Becher, T. (1989) *Academic Tribes and Territories.* Open University Press, Milton Keynes.

Beckett, J. V. (1988) *The East Midlands from AD1000.* Longman, London.

Bennett, R. J. (1989) Whither models and geography in a post-welfarist world?, in B. Macmillan, editor, *Remodelling Geography.* Basil Blackwell, Oxford, 273–90.

Bennett, R. J. (1990a) Decentralization, intergovernmental relations and markets: towards a post-welfare agenda?, in R. J. Bennett (ed) *Decentralization, Local Governments and Markets: Towards a Post-Welfare Agenda.* The Clarendon Press, Oxford, 1–28.

Bennett, R. J. (1990b) Decentralization and local economic development, in R. J. Bennett (ed) *Decentralization, Local Governments and Markets: Towards a Post-Welfare Agenda.* The Clarendon Press, Oxford, 221–44.

Bennett, R. J. and Thornes, J. B. (1988) Geography in the United Kingdom, 1984–1988. *The Geographical Journal* 154, 23–48.

Bensel, R. F. (1984) *Sectionalism and American Political Development, 1880–1980.* University of Wisconsin Press, Madison.

Berry, B. J. L. (1964) Approaches to regional analysis: a synthesis. *Annals of the Association of American Geographers* 54, 2–11.

Beynon, H. (ed) (1985) *Digging Deeper.* Verso, London.

Bhaskar, R. (1975) *A Realist Theory of Science.* Harvester Press, Brighton.

Bhaskar, R. (1979) *The Possibility of Naturalism.* Harvester Press, Brighton.

Bird, J. (1989) *The Changing Worlds of Geography.* The Clarendon Press, Oxford.

Blaikie, P. M. and Brookfield, H. C. (1987) Questions from history in the Mediterranean and western Europe, in P. M. Blaikie and H. C. Brookfield (eds) *Land Degradation and Society.* Methuen, London, 122–42.

Blauner, R. (1960) Work satisfaction and industrial trends in modern society, in W. Galenson and S. M. Lipset (eds) *Labor and Trade Unionism.* John Wiley, New York, 337–60.

Blomley, N. (1990) Federalism, place and the regulation of worker safety. *Economic Geography* 66, 22–46.

Bloomfield, B. (1986) Women's support group at Maerdy, in R. Samuel, B. Bloomfield and G. Boanas (eds) *The Enemy Within: Pit Villages and the Miners' Strike of 1984–5*. Routledge and Kegan Paul, London, 154–65.

Bodman, A. R. (1991) Weavers of influence: the structure of contemporary geographical research. *Transactions, Institute of British Geographers* NS16, 21–37.

Boorstin, D. J. (1965) *The Americans: The National Experience*. Cardinal Books, New York.

Bourne, L. S. (1989) On writing and publishing in human geography: some personal reflections, in M. S. Kenzer (ed) *On Becoming a Professional Geographer*. Merrill Publishing Company, Columbus, 100–12.

Brookfield, H. C. and Brown, P. (1963) *Struggle for Land*. Oxford University Press, Melbourne.

Brustein, W. (1988) *The Social Origins of Political Regionalism: France, 1849–1981*. University of California Press, Berkeley.

Bulmer, M. I. A. (1975) Sociological models of the mining community. *Sociological Review* 25, 61–92.

Bulmer, M. I. A. (1978) The character of local politics, in M. I. A. Bulmer (ed) *Mining and Social Change*. Croom Helm, London, 128–42.

Bunge, W. (1973) Ethics and logic in geography, in R. J. Chorley (ed) *Directions in Geography*. Methuen, London, 275–95.

Butler, D. R. (1989) Conducting research and writing an article in physical geography, in M. S. Kenzer (ed) *On Becoming a Professional Geographer*. Merrill Publishing Company, Columbus, 88–99.

Butzer, K. E. (1989) Cultural ecology, in G. L. Gaile and C. J. Willmott (eds) *Geography in America*. Merrill Publishing Company, Columbus, 192–208.

Champion, A. G. and Townsend, A. R. (1990) *Contemporary Britain: A Geographic Perspective*. Edward Arnold, London.

Chaplin, S. (1978) Durham mining villages, in M. I. A. Bulmer (ed) *Mining and Social Change*. Croom Helm, London, 59–82.

Cherow-O'Leary, R. (1987) *The State by State Guide to Women's Legal Rights*. McGraw Hill, New York.

Clark, A. H. (1949) *The Settlement of New Zealand by People, Plants and Animals*. Rutgers University Press, New Brunswick, NJ.

Clark, A. H. (1954) Historical geography, in P. E. James and C. F. Jones (eds) *American Geography: Inventory and Prospect*. Syracuse University Press, Syracuse, 71–105.

Clark, A. H. (1959) *Three Centuries and the Island*. University of Toronto Press, Toronto.

Clark, G. L. (1985) *Judges and the Cities*. University of Chicago Press, Chicago.

Clark, G. L. (1988) *Unions and Communities under Siege*. Cambridge University Press, Cambridge.

Clark, G. L. and Dear, M. J. (1984) *State Apparatus*. George Allen and Unwin, Boston.

Cliff, A. D. and Haggett, P. (1989) Spatial aspects of epidemic control. *Progress in Human Geography* 13, 315–47.

Cochrane, A. (1987) What a difference the place makes: the new structuralism of locality. *Antipode* 19, 354–63.

Cochrane, A. and Anderson, J. (eds) (1989) *Politics in Transition*. Sage Publications, London.

Collison, P. (1963) *The Cutteslowe Walls*. Faber and Faber, London.

Cooke, P. N. (1986) The changing urban and regional system of the United Kingdom. *Regional Studies* 20, 243–52.

Cooke, P. N. (1987) Clinical inference and geographic theory. *Antipode* 19, 69–78.

Cooke, P. N. (1989a) Locality, economic restructuring, and world development, in P. N. Cooke (ed) *Localities: The Changing Face of Urban Britain*. Unwin Hyman, London, 1–44.

Cooke, P. N. (1989b) Locality theory and the poverty of 'spatial variation' (a reply to Duncan and Savage). *Antipode* 21, 261–73.

Cooke, P. N. (1990) *Back to the Future*. Unwin Hyman, London.

Cosgrove, D. E. and Jackson, P. (1987) New directions in cultural geography. *Area* 19, 95–101.

Cowart, A. T. (1969) Anti-poverty expenditures in the American States: a comparative analysis. *Midwest Journal of Political Science* 13, 219–36.

Cox, K. R. (1970) Geography, social contexts, and voting behavior in Wales, 1961–1951, in E. Allardt and S. Rokkan (eds) *Mass Politics*. The Free Press, New York, 117–59.

Cox, K. R. (1989) The politics of turf and the question of class, in J. Wolch and M. Dear (eds) *The Power of Geography: How Territory Shapes Social Life*. Unwin Hyman, Boston, 61–90.

Crewe, I. (1986) On the death and resurrection of class voting. *Political Studies* 34, 620–38.

Crewe, I. (1989) Values; the crusade that failed, in D. Kavanagh and A. Seldon (eds) *The Thatcher Effect: A Decade of Change*. Clarendon Press, Oxford, 239–50.

Crick, M. (1985) *Scargill and the Miners*. Penguin, London.

Crocombe, R. G. (1972) Land tenure in the South Pacific, in R. G. Ward (ed) *Man in the Pacific Islands*. The Clarendon Press, Oxford, 219–51.

Crouch, C. and Marquand, D. (eds) (1988) *The New Centralism*. Basil Blackwell, Oxford.

Curtice, J. K. and Steed, M. (1988) Appendix 2 Analysis, in D. Butler and D. Kavanagh, *The British General Election of 1987*. Macmillan, London, 316–62.

Dahl, R. A. (1978) Democracy as polyarchy, in R. D. Gastil (ed) *Freedom in the World: Political Rights and Civil Liberties 1978*. G. K. Hall, Boston, 134–46.

Dahl, R. A. (1971) *Polyarchy: Participation and Opposition*. Yale University Press, New Haven, CT.

Danielsen, M. N. (1976) *The Politics of Exclusion*. Columbia University Press, New York.

Darby, H. C. (1962) The problem of geographical description. *Transactions, Institute of British Geographers* 30, 1–14.

Darby, H. C. (1968) *The Draining of the Fens* (third edition). Cambridge University Press, Cambridge.

Darby, H. C. (ed) (1973) *A New Historical Geography of England*. Cambridge University Press, Cambridge.

Dear, M. (1988) The postmodern challenge: reconstructing human geography. *Transactions, Institute of British Geographers* NS13, 262–74.

Derivery, D. and Dogan, M. (1986) Religion, classe et politique en France. *Revue Française de Science Politique* 35, 157–81.

Dickens, P. (1988) *One Nation? Social Change and the Politics of Locality*. Pluto Press, London.

Dickens, P. (1990) *Urban Sociology: Society, Locality and Human Nature*. Harvester Wheatsheaf, Hemel Hempstead.

Dickens, P., Duncan, S. S., Goodwin, M. and Gray, F. (1985) *Housing, States and Localities*. Methuen, London.

Dogan, M. (1969) A covariance analysis of French electoral data, in M. Dogan and S. Rokkan (eds) *Quantitative Ecological Analysis in the Social Sciences*. The M.I.T. Press, Cambridge, MA 285–98.

Downs, A. (1957) *An Economic Theory of Democracy*. Harper and Row, New York.

Downs, A. (1973) *Opening Up the Suburbs*. Yale University Press, New Haven.

Duncan, J. S. (1980) The superorganic in American cultural geography. *Annals of the Association of American Geographers* 70, 181–98.

Duncan, J. S. and Ley, D. F. (1982) Structural marxism and human geography: a critical assessment. *Annals of the Association of American Geographers* 72, 30–59.

Duncan, S. S. (1989) What is a locality? in R. Peet and N. J. Thrift (eds), *New Models in Geography: Volume Two*. Unwin Hyman, London, 221–54.

Duncan, S. S. and Goodwin, M. (1988) *Uneven Development and the Local State*. Polity Press, Cambridge.

Duncan, S. S. and Savage, M. (1989) Space, scale and locality. *Antipode* 21, 179–206.

Dunleavy, P., Gamble, A. M. and Peele, G. (eds) (1990) *Developments in British Politics 3*. Macmillan, London.

Dunleavy, P. and O'Leary, B. (1987) *Theories of the State*. Macmillan, London.

Eckstein, H. (1989) A comment on positive theory. *P S: Political Science and Politics* 22, 77.

Elazar, D. J. (1962) *The American Partnership*. University of Chicago Press, Chicago.

Elazar, D. J. (1970) *Cities of the Prairie*. Basic Books, New York.

Elazar D. J. (1984) *American Federalism: A View from the States* (third edition). Harper and Row, New York.

Elazar, D. J. and Zikmund, J. (eds) (1975) *The Ecology of American Political Culture: Readings*. Crowell, New York.

Eliot Hurst, M. E. (1985) Geography has neither existence or future, in R. J.

Johnston (ed) *The Future of Geography*. Methuen, London, 59–91.

Entrikin, J. N. (1991) *The Betweenness of Place: Toward a Geography of Modernity*. Macmillan, London.

Eyre, S. R. and Jones, G. R. J. (eds) (1966) *Geography as Human Ecology*, Edward Arnold, London.

Fenton, J. H. and Chamberlayne, D. W. (1969) The literature dealing with the relationships between political processes, socioeconomic conditions and public policies in the American states: a bibliographical essay. *Polity* 1, 388–404.

Ferejohn, J. A. (1974) *Pork Barrel Politics*. Standford University Press, Stanford.

Fincher, R. (1982) Urban redevelopment in Boston: rhetoric and reality, in K. R. Cox and R. J. Johnston (eds) *Conflict, Politics and the Urban Scene*. Longman, London, 220–40.

Findlay, A. M. and Graham, E. (1991) The challenge facing population geography. *Progress in Human Geography* 15, 149–62.

Fine, B. and Millar R. (eds) (1985) *Policing the Miners' Strike*. Lawrence and Wishart, London.

Fleming, J. Z. (1989) *City of Memphis v N.T.*: Before I built a wall I'd ask to know what I was walling in or walling out, and to whom I was like to give offense. *The Urban Lawyer* 21, 961–71.

Foord, J. and Gregson, N. (1986) Patriarchy: towards a reconceptualisation. *Antipode* 18, 186–211.

Forde, C. D. (1934) *Habitat, Economy and Society*. Methuen, London.

Freeman, T. W. (1960) *Ireland*. Methuen, London.

Freeman, T. W. (1961) *A Hundred Years of Geography*. Duckworth, London.

Gaile, G. L. and Willmott, C. J. (eds) (1989) *Geography in America*. Merrill Publishing Company, Columbus.

Gamble, A. M. (1988) *The Free Economy and the Strong State*. Macmillan, London.

Gamble, A. M. (1989) Thatcherism and the new politics, in J. Mohan, (ed) *The Political Geography of Contemporary Britain*. Macmillan, London, 1–17.

Ganz, A. (1985) Where has the urban crisis gone? *Urban Affairs Quarterly* 20, 39–57.

Gastil R. D. (1981) *Freedom in the World: Political Rights and Civil Liberties 1981*. Clio Press, Oxford.

Gatrell, A. C. (1984) The geometry of a research specialty: spatial diffusion modelling. *Annals of the Association of American Geographers* 74, 437–53.

Gatrell, A. C. and Smith, A. (1984) Networks of relations among a set of geographical journals. *The Professional Geographer* 36, 300–6.

Geertz, C. (1973) *The Interpretation of Cultures*. Basic Books, New York.

Gibbon, P. (1988) Analysing the British miners' strike of 1984–5. *Economy and Society* 18, 139–94.

Gibbons, M. T. (1990) Political science, disciplinary history and theoretical pluralism: a response to Almond and Eckstein. *P S: Political Science and Politics* 23, 44–6.

Giblin, B. (1984) Strategies politiques dans le bassin houiller du Nord de France. *Herodote* 33–4, 174–98.

Giddens, A. (1984) *The Constitution of Society*. Polity Press, Cambridge.

Giddens, A. (1985) *The Nation-State and Violence*. Polity Press, Cambridge.

Giddens, A. (1990) Structuration theory and sociological analysis, in J. Clark, C. Modgil and S. Modgil (eds) *Anthony Giddens: Consensus and Controversy*. The Falmer Press, London, 297–316.

Gilbert, A. (1988) The new regional geography in English- and French-speaking countries. *Progress in Human Geography* 12, 208–28.

Gilbert, D. (1988) Tradition and community: mining communities in South Wales and Nottinghamshire, in M. Heffernan and P. Gruffud (eds) *A Land Fit for Heroes: Essays in the Human Geography of Inter-War Britain*. Loughborough University, Department of Geography, Occasional Paper 14, Loughborough, 37–56.

Goffer, R. E. (1977) Essays in oral history, the butty system and the Kent coalfield. *Society for the Study of Labour History Bulletin* 34, 41–51.

Goodchild, M. F. and Janelle, D. F. (1988) Specialization in the structure and organization of geography. *Annals of the Association of American Geographers* 78, 11–28.

Goodman, G. (1985) *The Miners' Strike*. Pluto, London.

Gould, P. R. (1963) Man against his environment: a game theoretic framework. *Annals of the Association of American Geographers* 53, 290–7.

Gould, P. R. (1979) Geography 1957–77: the Augean period. *Annals of the Association of American Geographers* 69, 139–51.

Gregory, D. (1978) *Ideology, Science and Human Geography*. Hutchinson, London.

Gregory, D. (1985) Suspended animation: the stasis of diffusion theory, in D. Gregory and J. Urry (eds) *Social Relations and Spatial Structures*. Macmillan, London, 296–336.

Gregory, D. (1989a) Areal differentiation and post-modern human geography, in D. Gregory and R. Walford (eds) *Horizons in Human Geography*. Macmillan, London, 67–96.

Gregory, D. (1989b) The crisis of modernity? Human geography and critical social theory, in R. Peet and N. J. Thrift (eds) *New Models in Geography: Volume Two*. Unwin Hyman, London, 348–85.

Gregson, N. (1986) On duality and dualism: the case of time geography and structuration. *Progress in Human Geography* 10, 184–205.

Gregson, N. (1987a) Structuration theory: some thoughts on the possibilities for empirical research. *Environment and Planning D: Society and Space* 5, 73–91.

Gregson, N. (1987b) The CURS initiative: some further comments. *Antipode* 19, 364–370.

Griffin, A. R. (1962) *The Miners of Nottinghamshire 1914–1944: A History of the Nottinghamshire Miners' Unions*. George Allen and Unwin, London.

Griffin, A. R. (1971) *Coalmining*. Longman, London.

Griffin, A. R. (1977) *The British Coalmining Industry: Retrospect and Prospect*. Moorland Publishing, Buxton.

Griffin, A. R. and Griffin, C. P. (1977) The non-political trade union movement, in A. Briggs and J. Saville (eds) *Essays in Labour History, Volume 3*. Macmillan, London, 133–62.

Griffin, C. (1984) *Nottinhamshire Miners between the Wars: The Spencer Union Revisited*. Centre for Local History, University of Nottingham, Nottingham.

Griffiths, M. J. and Johnston, R. J. (1991) What's in a place? An approach to the concept of place, as illustrated by the British National Union of Mineworkers' strike, 1984–1985. *Antipode*, 23, 185–213.

Gudgin, G. and Taylor, P. J. (1979) *The Spatial Organization of Elections*. Pion, London.

Habermas, J. (1972) *Legitimation Crisis*. Heinemann, London.

Haggett, P. (1990) *The Geographer's Art*. Basil Blackwell, Oxford.

Hall, P. (1988) The intellectual history of long waves, in M. Young and T. Schuller (eds) *The Rhythms of Society*. Routledge, London, 37–52.

Hamnett, C. (1983) Regional variations in house prices and house price inflation, 1969–1981. *Area* 15, 97–109.

Hamnett, C. (1989) Regional variations in house prices and house price inflation in Britain, 1969–88. *The Royal Bank of Scotland Review* 159, 29–40.

Hamnett, C., McDowell, L. and Sarre, P. (eds) (1989) *The Changing Social Structure*. Sage Publications, London.

Harloe, M., Pickvance, C. and Urry, J. (eds) (1990) *Place, Policy and Politics: Do Localities Matter?*. Unwin Hyman, London.

Harrop, M. L. and Miller, W. L. (1987) *Elections and Voters*. Macmillan, London.

Hart, J. F. (1982) The highest form of the geographer's art. *Annals of the Association of American Geographers* 72, 1–29.

Hartshorne, R. (1939) *The Nature of Geography*. Association of American Geographers, Lancaster PA.

Harvey, D. (1975) Class structure in a capitalist society and the theory of residential differentiation, in R. F. Peel, M. Chisholm and P. Haggett (eds) *Processes In Physical and Human Geography: Bristol Essays*. Heinemann, London, 354–69.

Harvey, D. (1978) The urban process under capitalism: a framework for analysis. *International Journal of Urban and Regional Research* 2, 10–132.

Harvey, D. (1982) *The Limits to Capital*. Basil Blackwell, Oxford.

Harvey, D. (1985a) *Consciousness and the Urban Experience*. Basil Blackwell, Oxford.

Harvey, D. (1985b) The geopolitics of capitalism, in D. Gregory and J. Urry (eds) *Social Relations and Spatial Structures*. Macmillan, London, 128–63.

Harvey, D. (1989a) From managerialism to entrepreneurism: the transformation of urban governance in late capitalism. *Geografiska Annaler* 71B, 3–17.

Harvey, D. (1989b) *The Condition of Postmodernity*. Basil Blackwell, Oxford.

Harvey, D. (1989c) From models to Marx: notes on the project to 'remodel' contemporary geography, in B. Macmillan (ed) *Remodelling Geography*. Basil Blackwell, Oxford, 211–6.

Harvey, D. (1990) Between space and time: reflections on the geographical imagination. *Annals of the Association of American Geographers* 80, 418–34.

Hay, A. M. (1985a) Why we need postgraduate thesis research. *Environment and Planning A* 17, 1291–2.

Hay, A. M. (1985b) Some differences in citation between articles based on thesis work and those written by established researchers: human geography in the UK 1974–84. *Social Science Information Studies* 5, 81–5.

Hayek, F A (1944) *The Road to Serfdom*. University of Chicago Press, Chicago.

Hechter, M. and Brustein, W. (1980) Regional modes of production and patterns of state formation in western Europe. *American Journal of Sociology* 85, 1061–94.

Hirschmann, A. O. (1970) *Exit, Voice and Loyalty*. Harvard University Press, Cambridge MA.

Hobbes, T. (1651) *Leviathan*. (Republished 1968 by Penguin, London)

Hogan, R. (1985) The frontier as social control. *Theory and Society* 14, 35–51.

Holcomb, H. B., Kodras, J. E. and Brunn, S. D. (1990) Women's issues and state legislation: fragmentation and inconsistency, in J. E. Kodras and J. P. Jones III (eds) *Geographic Dimensions of United States Social Policy*. Edward Arnold, London, 178–99.

Holt, R. R. and Silverstein, B. (1989) On the psychology of enemy images: introduction and overview. *Journal of Social Issues* 45, 1–11.

Hudson, R. and Williams A. M. (1989) *Divided Britain*. Belhaven Press, London.

Hutcheson, J. and Taylor, G. (1973) Religious variables, political system characteristics, and policy outputs in the American states. *American Journal of Political Science* 17, 414–21.

Jackson, P. (1989) *Maps of Meaning: An Introduction to Cultural Geography*. Unwin Hyman, London.

James, P. E. (1942) *Latin America*. Cassell, London.

James, P. E. and Martin, G. J. (1979) *The Association of American Geographers: The First Seventy-Five Years*. Association of American Geographers, Washington DC.

Jessop, B., Bonnett, K., Bromley, S. and Ling, T. (1988) *Thatcherism: A Tale of Two Nations*. Polity Press, Cambridge.

Johnson, C. A. (1976) Political culture in American States: Elazar's formulation examined. *American Journal of Political Science* 20, 491–509.

Johnston, R. J. (1979) The spatial impact of fiscal changes in Britain: regional policy in reverse? *Environment and Planning A* 11, 1439–44.

Johnston, R. J. (1980) *The Geography of Federal Spending in the United States of America*. John Wiley, Chichester.

Johnston, R. J. (1981) The political element in suburbia: a key influence on the urban geography of the United States. *Geography* 66, 286–96.

Johnston, R. J. (1983a) Resource analysis, resource management and the integration of physical and human geography. *Progress in Physical Geography* 7, 127–46.

Johnston, R. J. (1983b) Politics and the geography of social well-being, in M. A. Busteed (ed) *Developments in Political Geography*. Academic Press, London, 189–250.

Johnston, R. J. (1984a) The region in twentieth century British geography. *History of Geography Newsletter* 4, 26–35.

Johnston, R. J. (1984b) A foundling floundering in World Three, in M. Billinge, D. Gregory and R. L. Martin (eds) *Recollections of a Revolution*. Macmillan, London, 39–56.

Johnston, R. J. (1984c) *Residential Segregation, the State and Constitutional Conflict in American Urban Areas*. Academic Press, London.

Johnston, R. J. (1984d) The political geography of electoral geography, in P. J. Taylor and J. W. House (eds) *Political Geography: Recent Advances and Future Directions*. Croom Helm, London, 133–48.

Johnston, R. J. (1985a) To the ends of the earth, in R. J. Johnston (ed) *The Future of Geography*, Methuen, London, 326–38.

Johnston, R. J. (1985b) Places matter. *Irish Geography* 18, 58–63.

Johnston, R. J. (1986a) The neighbourhood effect revisited: spatial science or political regionalism. *Environment and Planning D: Society and Space* 4, 41–56.

Johnston, R. J. (1986b) A space for place (or a place for space) in British psephology. *Environment and Planning A* 19, 599–618.

Johnston, R. J. (1986c) *On Human Geography*. Basil Blackwell, Oxford.

Johnston, R. J. (1986d) Four fixations and the unity of geography. *Transactions, Institute of British Geographers* NS11, 449–53.

Johnston, R. J. (1987) A note on housing tenure and voting in Britain, 1983. *Housing Studies* 2, 112–21.

Johnston, R. J. (1988a) Living in America, in P. L. Knox, E. H. Bartels, J. C. Bohland, B. Holcomb, and R. J. Johnston *The United States; A Contemporary Human Geopgraphy*. Longman, London, 237–259.

Johnston, R. J. (1988b) Theory and methodology in social geography, in M. Pacione (ed) *Progress in Social Geography*. Routledge, London, 1–30.

Johnston, R. J. (1988c) The political organization of US space, in P. L. Knox, E. H. Bartels, J. C. Bohland, B. Holcomb, and R. J. Johnston *The United States; A Contemporary Human Geography*. Longman, London, 81–109.

Johnston, R. J. (1989a) What's in a place? Some reflections on some recent trends in human geography, in L.-E. Borgegard (ed) *Samhallsplaneringens Informationsforsorjning*. Statens Institut for Byggnadsforskning, Gavle, Sweden, 31–46.

Johnston, R. J. (1989b) Spatial sciences: the ways forward? in L. H. van Wijngaard-en-Bakker and J. J. M. van der Meer (eds) *Spatial Sciences, Research in Progress*. *Nederlandse Geografische Studies* 80, 11–20.

Johnston, R. J. (1989c) *Environmental Problems: Nature, Economy and State*. Belhaven Press, London.

Johnston, R. J. (1989d) The individual and the world-economy, in R. J. Johnston and P. J. Taylor (eds) *A World in Crisis?* (second edition). Basil Blackwell, Oxford, 200–28.

Johnston, R. J. (1989e) Philosophy, ideology and geography, in D. Gregory and R. Walford (eds) *Horizons in Human Geography*. Macmillan, London, 48–67.

Johnston, R. J. (1989f) People and places in the behavioural environment, in F. W. Boal and D. N. Livingstone (eds) *The Behavioural Environment*. Routledge, London, 235–52.

Johnston, R. J. (1990a) The Institute, study groups and a discipline without a core? *Area* 22, 407–14.

Johnston, R. J. (1990b) The challenge for regional geography: some proposals for research frontiers, in R. J. Johnston, J. Hauer and G. A. Hoekveld (eds) *Regional Geography: Current Developments and Future Prospects*. Routledge, London, 122–39.

Johnston, R. J. (1990c) Lipset and Rokkan revisited: electoral cleavages, electoral geography and electoral strategy in Great Britain, in R. J. Johnston, F. M. Shelley and P. J. Taylor (eds) *Developments in Electoral Geography*. Routledge, London, 121–42.

Johnston, R. J. (1990d) Economic and social policy implementation and outputs: an exploration of two contrasting geographies, in J. E. Kodras and J. P. Jones III (eds) *Geographic Dimensions of United States Social Policy*. Edward Arnold, London, 37–58.

Johnston, R. J. (1990e) Local state, local government and local administration, in J. M. Simmie and R. King (eds) *The State in Action*. Belhaven Press, London.

Johnston, R. J. (1991a) Territoriality and the state, in G. B. Benko (ed) *Territory and the Social Sciences*. University of Ottawa Press, Ottawa.

Johnston, R. J. (1991b) The territoriality of law: an exploration. *Urban Geography* 12, 548–65.

Johnston, R. J. (1991c) *Geography and Geographers: Anglo-American Human Geography since 1945* (fourth edition). Edward Arnold, London.

Johnston, R. J. (1991d) A place for everything and everything in its place. *Transactions, Institute of British Geographers* NS16, 131–47.

Johnston, R. J., Allsopp, J. G., Baldwin, J. C. and Turner, H. (1990) *An Atlas of Bells*. Basil Blackwell, Oxford.

Johnston, R. J. and Gregory, S. (1984) The United Kingdom, in R. J. Johnston and P. Claval (eds) *Geography Since the Second World War: An International Survey*. Croom Helm, London, 107–31.

Johnston, R. J., Knight D. B. and Kofman, E. (1988) Nationalism, self-determination and the world political map: an introduction, in R. J. Johnston, D. B. Knight and E. Kofman (eds) *Nationalism, Self-Determination and Political Geography*. Croom Helm, London, 1–17.

Johnston, R. J. and Pattie, C. J. (1988) A nation dividing? *Parliamentary Affairs* 22, 37–57.

Johnston, R. J. and Pattie, C. J. (1990) The regional impact of Thatcherism: attitudes and votes in Great Britain in the 1980s. *Regional Studies* 24, 79–94.

Johnston, R. J., Pattie, C. J. and Allsopp, J. G. (1988) *A Nation Dividing?*. Longman, London.

Johnston, R. J., Russell, A. T. and Pattie C. J. (1991) Is Britain going green? *Journal of Rural Studies*.

Johnston, R. J., Shelley, F. M. and Taylor, P. J. (eds) (1990) *Developments in Electoral Geography*. Routledge, London.

Jonas, A. (1988) A new regional geography of localities? *Area* 20, 101–10.

Jones, J. P. III, (1990) Work, welfare and poverty among black, female-headed families, in J. E. Kodras and J. P. Jones III (eds) *Geographic Dimensions of United States Social Policy*. Edward Arnold, London, 200–17.

Jones, J. P. III and Kodras, J. E. (1986) The policy context of the welfare debate. *Environment and Planning A*, 18, 63–72.

Jones, N. (1986) *Strikes and the Media: Communication and Conflict*. Basil Blackwell, Oxford.

Judt, T. (1986) *Marxism and the French Left*. The Clarendon Press, Oxford.

Katznelson, I. (1982) *City Trenches*. University of Chicago Press, Chicago.

Kavanagh, D. and Seldon, A. (eds) (1989) *The Thatcher Effect: A Decade of Change*. The Clarendon Press, Oxford.

Kennedy, B. A. (1979) A naughty world. *Transactions, Institute of British Geographers* NS4, 550–8.

Kennedy, P. (1988) *The Rise and Fall of Great Nations*. Fontana, London.

Kenzer, M. (ed) (1989) *On Becoming a Professional Geographer*. Merrill Publishing Company, Columbus.

Kerr, C. and Siegel, A. (1954) The inter-industry propensity to strike: an international comparison, in A. Kornhauser et al. (eds) *Industrial Conflict*. McGraw Hill, New York, 189–212.

Key, V. O. (1949) *Southern Politics; In State and Nation*. A. A. Knopf, New York.

King, R. L. (1977) *Land Reform: A World Survey*. G. Bell and Sons, London.

Klingemann, H. -D. (1986) Ranking the graduate departments in the 1980s: towards objective political indicators. *PS* 19, 651–61.

Knight, D. B. (1988) Self-determination for indigenous peoples: the context for change, in R. J. Johnston, D. B. Knight and E. Kofman (eds) *Nationalism, Self-Determination and Political Geography*. Croom Helm, London, 117–34.

Knowles, K. G. J. C. (1952) *Strikes: A Study in Industrial Conflict*. Basil Blackwell, Oxford.

Kodras, J. E. (1986a) Labor market and policy constraints on the work disincentive effect of welfare. *Annals of the Association of American Geographers* 76, 228–46.

Kodras, J. E. (1986b) The spatial perspective in welfare analysis. *Cato* 6, 77–83.

Krieger, J. (1983) *Undermining Capitalism*. Princeton University Press, Princeton.

Lancelot, A. (1968) *L'Abstentionnisme Electoral en France*, A. Colin, Paris.

Laponce, J. A. (1980) Political science: an import-export analysis of journals and footnotes. *Political Studies* 28, 410–9.

Lee, D. and Evans, A. (1984) American geographers' rankings of American geography journals. *The Professional Geographer* 36, 292–9.

Lee, D. and Evans, A. (1985) Geographers' rankings of foreign geography and non-geography journals. *The Professional Geographer* 37, 396–402.

Leeds, A. (1984) cities and countryside in anthropology, in L. Rodwin (ed) *Cities of the Mind*. Plenum Press, New York, 291–312.

le Play, F. (1875) *L'organisation de la Famille*. Mame, Tours.

Lewis, J. and Townsend, A. R. (eds) (1989) *The North-South Divide*. Paul Chapman Publishing, London.

Lightman, G. (1990) *The Lightman Report*. Penguin, London.

Lijphart, A. (1977) *Democracy in Plural Societies*. Yale University Press, New Haven CT.

Lijphart, A. (1984) *Democracies: Patterns of Majoritarian and Consensus Government in Twenty-One Countries*. Yale University Press, New Haven CT.

Lijphart, A. (1989) Democratic political systems: types, cases, causes and consequences. *Journal of Theoretical Politics* 1, 33–48.

Lipset, S. M. and Rokkan, S. (1967) Cleavage structures, party systems and voter alignments, in S. M. Lipset and S. Rokkan, (eds) *Party Systems and Voter Alignments*. The Free Press, New York, 3–64.

McAllister, I. and Rose, R. (1984) *The Nationwide Competition for Votes*. Frances Pinter, London.

McDowell, L. (1989) Editorial – three years in (British) geography. *Area* 21, 34–5.

McDowell, L. and Massey, D. (1984) A woman's place? in D. Massey and J. Allen (eds) *Geography Matters!* Cambridge University Press, Cambridge, 128–47.

McDowell, L., Sarre, P. and Hamnett, C. (eds) (1989) *Divided Nation: Social and Cultural Change in Britain*. Hodder and Stoughton, London.

MacGregor, I. (1986) *The Enemies Within*. Fontana/Collins, London.

Magull, R. G. (1978) State and local antipoverty expenditures. *Public Finance Quarterly* 6, 287–343.

Mann, M. (1984) The autonomous power of the state: its origins, mechanisms and results. *European Journal of Sociology* 25, 185–213.

Marcus, M. G. (1988) New twists in the horns of an old dilemma. *Annals of the Association of American Geographers* 78, 540–2.

Markusen A. (1987) *Regions: The Economics and Politics of Territory*. Rowman and Littlefield, Totowa NJ.

Martin, R. L. (1989) The political economy of Britain's north-south divide, in J. Lewis and A. R. Townsend (eds) *The North–South Divide*. Paul Chapman Publishing, London, 20–60.

Massey, D. (1984a) *Spatial Divisions of Labour*. Macmillan, London.

Massey, D. (1984b) Geography matters! in D. Massey and J. Allen (eds) *Geography Matters!* Cambridge University Press, Cambridge, 1–11.

Massey, D. and Allen, J. (eds) (1988) *Uneven Re-development: Cities and Regions in Transition*. Hodder and Stoughton, London.

Massey, D. and Meegan, R. A. (1979) The geography of industrial reorganisation. *Progress in Planning* 10, 155–237.

Massey, D. and Meegan R. A. (1982) *The Anatomy of Job Loss*. Macmillan, London.

Mead, W. R. (1980) Regional geography, in E. H. Brown (ed) *Geography, Yesterday and Tomorrow*. Oxford University Press, Oxford, 292–302.

Monopolies and Mergers Commission (1983) *National Coal Board: A Report on the Efficiency and Costs in the Development, Production and Supply of Coal by the NCB*. HMSO, Cmd 8920, London.

Monroe, K., Almond, G., Gunnell, J., Shapiro, I., Graham, G., Berber, B., Shepsle, K. and Cropsey, J. (1990) The nature of contemporary political science: a roundtable discussion. *P S: Political Science and Politics* 23, 34–46.

Murphy, A. B. (1988) Evolving regionalism in linguistically divided Belgium, in R. J. Johnston, D. B. Knight and E. Kofman (eds) *Nationalism, Self-Determination and Political Geography*. Croom Helm, London, 135–50.

Murphy, A. B. (1990) Electoral geography and the ideology of place: the making of regions in Belgian electoral politics, in R. J. Johnston, F. M. Shelley and P. J. Taylor (eds) *Developments in Electoral Geography*. Routledge, London 227–41.

Murphy, T. P. (1971) *Science, Geopolitics and Federal Spending*. D. C. Heath, Lexington.

Nardulli, P. F. (1990) Political subcultures in the American States. *American Politics Quarterly* 18, 287–315.

Nayacakalou, R. R. (1961) The bifurcation and amalgamation of Fijian lineages over a period of fifty years. *The Fiji Society Transactions and Proceedings* 8, 122–33.

Newton, K. (1969) *The Sociology of British Communism*. Allen Lane, London.

North, J. and Spooner, D. J. (1982) The Yorkshire, Nottinghamshire and Derbyshire coalfield. *The Geographical Journal* 148, 22–37.

North Yorkshire WAPC (1985) *Strike 84–85*. North Yorkshire Women Against Pit Closures, Leeds.

O'Connor, J. (1973) *The Fiscal Crisis of the State*. St Martin's Press, New York.

Olson, M. (1982) *The Rise and Decline of Nations*. Yale University Press, New Haven.

Openshaw, S. (1989) Computer modelling in human geography, in B. Macmillan (ed) *Remodelling Geography*. Basil Blackwell, Oxford, 273–90.

Paasi, A. (1986) The institutionalization of regions: a theoretical framework for understanding the emergence of regions and the constitution of regional identity. *Fennia* 164, 105–46.

Palm, R. (1986) Coming home. *Annals of the Association of American Geographers* 76, 469–79.

Paterson, J. H. (1974) Writing regional geography, in C. Board et al. (eds) *Progress in Geography*, Edward Arnold, London, 1–26.

Paterson, J. H. (1984) *North America*. Oxford University Press, Oxford.

Pattie, C. J. and Johnston, R. J. (1990) One nation or two? The changing geography of unemployment in Great Britain, 1983–1988. *The Professional Geographer* 42, 288–98.

Pattison, W. D. (1964) The four traditions of geography. *Journal of Geography* 63, 211–6.

Peet, J. R. (1983) Relations of production and the relocation of US manufacturing industry since 1960. *Economic Geography* 59, 112–43.

Peet, R. (1989) World capitalism and the destruction of regional cultures, in R. J.

Johnston and P. J. Taylor (eds) *A World in Crisis?* (second edition). Basil Blackwell, Oxford, 175–99.

People of Thurcroft (1986) *A Village and the Miners' Strike.* Spokesman Books, Nottingham.

Phillips, A. W. (1958) The relation between unemployment and rate of change of money wage rate in the U.K., 1861–1957. *Economica* 25, 283–99.

Plotkin, S. (1987) *Keep Out: The Struggle for Land Use Control.* University of California Press, Berkeley.

Postan, M. M. (1966) Medieval agrarian society in its prime, in M. M. Postan (ed) *The Cambridge Economic History of Europe: I The Agrarian Life of the Middle Ages* (second edition). Cambridge University Press, Cambridge, 548–632.

Pred, A. R. (1984) Place as historically contingent process. *Annals of the Association of American Geographers* 74, 279–97.

Prince, H. C. (1971) Real, imagined and abstract worlds of the past, in C. Board et al. (eds) *Progress in Geography 3.* Edward Arnold, London, 1–86.

Przeworski, A. and Sprague, J. (1986) *Paper Stones: A History of Electoral Socialism.* University of Chicago Press, Chicago.

Pudup, M.-B. (1988) Arguments within regional geography. *Progress in Human Geography* 12, 369–90.

Ranney, A. (1971) Parties in state politics, in H. Jacobs and K. N. Vines (eds) *Politics and the American States* (second edition). Little, Brown and Co, Boston, 82–121.

Rees, G. (1985) Regional restructuring, class change and political action. *Environment and Planning D: Society and Space* 3, 389–406.

Rees, G. (1986) 'Coalfield culture' and the 1984–1985 miners' strike: a reply to Sunley. *Environment and Planning D: Society and Space* 4, 469–76.

Relph, E. (1976) *Place and Placelessness.* Pion, London.

Rhind, D. W. (1989) Computing, academic geography and the world outside, in B. Macmillan (ed) *Remodelling Geography.* Basil Blackwell, Oxford, 177–90.

Roberts, B. C. (1989) Trade unions, in D. Kavanagh and A. Seldon, (eds) *The Thatcher Effect: A Decade of Change.* Clarendon Press, Oxford, 64–79.

Robson, B. T. (1982) The Bodley Barricade: social space and social conflict, in K. R. Cox and R. J. Johnston (eds) *Conflict, Politics and the Urban Scene.* Longman, London, 45–61.

Rose, D. (1987) Home ownership, subsistence and historical change: the mining district of West Cornwall in the late nineteenth century, in N. J. Thrift and P. Williams (eds) *Class and Space: The Making of Urban Society.* Routledge, London, 108–53.

Rose, R. (ed) (1974) *Electoral Behavior.* The Free Press, New York.

Rose, R. and Urwin, D. (1975) *Regional Differentiation and Political Unity in Western Nations.* Sage Publications, Beverly Hills.

Rowntree, L. B., Foote, K. E. and Domosh, M. (1989) Cultural geography, in G. L. Gaile and C. J. Willmott, (eds) *Geography in America.* Merrill Publishing Company, Columbus, 209–17.

Rundquist, B. S. (1980) On the theory of political benefits in American public programs, in B. S. Rundquist (ed) *Political Benefits*. Lexington Books, Lexington, 227–54.

Rundquist, B. S. (1983) Political benefits and public policy: interpretation of recent US studies. *Environment and Planning D: Government and Policy* 1, 401–12.

Rundquist, B. S. and Ferejohn, J. A. (1976) Observations on a distributive theory of policy making: two American expenditure programs compared, in C. Liske, W. Jack and J. McCamart (eds) *Comparative Public Policy*. John Wiley, New York, 87–108.

Sack, R. D. (1980) *Conceptions of Space in Social Thought*. Macmillan, London.

Sack, R. D. (1983) Human territoriality: a theory. *Annals of the Association of American Geographers* 73, 55–74.

Sack, R. D. (1986) *Human Territoriality: Its Theory and History*. Cambridge University Press, Cambridge.

Samuel, R. (1986) Introduction, in R. Samuel, B. Bloomfield and G. Boanas (eds) *The Enemy Within: Pit Villages and the Miners' Strike of 1984–5*. Routledge and Kegan Paul, London, 1–39.

Samuel, R., Bloomfield, B. and Boanas, G. (eds) (1986) *The Enemy Within: Pit Villages and the Miners' Strike of 1984–5*. Routledge and Kegan Paul, London.

Sande, G. N., Goethals, G. R., Ferrari, L. and Worth, L. T. (1989) Value-guided attributions: maintaining the moral self-image and the diabolical enemy-image. *Journal of Social Issues* 45, 91–118.

Sarlvik, B. and Crewe, I. (1983) *Decade of Dealignment*. Cambridge University Press, Cambridge.

Sarre, P. (1987) Realism in practice. *Area* 19, 3–10.

Sarre, P., Phillips, D. and Skellington, R. (1989) *Ethnic Minority Housing: Explanations and Policies*. Avebury, Aldershot.

Savage, M. (1989) *The Dynamics of Working-Class Politics*. Cambridge University Press, Cambrige.

Sayer, A. (1984) *Method in Social Science*. Hutchinson, London.

Sayer, A. (1985) Realism and geography, in R. J. Johnston (ed) *The Future of Geography*. Methuen, London, 159–73.

Scarbrough, E. (1984) *Political Ideology and Voting*. Clarendon Press, Oxford.

Schattschneider, E. E. (1962) *The Semi-Sovereign People*. Dryden, Hinsdale, IL.

Sennett, R. (1973) *The Uses of Disorder*. Penguin, London.

Seyd, P. (1990) Radical Sheffield: from socialism to entrepreneurialism. *Political Studies* 38, 335–44.

Sharkansky, I. (1969) The utility of Elazar's political culture. *Polity* 2, 66–83.

Sharkansky, I. (1971) Economic theories of public policy: resource-policy and need-policy linkages between income and welfare benefits. *Midwest Journal of Political Science* 15, 722–40.

Sharpe, L. J. (1982) The Labour party and the geography of inequality: a puzzle, in D. Kavanagh (ed) *The Politics of the Labour Party*. George Allen and Unwin, London, 135–70.

Sharpe, L. J. and Newton, K. (1984) *Does Politics Matter?* The Clarendon Press, Oxford.

Sibley, D. (1981) *Outsiders in Urban Society*. Basil Blackwell, Oxford.

Siegfried, A. (1913) *Tableau Politique de la France de l'Ouest*, A. Colin, Paris.

Silverstein, B. and Flamenbaum, C. (1989) Biases in the perception and cognition of the actions of enemies. *Journal of Social Issues* 45, 51–72.

Skidelsky, R. (ed) (1988) *Thatcherism*. Basil Blackwell, Oxford.

Smith, D. (1988) Knowing your place: class, politics and ethnicity in Chicago and Birmingham, 1890–1983, in N. J. Thrift and P. Williams (eds) *Class and Space: The Making of Urban Society*. Routledge, London, 276–305.

Smith, D. (1989) *North and South: Britain's Growing Divide*. Penguin, London.

Smith, G. E. (1986a) Territoriality, in R. J. Johnston, D. Gregory and D. M. Smith (eds) *The Dictionary of Human Geography* (second edition). Basil Blackwell, Oxford, 482–3.

Smith, G. E. (1986b) Nationalism, in R. J. Johnston, D. Gregory and D. M. Smith (eds) *The Dictionary of Human Geography* (second edition). Basil Blackwell, Oxford, 312–4.

Smith, N. (1984) *Uneven Development*. Basil Blackwell, Oxford.

Smith, N. (1987) Dangers of the empirical turn: the CURS initiative. *Antipode* 19, 59–68.

Smith, S. (1990) Foreign and defence policy, in P. Dunleavy, A. M. Gamble and G. Peele (eds) *Developments in British Politics 3*. Macmillan, London, 246–68.

Smith, S. J. (1989) Society, space and citizenship. *Transactions, Institute of British Geographers* NS14, 144–156.

Soja, E. W. (1985) The spatiality of social life, in D. Gregory and J. Urry (eds) *Social Relations and Spatial Structures*, Macmillan, London, 90–127.

Soja, E. W. (1989) *Postmodern Geographies: The Reassertion of Space in Critical Social Theory*. Verso, London.

Sparks, L. (1990) Editorial – full circle? *Area* 22, 1–3.

Stead, J. (1987) *Never the Same Again: Women and the Miners' Strike 1984–85*. Semen's Press, London.

Steel, R. W. (1983) *The Institute of British Geographers: 1953–1983*. Institute of British Geographers, London.

Stinchcombe, A. (1990) Milieu and structure updated: a critique of the theory of structuration, in J. Clark, C. Modgil and S. Modgil (eds) *Anthony Giddens: Consensus and Controversy*. The Falmer Press, London, 47–56.

Stoddart, D. R. (1986) *On Geography*. Basil Blackwell, Oxford.

Stoddart, D. R. (1987) To claim the high ground: geography for the end of the century. *Transactions, Institute of British Geographers* NS12, 327–36.

Stonecash, J. and Hayes, S. W. (1981) The sources of public policy: welfare policy in the American States. *Journal of Social Policy* 681–98.

Storey, D. J. (1990) Evaluation of policies and measures to create local employment. *Urban Studies*, 27, 669–84.

Sunley, P. J. (1986) Regional restructuring, class change and political action: a comment. *Environment and Planning D: Society and Space* 4, 465–8.

Sunley, P. J. (1988) Broken places: towards a geography of the 1926 coal dispute, in M. Heffernan and P. Gruffud (eds) *A Land Fit for Heroes: Essays in the*

Human Geography of Inter-War Britain. Loughborough University, Department of Geography, Occasional Paper 14, Loughborough, 5–36.

Sunley, P. J. (1990) Striking parallels: a comparison of the geographies of the 1926 and 1984–85 coalmining disputes. *Environment and Planning D: Society and Space* 8, 35–52.

Taaffe, E. G., Morrill, R. L. and Gould, P. R. (1963) Transport expansion in underdeveloped countries: a comparative analysis. *Geographical Review* 53, 503–29.

Tajfel, H. and Turner, J. C. (1979) An integrative theory of intergroup conflict, in W. G. Austin and S. Worchel (eds) *The Social Psychology of Intergroup Relations*. Brookes/Cole, Monterey, CA.

Tabb, W. K. (1984) Urban development and regional restructuring: an overview, in L. Sawers and W. K. Tabb (eds) *Sunbelt/Snowbelt*. Oxford University Press, New York, 3–18.

Taylor, A. (1984) *The Politics of the Yorkshire Miners*. Croom Helm, London.

Taylor, P. J. (1982) A materialist framework for political geography. *Transactions, Institute of British Geographers* NS7, 15–34.

Taylor, P. J. (1985) The value of a geographical perspective, in R. J. Johnston (ed) *The Future of Geography*. Methuen, London, 92–110.

Taylor, P. J. (1989) *Political Geography: World-Economy, Nation-State and Community* (second edition). Longman, London.

Taylor, P. J. and Johnston, R. J. (1979) *Geography of Elections*. Penguin, London.

Thirsk, J. (1973) Field systems of the East Midlands, in A. R. H. Baker and R. A. Butlin (eds) *Studies of Field Systems in the British Isles*. Cambridge University Press, Cambridge, 232–80.

Thrift, N. J. (1983) On the determination of social action in space and time. *Environment and Planning D: Society and Space* 1, 23–58.

Tiebout, C. M. (1956) A pure theory of local expenditures. *Journal of Political Economy* 64, 416–24.

Todd, E. (1985) *The Explanation of Ideology: Family Structures and Social Systems*. Basil Blackwell, Oxford.

Todd, E. (1987) *The Causes of Progress: Culture, Authority and Change*. Basil Blackwell, Oxford.

Tresch, R. W. (1975) State governments and the welfare system: an econometric analysis. *Southern Economic Journal* 42, 33–43.

Tuan, Y.-F. (1982) *Segmented Worlds and the Self*. University of Minnesota Press, Minneapolis.

Turner, B. L. II (1988) Whether to publish in geography journals. *The Professional Geographer* 40, 15–8.

Turner, B. L. II and Meyer, W. B. (1985) The use of citation indices in comparing geography programs: a comparative study. *The Professional Geographer* 37, 271–8.

Turner, J. (1989) The disintegration of American sociology. *Sociological Perspectives* 32, 419–33.

Turner, J. H. and Turner, S. P. (forthcoming a) *American Sociology: Its History, Structure and Substance*. Polish Scientific Publishers, Warsaw.

Turner, S. P. and Turner, J. H. (forthcoming b) *The Impossible Science: An Institutional History of American Sociology.*

Ullman, E. L. (1954) Amenities as a factor in regional growth. *Geographical Review* 44, 119–32.

Urry, J. (1981) *The Anatomy of Capitalist Societies: The Economy, Civil Society and the State.* Macmillan, London.

Urry, J. (1986) Locality research: the case of Lancaster. *Regional Studies* 20, 233–42.

Waddington, D., Wykes, M. and Critcher, C. (1990) *Split at the Seams? Community, Continuity and Change after the 1984–5 Coal Dispute.* The Open University Press, Milton Keynes.

Walker, R. A. (1981) A theory of suburbanization, in M. J. Dear and A. J. Scott (eds) *Urbanization and Urban Planning in Capitalist Societies.* Methuen, London, 383–430.

Walker, R. A. (1989) What's left to do? *Antipode* 21, 133–65.

Wallace, H. (1990) Britain and Europe, in P. Dunleavy, A. M. Gamble and G. Peele (eds) *Developments in British Politics 3.* Macmillan, London, 150–74.

Waller, R. J. (1983) *The Dukeries Transformed.* Clarendon Press, Oxford.

Ward, D. (1971) *Cities and Immigrants.* Oxford University Press, New York.

Watts, M. (1983) *Silent Violence.* University of California Press, Berkeley.

Whitehand, J. W. R. (1984) The impact of geographical journals: a look at the ISI data. *Area* 16, 185–7.

Whitehand, J. W. R. (1985) Contributors to the recent development and influence of human geography: what citation analysis suggests. *Transactions, Institute of British Geographers* NS10, 222–34.

Whitehand, J. W. R. (1990) An assessment of *Progress. Progress in Human Geography* 14, 12–23.

Whittlesey, D. F. (1956) Southern Rhodesia; an African compage. *Annals of the Association of American Geographers* 46, 1–97.

Williams, R. (1976) *Keywords.* Fontana, London.

Winterton, J. and Winterton, R. (1989) *Coal, Crisis and Conflict: The 1984–85 Miners' Strike in Yorkshire.* Manchester University Press, Manchester.

Witham, J. (1986) *Hearts and Minds: The Story of the Women of Nottinghamshire in the Miners' Strike, 1984–1985.* Canary Press, London.

Wittfogel, K. A. (1957) *Oriental Despotism.* Yale University Press, New Haven.

Wohlenberg, E. H. (1976a) Interstate variations in AFDC programs. *Economic Geography* 52, 254–66.

Wohlenberg, E. H. (1976b) Public assistance effectiveness by states. *Annals of the Association of American Geographers* 66, 440–50.

Wohlenberg, E. H. (1976c) An index of eligibility standards for welfare benefits. *The Professional Geographer* 26, 381–84.

Wohlenberg, E. H. (1980) Correlates of equal rights amendment ratification. *Social Science Quarterly* 60, 676–84.

Wright, G. C. (1975) Interparty competition and state social welfare policy: when a difference makes a difference. *Journal of Politics* 37, 796–803.

Wrigley, N. (1983) The half-life of an *E & P*. *Environment and Planning A* 15, 571–6.

Wrigley, N. (1985) Citation classics in urban and regional research. *Environment and Planning A* 17, 145–9.

Wrigley, N. (1988) Editorial: coming on stream. *Transactions, Institute of British Geographers* NS13, 387–8.

Wrigley, N. (1990) Editorial: the environment resurfaces. *Transactions, Institute of British Geographers* NS15, 3.

Wrigley, N. and Matthews, S. (1986) Citation classics and citation levels in geography. *Area* 18, 185–94.

Wrigley, N. and Matthews, S. (1987) Citation classics in geography and new centurions: a response to Haigh, Mead and Whitehand. *Area* 19, 279–84.

Young, H. (1990) *One of Us: A Biography of Margaret Thatcher.* Pan Books London.

Young, I. (1985) South Wales, in I. Jedrzejczyk, R. Page, B. Prince and I. Young (eds) *Striking Women: Communities and Coal.* Pluto Press, London, 9–27.

Zelinsky, W. (1961) An approach to the religious geography of the United States: patterns of church membership in 1962. *Annals of the Association of American Geographers* 51, 161–93.

Zelinsky, W. (1973) *The Cultural Geography of the United States.* Prentice-Hall, Englewood Cliffs NJ.

Zelinsky, W. (1975) The demigod's dilemma. *Annals of the Association of American Geographers* 65, 123–43.

Index